# GENIUS LOCI

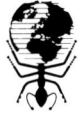

# GENIUS LOCI

## AN ESSAY ON THE MEANINGS OF PLACE

JOHN DIXON HUNT

REAKTION BOOKS

*For Josephine*

Published by
Reaktion Books Ltd
Unit 32, Waterside
44–48 Wharf Road
London N1 7UX, UK

www.reaktionbooks.co.uk

First published 2022
Copyright © John Dixon Hunt 2022

Printed and bound in India by Replika Press Pvt. Ltd

A catalogue record for this book is available from the British Library

ISBN 978 1 78914 608 0

# Contents

Architecture is the very mirror of life.
You have to cast your eyes on buildings
to feel the presence of the past, the spirit of a place.

I. M. PEI

# Preface

*Genius loci* was a Latin term that, although still used, has morphed: into an English 'genius of place', then into an emphasis on 'spirit of place' or, even more literally, 'nature of place'. The Latin term survived in use, by artists such as Paul Nash when writing his memoir in the early twentieth century, or in discussions by designers such as Ian McHarg in *Design with Nature* (1969). But some people, as we will see in Chapter Two, think *genius loci* simply does not exist, and attribute it to whatever an individual brings to a site. That was happily described by W. H. Auden, aged sixty: 'sites [are] made sacred by something read there,/ a lunch, a good lay, or sheer lightness of heart.' The sense that sites are indeed sacred can result from such individual responses, but also, as I hope to argue, from an accumulation of notions and ideas that cling to and eventually describe a place, beyond individual whim or happenstance. Sometimes a meaning of place is implied without invoking any term at all, for most people nourish a sense of some local significance that they know well or discover suddenly, as Auden announced, in a new location. The phenomena of a place can be recognized and described, drawn or photographed, and even composers will signal or 'describe' in their music some aspect of the physical world. But phenomena may themselves readily suggest something beyond the actual and so reach for, or discern, numinous possibilities, hence the Greek term *noumena*. The topic of *genius loci* can be approached in a variety of ways, which the succeeding essays attempt, for it constitutes an important way of being in the world: less what a place is necessarily than how we recognize, define and use it, and thus how we relish its particular importance.

The term *genius loci* was coined and widely used by the Romans, applied to their temples, streets, houses and topographical features such as rivers, springs or mountains. It alluded to the presence of deities or famous ancestors who now people these places, where they might be worshipped, thus giving meaning to the localities. It survived in the Renaissance, by now as a metaphor for meanings of place, as when garden designers incorporated classical statues and inscriptions into their designs, or when poets continued to find in classical mythology a useful way of animating their verses on place. But other modern approaches to the actual world, such as those of geologists, geographers, topographers or travel writers, find useful the need to describe places in terms that both elucidate and metaphorize them.

Groups of people may share the same understanding of a place, but individuals can also devise their own interpretations. Geologists and geographers work with the facts of place, phenomena, objective ideas, and these can be borrowed by non-specialists: Auden's 'In Praise of Limestone' is a splendid example.[1] Limestone is celebrated because, when the poet tries 'to imagine a faultless love/ Or the life to come, what I hear is the murmur/ Of underground streams, what I see is a limestone landscape'. The pun on 'faultless' is a measure of the poem's opening, where limestone is hailed as the geology that 'inconstant ones/ Are consistently homesick for'. That geology is then opposed to clays and gravels, or to granite wastes, that respectively lure 'saints-to-be' or 'intendent Caesars'. And beyond that instinct to link character and action to geology is the very slip-page of the word 'landscape': from the facts and lie of the land into metaphoric ways of description, as in the 'landscape of fear', or that 'of success'.

The idea of *genius loci* may be a question of how a person identifies with a site – his home, his local surroundings, his nationality – some of which can be tangible, such as smell, sound and above all language. Places can be, we might say, 'inhabited' in profound ways. Sometimes it is simply that certain places usefully activate parts of ourselves that we had not realized before or elsewhere. We acquire a sense of place through a variety of conscious and unconscious contacts – what we read, what we see in art or photography, where we go, or even what we miss in a given site – and by comparisons that we make between places. We rely on a miscellany of ideas and associations.

The essays in this book consider, first, the narrative of the phrase *genius loci* and why it has changed over time into something less pious and mythological, a more vernacular description, despite still holding true to the wish to seize on something distinctive about a place. Then two twentieth-century French writers argue and find different ways to accept, even when they refuse to believe it, that a *genius loci* exists. After that it seemed useful to focus on one particular place that others have visited, written about and drawn: I chose the island of Torcello in the Venetian lagoon, where a *genius loci* seems palpable, even if visitors seem to expand their recognition of one momentous structure, the basilica, into a more general apprehension of the surrounding landscape.

Painters and writers have alternative ways of grasping and explaining *genius loci*, so two essays explore how artists, such as Turner and the Nash brothers, find ways to signal the mysteries of place, and then poets, who have since ancient times been among the most eager to celebrate places. While travel books do not necessarily focus on *genius loci*, wishing rather to elaborate on facts and specific understandings of place, we examine the work of five writers with very poetic instincts who have written about different places, to find a sense of their mystery and potent significance; all those writers were in one way or another strangers in the places they chose to understand. They may not rely on, or even invoke, the term *genius loci*, but they are still fascinated by how we understand and explain what a place, or a whole country, means. 'Meaning', though, is a slippery term. While it is often assumed that we need words to explain meaning (what the French say with '*Qu'est-ce que vous voulez dire?*'), it may involve a less articulate *saying* to suggest, to point to, what is nonetheless a significant understanding.

Finally, it is possible to see that all these various resources – geology, topography, words, drawing, photography, science – can be gathered to sustain, at their best, the making of place, what we now term landscape architecture, for it may be assumed that designers have in mind how to create or draw out a 'meaning' of the site they design. This, the longest chapter, both explores present-day examples of *genius loci* and delves back into some early designs, in which it is still possible to see this notion at work or at play. A conclusion accepts the ambiguities of *genius loci*, but equally of understanding its potency of place.

# ONE

# The *Genius Loci* of the Ancients and Its Modern Revisions

Footfalls echo in the memory
Down the passage which we did not take
Towards the door we never opened
Into the rose-garden.

T. S. Eliot, from 'Burnt Norton' (1936), no. 1 of *Four Quartets*

I taly, wrote Gilbert Highet, 'is a land full of presences'; he went on to explore how seven different Latin poets wrote about its landscapes.[1] The ancient Romans generally registered those presences by acknowledging a wide range of deities, male and female. Their *genius* had an impact on all aspects of life, and the Romans filled their homes, gardens, hearths and crossroads with images of *lares*, spirits, gods and minor divinities who 'explained' the meanings of sites or geographical features.[2] Pliny the Elder's huge *Natural History* distinguished between the work of agriculture and gardening and, by implication, the people who did the work in each: Tellus, goddess of earth and fields, is distinguished from Pomona, deity of gardens, because the former involved hard work and the latter shows her 'gifts' straightforwardly. Gardens, he noted, always have a 'certain sense of sanctity', to which the resident deities contributed. Roman domestic gardens were peopled accordingly with statues of the various deities: there were many Venuses, nymphs for fountains and springs, and Muses galore, some male, some female, among them Polyhymnia, Clio and Urania.[3]

The deities of ancient Rome continued to feature in Christian Europe, although now as representations, metaphorical or symbolic, of classical gods and goddesses. The famous garden of Rousham in Oxfordshire had a Vale of Venus, where her statue presided over the grottoes that descended the hillside. A little later, Stourhead in Wiltshire had a reclining nymph placed in its grotto (illus. 1), while a standing river god signalled the source of the River Stour. But, to make sure that visitors understood the nymph, Alexander Pope's version of what he called a 'beautiful antique' inscription was inscribed before her:

> Nymph of the grot these sacred springs I keep
> And to the murmur of these waters sleep;
> Ah spare my slumbers gently tread the cave,
> And drink in silence or in silence lave.[4]

But the incidence of female images (whether Roman, Renaissance or later) suggested that, even if men designed gardens (local stewards or head gardeners, before the days of landscape architects), the work and the pleasures were shared equally by women.[5] Their contribution to or shaping of *genius loci* would probably have been local or even personal.

The invocation of gods that presided over place took many forms in Roman poetry as well as in statuary, although we may wonder whether Margaret Atwood's modern remark did, even then, apply: 'There are lots of gods. Gods always come in handy, they justify almost anything.'[6] The Romans' phrase *genius loci* was then a precise term, although it is now (while still used today) somewhat vaguer. Catullus hails 'Neptune, god of water' when he seeks to glorify the lake at his beloved Sirmio on Lake Garda; Virgil,

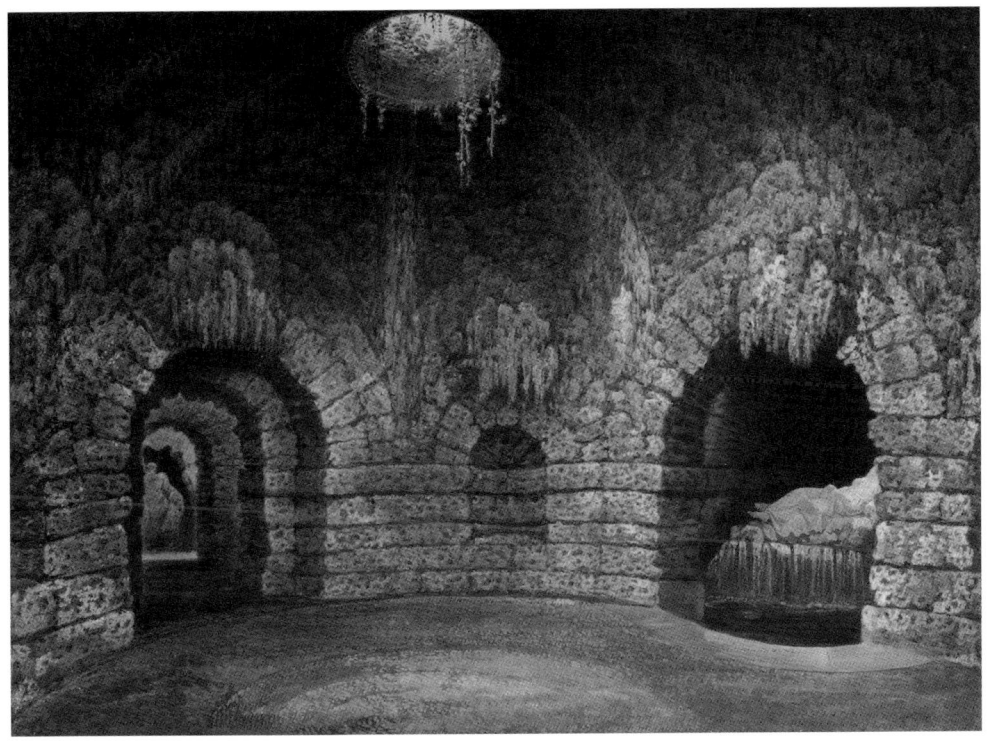

whose *Aeneid* frequently invoked spirits of place, was himself in the Renaissance deemed a presiding genius whose 'name exalts the place', Naples, marked now only by remnants of his supposed tomb; Horace invoked Mercury to cherish the 'little spot of land' of his Sabine farm. In *Amores*, Ovid writes warmly of his birthplace and, although without noting any genius, implies its richness in associations and in his own genius: 'Some stranger, looking at the little city walls/ Of Sulmo, rich in rivers, small in acres/ may say "Diminutive you are, and yet you bore/ a mighty poet – therefore you are great,"' and the modern Sulmona boasts both medieval and later statues of him. Yet it is his *Metamorphoses* that reveals how other Romans would have understood *genii locorum*, for its verses celebrate the origins of natural items: Narcissus changes into a flower, Daphne transforms into laurel, nymphs preside in a grotto,

1 Nymph in Stourhead grotto, watercolour by Francis Nicholson.

*13*

giants change into mountains. In Campania, for example, serpents were often invoked to signal a special topography, and one wall painting (illus. 2) in Herculaneum shows the god Harpocrates approaching an altar around which is coiled a snake that eats the food placed there; the inscription reads '*Genius huius loci montis*' (the genius of this place, the mountain). Another, in a garden destroyed by the eruption of Vesuvius, had a painting of a household shrine, also with a snake, of Bacchus standing on the summit of the volcano.

What these ancient writers chose to identify, explain and celebrate are still essential instincts today, whether or not we use their term and despite the fact that we no longer deal with their gods, for the *idea* of *genius loci* has enjoyed a long life, even if that particular formulation did not survive. Susan Stewart's *The Ruins Lesson* (2020) displays a multitude of writings where figures of 'presences' animate locations from ancient ruins to the landscapes and poetry

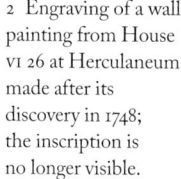

2 Engraving of a wall painting from House VI 26 at Herculaneum made after its discovery in 1748; the inscription is no longer visible.

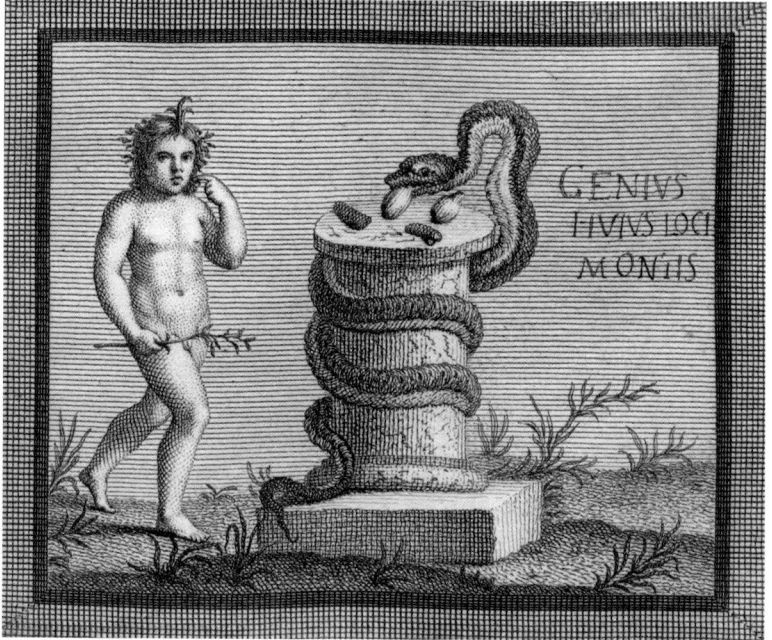

of the Renaissance.[7] Alexander Pope invoked the phrase to describe landscape gardening, and, as Chapter Five makes clear, Romantic and contemporary poets, like their Roman predecessors, dwelled often on what makes a place meaningful, usually a site of some special significance to them personally.

The word *genius* was absorbed into the language of early Christianity, just as relics of Roman buildings were incorporated into new places of worship. Highet notes that a winged spirit morphed into the Christian idea of an angel, and, one must suppose, the snake into the Devil.[8] During the Renaissance, with designers and clients still familiar with classical references, the metaphorical imagery was realized in garden imagery, where sites must be marked and defined. In the Medici villa of Pratolino in Tuscany, the huge statue of the Apennines, based perhaps on an engraving for Ovid's *Metamorphoses*, shows a giant being turned bit by bit into mountain stone, to celebrate the villa's situation on that range of the mountains (illus. 3). River gods 'performed' at the Villa Lante in Bagnaia, and later, at Versailles, a statue of Apollo, the sun god, presided over the gardens for Louis xiv, the 'Sun King'. Since Apollo was also the leader of the Muses, his presence there announced the enormous role that the arts played in its design.

Since then, as we have seen, the Latin phrase *genius loci* has morphed somewhat. While ancient gods no longer function as indicators or celebrators of sacred places, present-day sites still invite both collective and personal understandings of their significance, so that the presence – or the fossil – of Roman notions of significant or sacred sites still resonates. A recent book of essays by Susan Owens, *Spirit of Place: Artists, Writers and the British Landscape* (2020), focuses less on meanings of place than on what places and their visitors share by way of a variety of concepts: mystery, discovery, feeling and, indeed, 'presence'.

The extent of this classical understanding of place and what it signified is considerable, and is tackled here mainly to establish how much this fossil of marking or designing a place has continued and been altered in the modern world with its habit of alluding to, if not wholly believing in, the language of the ancient *genius loci*.[9] For the Roman *genius loci* would not serve very usefully in later times of monotheistic cultures, so it was changed into both local languages and less mysterious understandings of the things that constituted place.

A midway point in this shift from the Latin to an English usage can be seen when in 1746 Mark Akenside wrote, and later annotated, his 'Hymn to the Naiads', ancient figures said to inhabit rivers, springs and waterfalls. Akenside's extensive notes on this poem review classical texts from Greek (Homer, Hesiod, Callimachus, Apollodorus) and Latin (Virgil, in particular, and Ovid's *Metamorphoses*); these sustain his sense of the significance of the naiads, although he writes that 'the mere genealogy or the personal adventures of the heathen gods [are] but little interesting to the modern reader.' It had certainly been 'convenient', he nevertheless observes, 'to employ these ancient divinities . . . in personifying natural causes, and representing the mutual agreement or opposition of the corporeal and moral powers of the world'. He thus saw naiads as 'allegorical deities, or *powers of nature*' (my italics); the nature so emblematized is the interaction of sun and running water, which give 'motion to the air' and to 'summer breezes'.[10]

Not surprisingly in a nation then sustained by the enquiries of the Royal Society, Akenside also links and explains naiads in terms of the current understanding of how air moves, to the extent that the classical repertoire becomes a metaphor for the physics of atmospheric effects. Thus a note on 'sallying streams' in line 49 of his 'Hymn' explained that

The state of the atmosphere with respect to rest and motion is, in several ways, affected by rivers and running streams; and that more especially in hot seasons: first, they destroy its

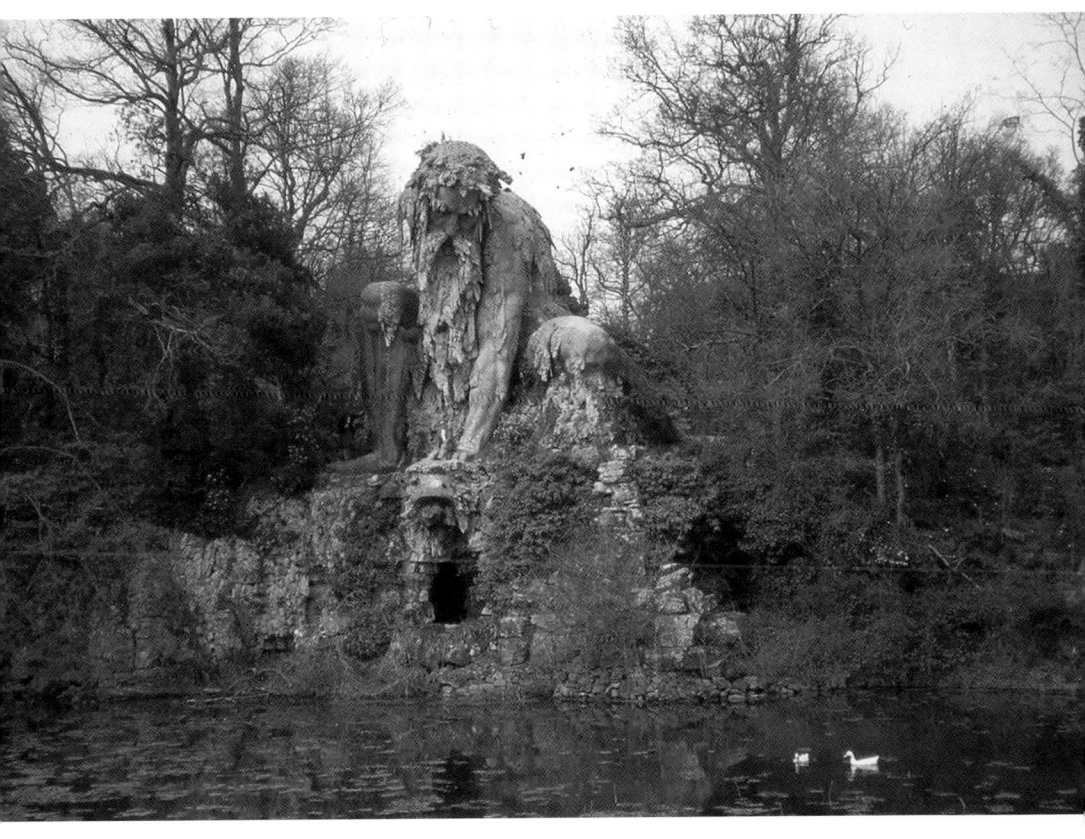

equilibrium, by cooling those parts of it with which they are in contact; and secondly, they communicate their own motion: and the air which is thus moved by them, being left heated, is of consequence more elastic than other parts of the atmosphere, and therefore fitter to preserve and to propagate that motion.

3 Giambologna, the Apennine Colossus, Villa Pratolino, 1570–80.

More than fifty years after this, in 1802, lines of Akenside's poem were nevertheless adopted by J.M.W. Turner to gloss his watercolour of *The Falls of the Clyde* (Walker Art Gallery, Liverpool; today this site is referred to as the Falls of Clyde), where the nymphs occupy one of the banks and signal their presence as 'powers of nature' (illus. 4). Then, almost thirty years later, Turner returned to paint the same scene, now in oils (Lady Lever Art Gallery, Port Sunlight), but he virtually eliminated the naiads, relying on his own painterly skills, not classical and metaphorical figures, to render the site's atmospherics (illus. 5).

William Blake also noted, but lamented, the demise of any substantial notion of *genius loci* in *The Marriage of Heaven and Hell* in the late 1790s (illus. 6). The 'ancient poets animated all sensible objects with Gods and Geniuses, calling them by the name and adorning them with the properties of woods, rivers, mountains, lakes, cities, and nations.' But he continued by blaming its demise on an established 'system' that had 'enslav'd the vulgar by attempting to realize or abstract the mental deities from their objects. Thus began priesthood – choosing forms of worships from [that is, as opposed to] poetic tales ... Thus men forgot that all deities reside in the human breast.' Abstraction, formal theology, system,

4 J.M.W. Turner, *Falls of the Clyde*, 1802, watercolour.

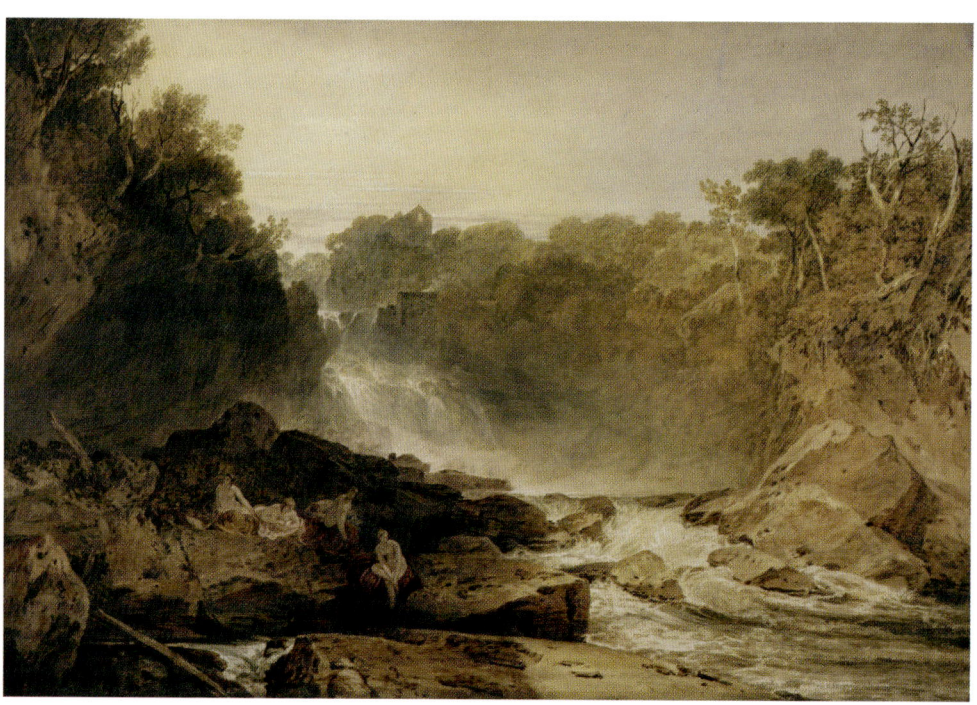

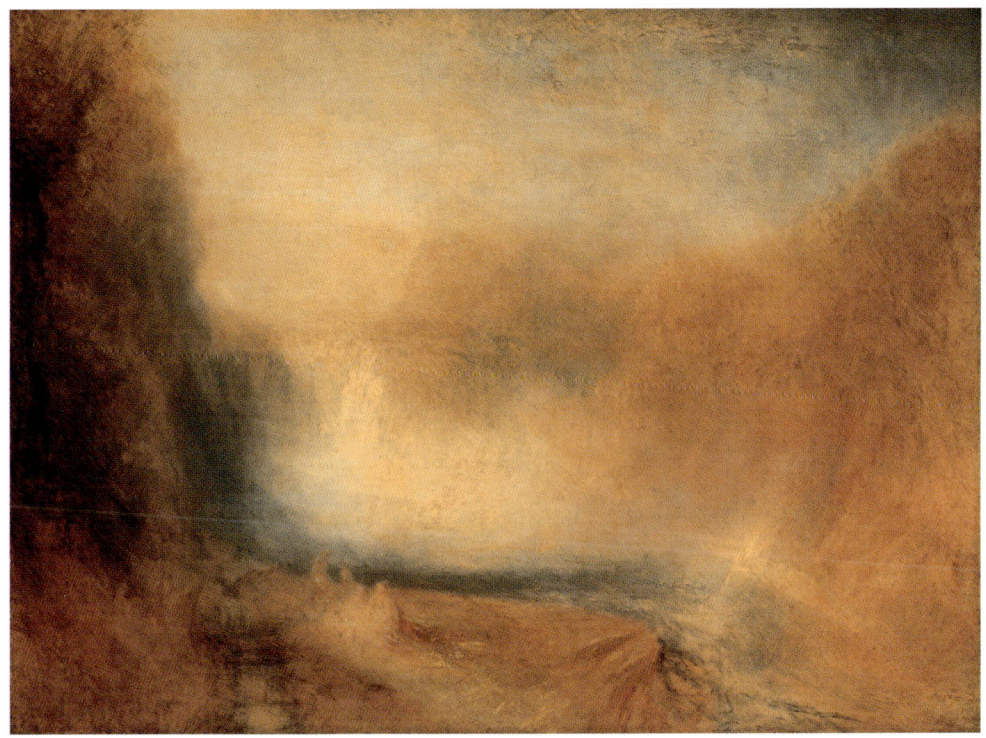

objectivization – all were anathema to Blake; only individuals might attempt a true vision of perfection, a state that the next section of his poem finds supremely difficult. Nonetheless, as late as 1841 the second edition of George Field's *Chromatography* still sought to explain how 'ancient poets . . . mythologically' saw light and shade depicted as Lucifer, Phosphorous and Hesperus.

5 J.M.W. Turner, *Falls of the Clyde*, *c.* 1845, oil on canvas.

Yet the idea, if not the Latin language, did not entirely disappear, when it was absorbed to allow a local understanding of place. In 1731 it was Englished by Alexander Pope as 'Genius of *place*' in his epistle addressed to Lord Burlington on the role and requirements of a landscape gardener. The new emphasis served to insist on the need to attend to local language and local topographies, not the abodes of foreign gods:

The ancient Poets animated all sensible objects
with Gods or Geniuses, calling them by the names and
adorning them with the properties of woods, rivers,
mountains, lakes, cities, nations, and whatever their
enlarged & numerous senses could percieve.

And particularly they studied the genius of each
city & country, placing it under its mental deity.

Till a system was formed, which some took ad-
vantage of & enslav'd the vulgar by attempting to
realize or abstract the mental deities from their
objects: thus began Priesthood.

Choosing forms of worship from poetic tales.
And at length they pronounced that the Gods
had orderd such things.

Thus men forgot that All deities reside
in the human breast.

Consult the *Genius* of the *Place* in all,
That tells the Waters or to rise or fall,
Or helps th' ambitious Hill the Heav'ns to scale,
Or scoops in circling Theatres the Vale.

*Opposite:*
6  William Blake
on *genius loci* from
a plate in *The Marriage
of Heaven and Hell,*
*c.* 1794.

But then, with a syntactic sleight of hand, the topography also addresses what is clearly a different sort of genius, when Pope now sees the 'you' as the designer, who

Calls in the Country, catches opening Glades.
Joins willing Woods, and varies Shades from Shades,
Now breaks, or now directs, th' intending Lines;
*Paints* as you plant, and as you work, *Designs*.

Given that Pope's addressee was the architectural connoisseur Burlington, whose gardens at Chiswick had been in part designed by William Kent, a friend of Pope's, his lines continue with instructions for such a designer, and end with a triumphant appeal to one of the grandest of early eighteenth-century gardens, where Kent also designed pavilions and temples. A designer must begin by appreciating what materials he has to deal with on the site, so that

Parts answ'ring Parts, shall slide into a Whole,
Spontaneous Beauties all around advance,
Start, ev'n from *Difficulty*, strike, from *Chance*;
*Nature* shall join you; *Time* shall make it grow
A Work to wonder at – perhaps a Stowe.

There a garden (Stowe) can be brought into prominence by an observant and talented place-maker, whose art draws out, or rather re-creates, the genius of that site in all its topographical and cultural complexity.

Yet Pope was perhaps ahead of his times in linking landscape art with the materials of nature in 1731. His genius of place merges physical properties with whatever new forms a good designer can instil into it, something that a visitor might see as a 'spirit' of that modified place. But in matters of landscape architecture, many still clung to visual equivalents of ancient lore. What Akenside and later Turner had celebrated with their naiads had been paralleled by endless copies of Renaissance statues and inscriptions that recalled the presence, inspiration or metaphoric power of ancient deities, and continued to do so.

Pope's was an eighteenth-century attempt to 'rescue' genius of place from a judgement that would see it as no longer relevant, or even nonsensical. Kent, in common with other designers, would continue to rely on the apparatus of Renaissance garden devices that he had seen during his years in Italy.[11] There statues of river gods, based maybe on excavated Roman originals, were installed around water basins and streams, and at the Villa d'Este terracotta plaques illustrating Ovid's poetic metamorphoses were featured along the walk of a hundred fountains. It is doubtful that Kent would have visited or known of Bomarzo, but rocks in its woodlands were carved during the sixteenth century to represent nymphs, giants and various monsters (illus. 8).

Such specific references continued in the following centuries. Eighteenth-century English gardens such as Stowe and Stourhead were peopled with imagery that sought to direct visitors' reception of those places. At Stowe, Kent installed full-length statues of Greek masters (a great lawyer, a poet, a philosopher and a warrior) in his Temple of Ancient Virtue, while on the opposite side of the aptly named River Styx his Temple of British Worthies placed fourteen busts – including that of Pope – in quasi-gothic niches. The *gothick* touch suggested that a major influence on British culture was seen to derive from its later, indigenous past of geniuses. Yet Kent was also quick – perhaps at the instigation of Pope – to recognize

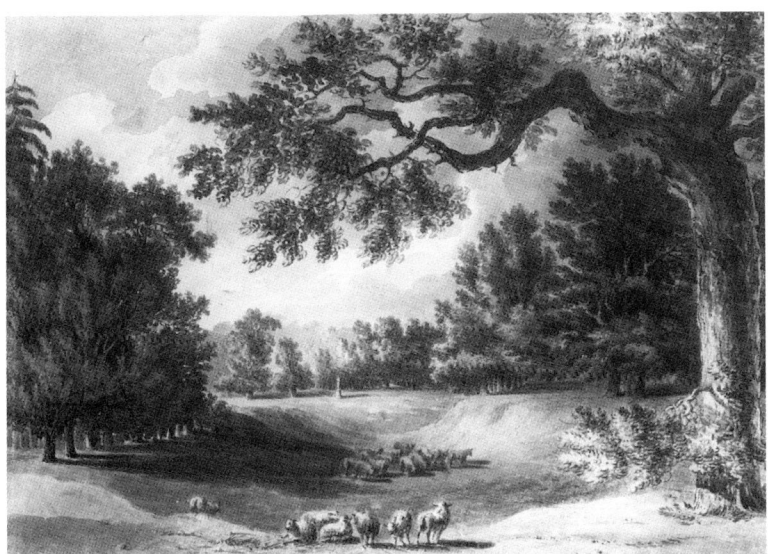

7 J. C. Nattes,
drawing of the
Grecian Valley
at Stowe, 1802.

the satiric potential of such emblems: a ruined Temple of Modern
Virtue, with a decapitated head of the prime minister Robert
Walpole, was placed alongside Ancient Virtue, while on the rear
of British Worthies an engraved memorial lauded another exem-
plary genius, which turns out to be an otter hound called Ringwood!
Yet, in its way, it was a perfect recognition of one suitable genius
for an estate where hunting was a major activity.

But one segment of Stowe reveals how Lancelot 'Capability'
Brown later saw the future of place-making (his preferred term)
without relying on a conspicuous agenda of classical references
or imagery. The Grecian Valley was created in the late 1740s when
the estate acquired new land across an adjacent road and could
extend its gardens (illus. 7). It is still one of the most wonderful
moments at Stowe. The Temple of Concord and Victory (its
designer a matter of some dispute, but Brown himself has been
plausibly suggested) presides over the bend or dog-leg of the valley;
its open glade, L-shaped, seems natural but is carefully shaped and
planted, virtually clear of any ornament besides the Greek Temple

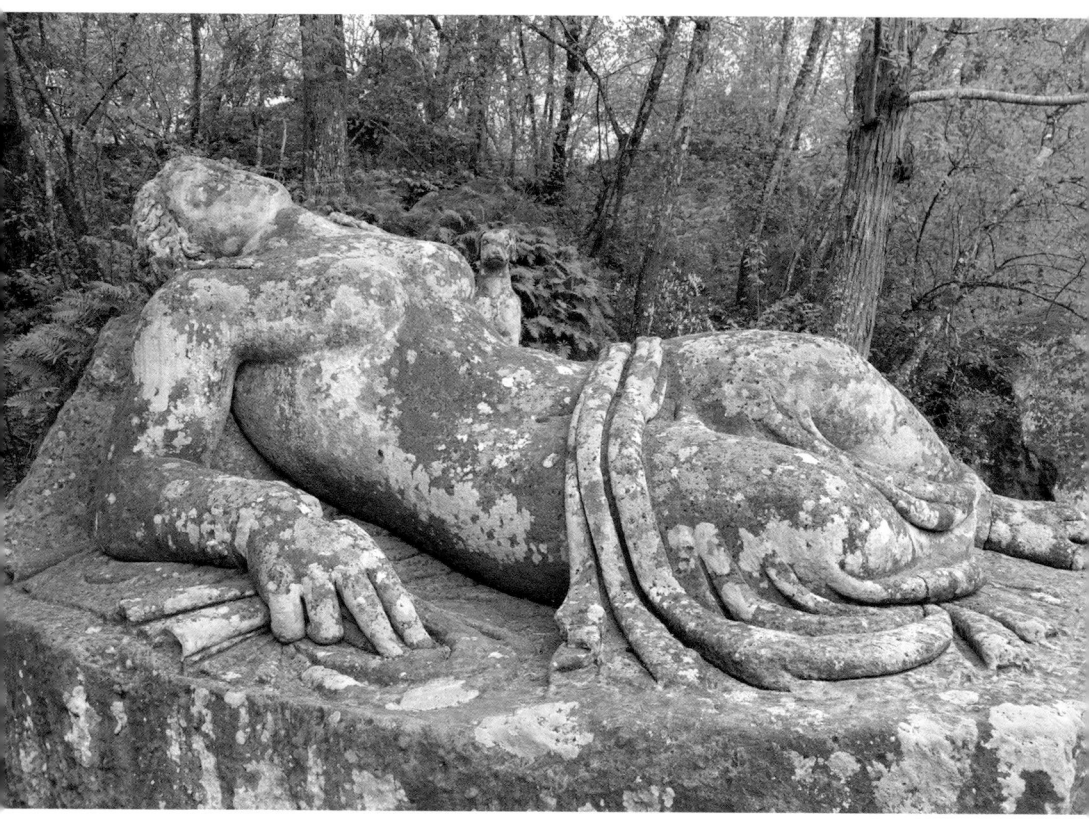

at its head. Lines of trees, some clumps, meandering paths and a few scattered statues, intended more as decoration than as ways to give meaning to this site, compose the scene.

Two items there are significant: one is Lord Cobham's Pillar, seen to the right from the Temple steps, which acknowledges the contemporary family ownership of the estate; the second is hidden at the bottom of the valley, where it was relocated in 1764. It was originally a Gibbs temple in the centre of the early garden and dedicated to the genius of Diana, but, once moved to its final site, was renamed with an archaic name and dedicated to an equally archaic mode of poetry, as the Fane of Pastoral Poetry. In retrospect, it seemed an apt gesture to signal that there was little need to identify the site as having any precise meaning, instead celebrating a far more picturesque corner of an already famous and busy garden. Still later at Stourhead, a River God and a sleeping Nymph adorn the grotto, to signal the source of the River Stour.

Emblematic gestures to ancient recognitions of *genius loci* became less and less significant or relevant in English gardens. A simple way to grasp both the lingering hold and the decline of such emblematic images is to compare Gilbert West's long poem on *Stowe* (1732) with William Gilpin's *Dialogue on Stowe* (1748), his first writing or 'observation' about places. West begins by appealing to the 'guardian Phoebus', and his rhetorical verses are explained in footnotes, which note, for example, how 'Statues of *Apollo*, the *Nine Muses*, and the *Liberal Arts* and Sciences [were] placed round the *Parterre*'; Virgil is cited in the Gibbs Building, and a reference to him is transcribed in a footnote; Naiads, 'laughing Dryads and Hymenaeals', Juno and Venus, all people the landscape, along with a host of 'instructive Emblems'.

Sixteen years later, Gilpin (now in prose) conducts two visitors around a landscape that is still increasingly studded with similar and even newly installed emblematic pieces, but where different responses by the visitors make it clear that Stowe is as much a site in which each visitor will have various responses to the constructed views; the picturesque underpins much of the visitors' progress when they pause, look and describe. Their reactions are – as befits a dialogue – often different (sensible of the other's point of view). One prefers to admire the artistry of the sculptures, not the imagery of 'Semi-Gods, or canonized Heroes'. The other is more attentive to the significance of local topographical views and meanings. In a subsequent prose version of 1751, where the dialogue form is displaced into a straightforward narrative of the visit, lengthy footnotes identify and explain, for example, the four statues in the Temple of Ancient Virtue, and one of them sees the ruins of Modern Virtue as a contrasting rebuke to the adjacent classical rotunda and its occupants. Yet one of the visitors is still tempted at the Temple of Contemplation to indulge his 'enthusiasm' for 'Genius of the Place', although his companion abandons him at that point. In all, Stowe is understood in 1751 more through *how* two visitors understand the landscape than how they identify visual or verbal items, let alone find meanings for presiding deities in the garden items or the garden as a whole. The reliance on a vocabulary of shared ideas and assumptions surrenders to an understanding of what this designed place signifies to each of them individually.

The underlying fracture between emblematic and expression is taken up explicitly by Thomas Whately's *Observations on Modern Gardening* (1770). His section 'On Character' of place (pp. 150ff) in fact makes further distinctions: beyond emblematic characters, there are also what he terms imitations and originals. An imitative character allows the representation *in a garden* of some scene that 'has been celebrated in description, or is familiar in idea, namely what we have already witnessed in print or paint'. But gardening, Whately writes, also 'aspires to more than imitation', in part by securing that when a design moves beyond representing something already in existence it asks of its visitor an 'original' experience, not requiring examination and explanation of what is encountered, but 'obvious at a glance, and instantaneously distinguished *by our feelings*' (my italics). Yet the 1790s still saw (at least in novels) an amazing, if frequently satirical, exposé of ways in which gardens would feature emblematic structures, with allusions to the way Ovid's *Metamorphoses* suggested random features with few purposeful gestures to a suitable *genius loci*.[12]

The next declension of the topic and what it points to is the emergence of the idea of 'spirit of place'. The word 'spirit' defines itself in part against the idea of body, a feeling not visible but assumed to be a guiding force of somebody's apprehension of place as of a person. It can be an ambiguous word – sometimes sensed, or recognized, in a site, sometimes a psychological or phenomenological response in the visitor, which can also be explained and may even become identified with the place itself, even serve as a metaphor for a site. Phenomenology is, at root, a finding of words to explain phenomena, and an appeal to 'spirit' allows a plausible formulation of meaning for places.

It was the phrase 'ruling spirit of place' that John Ruskin used when writing to his former Oxford tutor about his understanding of Chamonix in the Alps in the 1840s. It was an area that he loved; he would visit many times, even tried to purchase a property there, and spent hours sketching its glaciers, the Mer de Glace within its frenzied interior or from a distance, the pinnacles (*aiguilles*) of Mont Blanc and the meadows through which he climbed to sketch them. He learned to read its geology and sought to capture its forms in his watercolours. He researched local history, and also relied on his long-term guide, Joseph Marie Couttet, to inform him about the area. His evangelical upbringing saw all this material and natural world as evidence that a divine mind ruled there, and he would never have considered identifying its genius of place through the metaphor of pagan deities. 'The noblest scenery of that earth', he wrote while still an undergraduate, 'has been appointed to be the school . . . of minds.'[13]

Nor were the French Alps the only place where Ruskin found a 'ruling spirit': he did also in northern France (notably Rouen and Abbeville), Switzerland and its cities, and above all Venice and Verona. To the Venetian Count Zorzi he declared himself a 'foster-child of Venice', which has 'taught me all that I have rightly learned of the arts which are my joy'. In all these places he both drew and learned to hear the 'voice', as well as the shapes and forms of buildings that 'spoke' to him. Both were words he used to acknowledge how places communicated with him, a modern version of the rhetorical *prosopopoeia*, a figure of speech in which an imaginary, absent or deceased person is represented as speaking to its visitor about a particular place. A biblical example would be when Moses is instructed by God: 'Take off your sandals, for the spot on which you are standing is holy ground' (Exodus 3:5).

One who taught Ruskin to listen to those voices was Turner, from whom he learned to see how places were depicted, not so much to imitate the older artist's painterly technique, but to understand how he saw and represented different places. Without invoking the term *genius loci*, Ruskin came to term this 'Turnerian topography', where the skill of looking was matched with a poetic imagination: not just what a daguerreotype could depict, but what the imagination grasped as the essence of a specific scene and moment. The careful scientific approaches of Ruskin certainly sustained his examination of place and its potent meanings, yet it did not hamper his underlying recognition of its spirit.

The next declension of the term was to emphasize the empirical, even positivistic realities of places. The skills of geologist and geographer and the usefulness of photographic rather than drawn imagery came to dominate many approaches to understanding what a place meant. Avi Friedman is a late example of this approach in his book *The Nature of Place* (2011), subtitled 'A search for authenticity'. The title seems to be tautology, for a place has to be accessed through an examination of its character or 'nature', its materials, cultural uses and daily occurrences, which in its turn implies knowing about the place in question. The nature of a site can be itemized and analysed, but declines any supernatural or even spiritual significance in how a place is understood. Friedman gets to the heart of things via description and photography of the facts of buildings and housing (on which he has also written widely), of public sculpture, cooking, vistas, children's play equipment. These can be common-sense apprehensions of spirits of place that we often assume and absorb. There are some chapters that do also address the 'spirit of place': the Italian town of Assisi is shown by images of its basilica, and the 'heart' of an English city such as York is compared to five Continental squares or streets. But essentially the book moves easily among the tangible aspects of place and by comparisons with alternative locations. We know the authentic Amsterdam by its canals in comparison/contrast with those of Venice or Bruges; we know how to distinguish Tel Aviv from Toronto by what we see in each.

But Friedman's approach eschews any sense that *genius loci* might admit any idea beyond the finite and ontological. Although he works within the general framework of cultural geographers, he lacks the appeal and indeed fervour of a writer such as J. B. Jackson, whose writings on 'everyday America' provide a perspective on the landscape. Jackson writes of places 'with which we have daily contact . . . where we live and work and celebrate together'. It is that notion of contact and celebration that colours his regard for places, yet one that avoids any sentimental explanation. Jackson's example will prove a useful guide later to how we characterize each place we know or visit by understanding its vernacular architecture, how people live and behave there, their language, both old and contemporary history, and local customs.

Yet such larger, general assumptions about the meaning of places depend on the fact that each visitor, every traveller, will have his or her own specific means of entering into the nature of a place. Some consensus emerges in the accumulation of individual responses, and these may enable a spirit (or even a genius) of place to be communicated. But the peculiarity of individual responses is nonetheless based, first, on a person's desire to grapple with the specifics of a place (rather than ignore them, as some do), and, second, on the skill and willingness to observe, read and learn. Do we in fact simply accept what we see as common sense that needs no articulation, and therefore bother little with understanding the nature of a place? Is there anything like a spirit or genius to be identified there? When Pico Iyer writes in *A Beginner's Guide to Japan* (2019) that on 'departing a Japanese garden', he still hopes 'to carry some of its pruned silences out into the streets; [for] the only thing you need to leave behind is yourself', he is instinctively linking an actual garden with his own imaginative memories. These questions will sustain the remaining discussions here of painters, travel writers and poets, each of which – as to genre and to individual – explores the genius of places.

We approach so much understanding through what we see or read. A couple of modern responses to *genius loci* provide a succinct introit to this approach: Giuseppe di Lampedusa's novel *The Leopard* (1958) and, more recently, a short poem on a garden, also in Sicily, a country that Lampedusa's hero characterizes for its 'violence of landscape, cruelty of climate, continual tensions in everything' (p. 178), and where its people have 'a very strong collective memory' and 'think themselves perfect, their vanity stronger than their misery' (pp. 179, 183). In novel and poem, characters examine what special places might hold for them, and each registers some elegiac sense that a wonderful place and even a moment are tensed against the realities of current politics, both personal and public.

*Genius loci* matters greatly in *The Leopard*.[14] All novels work at varying degrees to make their settings meaningful for their characters and illuminating to their readers. But Lampedusa espoused a strong wish to present events in time and place from a uniquely personal and historical perspective – the world of the Risorgimento (the movement for the unification of Italy) and its impact on his aristocratic family in Sicily. Yet several remarks by the 'author' Lampedusa place those events in the years after the novel's end, including a bomb manufactured in Pittsburgh, Pennsylvania, that would demolish in 1943 the 'artfully twisted metalwork, fabrics and silken tapestries dyed with colour derived from earth and plant juices' in one of the Prince's country houses, which had hitherto been 'peaceful', 'unchanged', 'undisturbed by the noisy whirlwind of civil dissent' (pp. 225, 247–8, 63–6).

The novel is set in 1860, and its hero, Don Fabrizio Corbera, prince of Salina, faces crises political, social and personal as he navigates the upheavals of family, religion and national unity. It is factual, yet attentive, as the author wrote himself, to 'all the nuances, historical, social, economic and amatory' (p. xxix). But Lampedusa also makes wonderfully potent how that main character responds to the places where he loves and lives, not always with admiration, often with fear or dismay, but sustained by an acute sense that some sites mattered for how they spoke intimately to him, how they sustained his best and happiest moments. Anything that is important, authentic, is necessarily tensed against anything that is not essential.

The prince's estate at Donnafugata, with its decayed garden and the adjacent 'archaic and aromatic' countryside (p. 101), is the centre of the world he loves. Yet he finds it precarious, having a sense that such charged and mysterious places – actual as well as spiritual – have to be appreciated most when challenged or under threat. The prince's whole life is lived – sometimes literally – under divine surveillance and protection. As an amateur astronomer he gazes through powerful telescopes in his Palermo observatory, 'accustomed to scrutinizing limitless outer space and to probing vast inner abysses', 'absorbed in abstract calculations and the pursuit of the unreachable' (pp. 241 and 251). His invocation of the planet Venus, 'wrapped in her turban of autumn mist . . . always faithful, always waiting for Don Fabrizio on his early morning outings' (p. 238), seems mysteriously to visit him as he lies dying in a hotel room in Palermo after collapsing at the railway station following a distressing return from Naples.

But Earthly rites also sustain the prince: the 'Glorious and Sorrowful Mysteries' of the 'daily recital of the Rosary', the services and *Te Deum* greeting him on the family's arrival at Donnafugata, the visit (as a very privileged male) to a closed convent; then the mythological figures on the tiles of his palace in Palermo, the 'troops of Tritons and Dryads' on its ceilings 'bent on glorifying the House of Salina', with 'thunderous Jove and frowning Mars and languid

Venus' supporting the 'armorial shield of the Leopard'. The place breathes 'the life of the spirit in its most sublimated moments, [yet] moments that are most like death' (p. 41). 'Order and disorder' (p. 5) haunt him, like the brooch of a 'little Medusa with ruby eyes' pinned on his black cravat (p. 29).

It is the same ancient deities that people the prince's garden at Donnafugata, after another wearisome journey from Palermo – a 'nauseating place' (p. 54) – over three days of heat and discomfort:

An hour later [after hearing a funeral bell tolling in the Mother Church] he awoke refreshed and went down into the garden. The sun was already low and its rays, no longer overwhelming, were lighting amiably on the araucarias, the pines, the lusty ilexes which were the glory of the place. From the end of the main alley, sloping gently down between high laurel hedges framing anonymous busts of broken-nosed goddesses, could be heard the gentle drizzle of spray falling into the fountain of Amphitrite. He moved swiftly towards it, eager to see it again. The waters came spurting in minute jets, blown from shells of Tritons and Naiads, from noses of marine monsters, spattering and pattering on the greenish surface, bouncing and bubbling, wavering and quivering, dissolving into laughing little gurgles; from the whole fountain, the tepid water, the stones covered with velvety moss, emanated a promise of pleasure that would never turn to pain. Perched on an islet in the middle of the round basin, modelled by a crude but sensual hand, a vigorous smiling Neptune was embracing a willing Amphitrite; her navel, wet with spray and gleaming in the sun ... Don Fabrizio paused, gazed, remembered, regretted. He stood there a long while. (pp. 72–3)

The prince is himself not without his amorous encounters, so this place and its sexy garden deities please him, even when, as he would be obliged to do in confession, he regretted them. In a letter to his adopted son, Lampedusa wrote, 'I believe the whole [novel] is not without its elegiac poetry' (p. xii). *Genius loci* is rarely a place where sadness does not mingle with its pleasures.

Much later, in the ancient Greek city of Akrai in Sicily, a modern visitor stumbles on an old garden, where deities and memorials of a lost *genius loci* existed. Yet a recent owner has wilfully set out to destroy all the sculptural images, because when trespassers once came 'to see the gods/ Caved on his rocks', they stole his nectarines and figs, but then found they could not 'plunder/ The images of meaning'. So its owner,

> jealous of their interest,
> Or thinking that the deities
> Spoke more to strangers, so smashed the stone
> Beyond the malice of the weather.

This leaves the modern visitor, although 'hushed in the fecundity of grove,/ In the recovered *hortus* of bird/ And rabbit', unable 'to trace their lineaments – Presiding spirits of the place he loved'.[15] These are fictional confrontations with imagined places where the loss, regretted and yet inevitable, of a deep understanding of place – sometimes ancestral, sometimes personal – occurs.

The next chapter insists on approaches by which we can move beyond, or harness, personal and imaginative responses. One way, by a French geographer who has written about Japanese garden art, is to explore and then record phenomenological encounters with them. Another, more astringent French philosopher, refusing the belief that there is anything like *genus loci*, is forced back upon explaining that what we know about a place is derived from what we bring to it from our readings, association and knowledge.

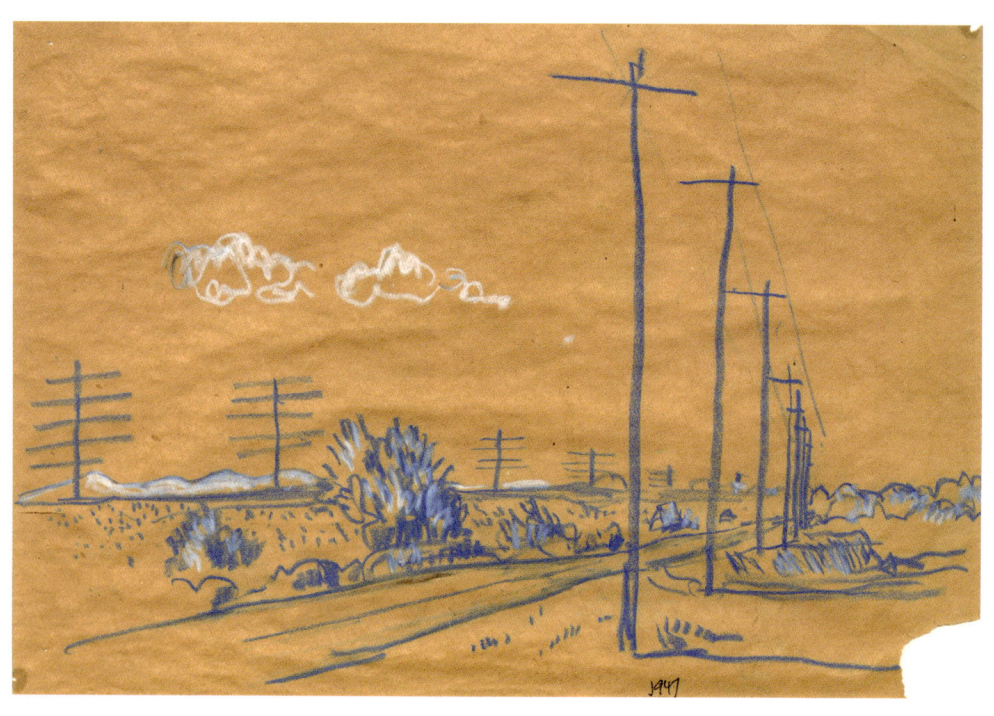

# TWO

# Does *Genius Loci* Exist?

To look is to see only a fraction of what one is looking at.
Even in the most vigilant eye, there is a blind spot.
Teju Cole, *Blind Spot* (2017)

In the 1990s the French philosopher Alain Roger challenged the very notion of *genius loci*, and invoked in support an essay by the geographer Augustin Berque. Their dialogue bears revisiting, not least because it suggests how the dispute, such as it was, may usefully be resolved. It is perhaps unsurprising that it was the French who became involved, given both the high-octane level of French theory and, perhaps more crucially, their interesting fascination with the word *lieu* (place) in French and its useful coinage of the phrase *haut lieu* (literally, high place). *Haut lieu* does not indicate altitude, but rather attitude, association, perspective, a sense of some essence; thus an understanding or assumption of some significance in a place, so drawing attention to how its special meaning is shared by observers.[1]

Yet their exchange, and other essays that followed in the wake of their arguments, notably by Michel Collot, has still not entirely put to rest the question as to whether *genius loci* exists and, if it does or could, how it is manifested, and in what form. Is it what users

9 J. B. Jackson, *Telegraph Poles*, 1947, drawing.

and visitors bring to places, for only then does such a *genius* 'exist'? Does it rely on the extensive enquiries in phenomenology that Berque and later some of Collot's sources invoke? If so, how does it get communicated? Philosophical propositions and arguments are extremely useful, but in front of an actual place, do we just weigh it in our minds, draw it or write it (since we are not intending physically to change the site)? More likely, and for most people, our senses experience the sounds and smells, the wind on our skin, the tactility of surfaces and materials. While I have profited from various readings, and presumably it is those that I can bring to a place where I want to grasp its particular character, is all I can do to write (or draw, maybe photograph) my sense of place, with the place itself unchanged? Good description of a place is always vital, but can that be sufficient? Perhaps it is only landscape architecture, or place-making, that can provide a visual and palpable version of a site for us to understand more fully. But that is to anticipate.

Roger's *Court traité du passage* (1997) denies any notion of 'le génie du lieu' (pp. 20ff). He does this, in essence, by mocking a Romantic passage in *La Colline inspirée* (1913) by Maurice Barrès, who entitled a section 'Il est des lieux où souffle l'esprit' (There are places where the spirit breathes). Barrès was discussing Mont Sainte-Victoire, a site that has elicited a considerable verbal and visual response. Barrès himself sees the place as pulling 'the soul out of its lethargy, [a site] enveloped in mystery, elected for all eternity as the seat of religious emotion'; an abrupt rock that, as one approaches through a valley of bloody territory ('*terres sanglantes*'), is 'bathed in Dantesque horror'. Barrès's paragraph ends with a sequence less overblown and more attentive to atmosphere that might appeal to those not overwhelmed by recollections of Dante: 'How often, by chance in a happy and moving day, have we not encountered the edges of a wood, a summit, a spring, a simple grassy space, that asks us to stop thinking and listen to something more profound than our heart! Silence! the gods are here.' That appeal depends largely on a sense that it is the individual who may respond to a variety of potent places, and even then by its appeal to silence over words. Barrès's gesture to 'the gods' is a fossil of an antiquated tradition.

Asking of Barrès whence came this power of place (*'puissance de ces lieux'*), Roger allows that, since he is himself not inclined to any mythical incantation, he must assume that these *'génies'* are neither natural nor supernatural, but cultural. They are created by the assumptions and habits of each visitor, hence an *'artialisation de la nature'*, a term he borrows from Michel de Montaigne that sees nature as being rendered and understood through a person's knowledge of many arts, including those of rhetoric. So we need to see *who* is viewing Sainte-Victoire, and what he or she may think, not just through the eyes of Dante, but also through those of Paul Cézanne, who painted a number of views there, just as Le Butte Montmartre is seen by Maurice Utrillo, or the port of Rouen by Albert Marquet. Therefore this Sainte-Victoire can only be Barrès's, supported by whatever he had read and seen.

Roger's invocation of remarks from Montaigne is intriguing. It sustains his own view that genius of place simply does not exist, and that endless commentary has confused the topic exceedingly: hence he borrows Montaigne's *'artialisation'* of nature. Yet he plays down the ironies of Montaigne. The sixteenth-century essayist was writing 'On some lines of Virgil' and arguing that endless commentary by 'schoolmen' had obscured the clarity of Virgil's words and ideas (Book III.5). He begins by writing that 'The more our moral thoughts are abundant and solid the more engrossing they are and oppressive.' He goes on to note that if he were in 'the trade of schoolmen', he would *'naturaliserois l'art autant comme ils artialisent la nature'*.[2]

*Artialisation* was a neologism, coined by Montaigne himself, and Roger (as later Berque, who changes it to *'artéfaction'*) finds modern French equivalents. But the original emphasis then and now on *art* can be ambiguous: it does not only or even mean the art of poetry or painting, but more generally the arts of rhetoric, which the schoolmen practised. Roger, in discussing Barrès's enthusiastic description of Mont Sainte-Victoire, in which he invokes bloody territories and Dante, might himself also have cited Cézanne, but it is less the artistic references than Barrès's excessive inflation in describing the natural site artificially, what Montaigne termed the 'oppression' of our moral thoughts. Barrès at the end does lower the rhetoric when describing how people might enjoy some moments of *genius loci*. Yet Montaigne slyly allows a plausible alternative. While he worries that nature can be smothered in words and rhetorical arts, he prefers a view of nature (that is, both human nature and topographical nature) that is more straightforward and simple, *'naturaliser'* (but not simplified).

There is, then, a perspective of nature that emerges *between* extensive enthusiasm and objective or positivist response. Maybe it can be understood as emerging between the imagination of the viewer – Blake's notion that 'all deities' can now reside only 'in the human breast' – and how it is in some fashion triggered by actual places and by what ordinary people can bring to moments and places of significance for them. It suggests what Clifford Geertz argued in *Local Knowledge* (2000) that an 'ethnology of thought', demonstrating 'the explanatory power of setting *sui generis* phenomena in echoing connection', can be an alternative.[3] This, though with some reservations, is what Berque offers. For in a footnote Roger cites Berque's essay the previous year in the journal *Le Débat* that had argued that *'En lui-même, le génie du lieu n'existe pas.'* But that misses a useful small and earlier book by Berque of 1990, the topic of which, *Médiance*, offers a slightly different perspective.

Genius of place may, indeed, not exist in itself (*'en lui-même'*), especially for a determined rationalist or ontologist. Yet Berque sees clearly that a simple, objective assessment of place can be insufficient, and therefore needs some account of *how* it is allowed to be plausible or meaningful to its viewers. That may involve words, or (although Berque does not do this) drawings/images, which could 'shape' a viewer's perception of the site depicted *à la* Montaigne. The core of his argument is set out in a table of definitions (p. 48).

Its first definition is of 'milieu'. A *lieu* is a specific place or site that is both physical and phenomenological. That is to say that *mi*lieu is the relation of a place to what a person is in the midst of, and that this *relationship* has to be stated, explained, not simply taken for granted, nor seen as being there '*en lui-même*'. Next, Berque defines 'environment' as a physical or factual *milieu* that includes artefacts, social relationships and nature, which are not necessarily original elements of that place, for indeed it is rare these days to encounter a place without such social infrastructure. Hence he draws on the term *médiance* (his third definition) as the *sens* (apprehension) of a milieu that at the same time attends (*tendence*) to its objectivity as well as its perception or reception by a human being. It draws on what in English might be a 'mediation', something that is shared, a middle place ('*médial: relative au milieu*', his next definition). The final two definitions, the base of his argument, are '*mésologie*' and '*trajection*': the first, the study of ambivalent *milieux*; the second, of a 'combination' of subjective and objective, physical and phenomenological, ecological and symbolic, which all together produce that *médiance*.

Now this may be – I must confess it was for me at first reading – a laborious way to confront the scepticism of Roger. It echoes Montaigne's distrust of making nature artificial rather than treating art naturally. Yet it does help. For it works to elucidate a clearly important fact: that our responses to place are composed both by what is there (obviously) and by what we bring to it, and so what we *say* about it (less obvious, yet dependent on our sense of that personal contribution). While not couched in a similar way, it recalls Ruskin's explanation of 'Turnerian Topography' in *Modern Painters*. It was clear that Turner did not paint something that was what a daguerreotype would have recorded, but brought his own instinct and imagination to bear on an otherwise carefully observed topography.[4]

Berque's small book is, as he says, a manifesto, not a treatise. This intriguing work invites more discussion of the crucial, if ambivalent, notion of *genius loci*, not that Berque himself uses the Latin term. For him 'nature' is central to any discussion of landscape and, since he is himself no designer, he ends by invoking two texts by those who were, both of which, as he puts it, 'support in certain ways my concerns': Antoine-Joseph Dézallier d'Argenville's *La Théorie et la pratique du jardinage* (1709; second edn 1713), and 'Notes on the Art of Gardens' by the eleventh-century Japanese author Tachibana no Toshitsuna. This move to cite designers obviously extends his argument beyond what non-designers might appreciate, but is useful as a means of showing what assumptions people who experience designed spaces as well as designers need to recognize.[5]

The passages cited from those two older texts argue for slightly different ways in which a landscape acquires meaning. The Frenchman asks that topography should be the basis on which the garden is planned and laid out, hence placing great emphasis on what is, a priori, existing and known; this involves – given the moment at which Dézallier d'Argenville wrote – some collective understanding of those means and what they signified and how they were used by a designer, for his readers then would probably have shared more assumptions about his remarks than would later generations. The Japanese writer makes the same point, but requires that the maker comprehend the 'principles', by examining all the possibilities that promote its character (*fuzai*), which requires and combines an understanding of the nature of the ground with the modes by which 'stones' (that is, garden-making) are raised, positioned and combined. Both garden theorists accept that their work is conditioned by what preceded it in space (topography) and in thinking (principles).

The difficulty I have here is how those who are *not* professional designers might respond. They would attend, albeit unconsciously, to the *numen* of places, and also tend to gather this in a process of moving through different environments; some of these places are clearly human-inflected (paths, woodland, lines of trees), but they are not 'designed'. Berque's quotations from Toshitsuna are, as he says, principles of creative practice ('*les principes de l'expression créatrice*'), and necessary to any designer. Yet they leave unexamined how the non-creator would respond in periods either when there was a general, more widely understood acceptance of design principles or when that shared knowledge and taste were less widespread.

Today, even for those who frequent gardens and parks and may be extremely knowledgeable, it is doubtful that what Toshitsuna expects of a designer is likely to hold for them (here I translate from Berque's French version of the original manuscript). First, a sense of place and a skill or taste for the physical and cultural milieu, with a profound grasp of the latent social order and the resources available; then a strict understanding of the ecosystem and a care not to disturb it in the course of construction; this place-making ultimately deploys a local site of social value, while ensuring that the new forms of garden are invented ('*un foyer nouveau du sense de ce milieu*'). Both those practitioners accept that their work, once made available to others, will imply or even somehow impose a sense of place on its users.

To see and register Berque's '*artéfaction*' (p. 124) will depend on how much visitors – not just designers – can see *making art* in their responses to gardens, parks and designed landscapes. That 'art' will be the result not only of designers, but of planners and the accidents of cultural circumstance that are folded into a site by an alert and imaginative architect and later by its users; this certainly must include J. B. Jackson's attention to the vernacular landscape, where (to cite Montaigne once more) 'beautiful minds' may handle and exploit languages of description and place. In its turn this may help with places consisting of more or less unmediated 'nature', places that are not specifically designed but that have emerged incrementally and culturally over the years.

It also requires a more informed audience, however, and in a world of much confusion over climate, ecosystems and social beliefs that knowledge is harder to come by. Writing or depicting landscape, both made and found, is crucial (*artéfaction*, indeed), but these interventions have to influence and permeate others' minds and imaginations precisely so that they might find the modern equivalent of the Roman *genius loci*. This would be the power and mystery of place, not simply the obvious places where we respond to images, captions and conspicuous signs of meanings (such as the *locus amoenus*, pleasant places in parks or gardens, 'lovesome things, god wot'), but also places in the much larger world outside them that are not only the result of landscape intervention. Underneath all *genius loci* is a remnant of the Roman wish to engage with religion-spiritual meaning. That still pertains, even in a world where such intimations take different forms.

THE FRENCH, as already noted, have been particularly attentive to ideas and approaches to place. So it is worth pursuing further the reflections of Roger and Berque. Michel Collot has for some time been leading a seminar in Paris on '*une géographie littéraire*', where he and his colleagues revisit and enlarge on a concept of how we respond by writing about place.[6] Collot invokes a serious body of writing on phenomenology, notably that produced by Maurice Merleau-Ponty, and he does move his enquiries into what may be written about specific landscapes, but the evidence, although widely researched, still rests on verbal accounts of landscape. That can be extremely useful, especially since Collot ransacks theoretic and philosophic writings to good effect. But what I miss is how this discussion determines, effects or affects our own vital experiences with landscape outside those Paris seminars. Those are necessarily conducted in words, but we must foreground places themselves – in images, photographs and how the writing itself may translate place into words and then into acknowledgements of a specific instance of *genius loci*. Such writing will seek to address how those witnesses of place can express or know their reactions, and it offers the chance to be less philosophical in responding to actual sites.

Roger and Berque saw *artialisation de la nature* as the clue to how we come to read meanings into places, because we bring our experiences of what we read and what we see in art to bear on that response, along with other instincts. Collot uses what he terms 'literary geography' as a means to explain and extend those readings. So it is not how we contribute to them, but how we explain their resonances; a sympathetic understanding of this literary geography will inevitably affect our reactions to place. It augments traditional geographical research that normally focuses on spatial analyses of natural and human phenomena, area studies of places and regions, studies of how humans occupy the land and shape it, and the Earth sciences: in all those, research has to be put into words (and images). Collot, writing some years after Roger and Berque, to whom he refers, is nevertheless interested in how landscapes are experienced, which effectively means finding ways to talk, write or draw those experiences. Even without much immersion in literary geography, we can become acquainted with how places have been articulated in writing, and bring to an understanding of place an arsenal of capabilities. Few people are without curiosity, and few without some skill to engage. Yet it is an aptitude that can and should be cultivated.

Collot has explored a variety of others' capabilities in that respect, and in his essay 'Le Génie des Lieux' he addresses the work of Michel Butor.[7] Butor's work is huge, much preoccupied with maps, as he himself confessed, and with travel on foot and by train, car and aeroplane, all of which become involved in what he writes;

he invented what he calls *Itérologie*, or 'word-travel'. His essay 'Génie' in *Alphabet d'un apprenti* (2003) declares that what distinguishes one place is its difference from others (no surprise there, surely); this involves not only one thing visited and thought about, but a mental comparison of one place with any other. But he continues by writing that what distinguishes one place from another is the particular effect it has *on us* ('*ce qui fait qu'il a sur notre esprit une emprise particulière*').[8] In *L'Horticulteur itinérant* (2004), Butor finds that the genius of place is determined less by the site or by how we look, than by the art of composition (both verbal and visual) that compares different places and adjudicates their elements (pp. 205–6). That – for Collot – confirms his sense that this is the essential Butor.

This is not a mere *description* of such explorations, but a place absorbed into the space of a page, a literary geography, where what matters are the writer's voice and mode of approach. This is clear from the *mis-en-page* of such books as Butor's *Étude pour une representation des États-Unis* (1962), where maps and text are presented in dialogue with each other. 'Certain places are particularly active,' Butor writes, 'revealing parts of ourselves that we do not know; that is what I term the "genius", relying on the Latin tradition. Often, it is because places are fashioned by humans, the materialization of a culture and period.'[9] Thus places 'speak' to us, because we 'read' their voices into their phenomena, and that elicits for us a sense of place: 'We know that a visit to Delphi reveals Apollo' (p. 202). Honoré de Balzac, likewise, is quoted to the effect that 'Landscape holds ideas that make us think' (p. 17), but it is surely we who extract those ideas, nor are 'ideas' the only thing to extract. Yet these intimations of place are, Butor insists, rarely personal, but rather proceed from the words of others (p. 207), which articulate what landscape 'thinks'. Landscape is more than an object approached from outside; it is a site where a close relationship is established between it and humans, and that needs its own history

– what Fernand Braudel wanted to call a *géohistoire*, for history has to be spoken or written as well as visited.[10]

Collot seems to argue for a much more engaged understanding of place than Berque's ascription of it to phenomenology. Collot bases much of his writing on famous works of phenomenology by Edmund Husserl, Martin Heidegger and Merleau-Ponty; but he too is less concerned to confront actual sites and their *genius loci* head on. And that returns us to landscapes. Another of his books, *La Pensée-paysage* of 2011, argues for thoughts to be made palpable in word as well as image; so he provides illustrations of paintings (many abstract), photographs and examples of land art, where place and captions intersect. He has also published a series of prose poems, which will be taken up in Chapter Five.

Land art has been a useful way to understand landscape architecture, partly because its medium is landscape itself, a much more direct reception of some *genius loci*.[11] It can be photographed, of course, and explained or drawn, which is how it is often revealed, since some sites are hard to reach. I have never been to Robert Smithson's *Spiral Jetty* (1970), but my descent once into Michael Heizer's *Double Negative* (1969–70; illus. 10), through the scattered detritus of its fallen walls, gave me a strong sense of how the space had been excavated and this moment of the desert revealed. Such experiences can be useful in responding to those that are not as 'extreme' as Heizer's, for they teach a visceral response. However, much land art lacks any sense of inhabitation, out of which deep intimacy with a place and some *genius loci* may emerge; that would be an involvement that I do not take from most land artists, however much I like their work.

One of the most interesting attempts to understand what a place means comes in J. B. Jackson's exploration of vernacular or non-elite places. This is partly because he avoids what Montaigne had termed '*artialisent de la nature*', but also because in his chosen sites he practises an ethnography of thought and, like Geertz,

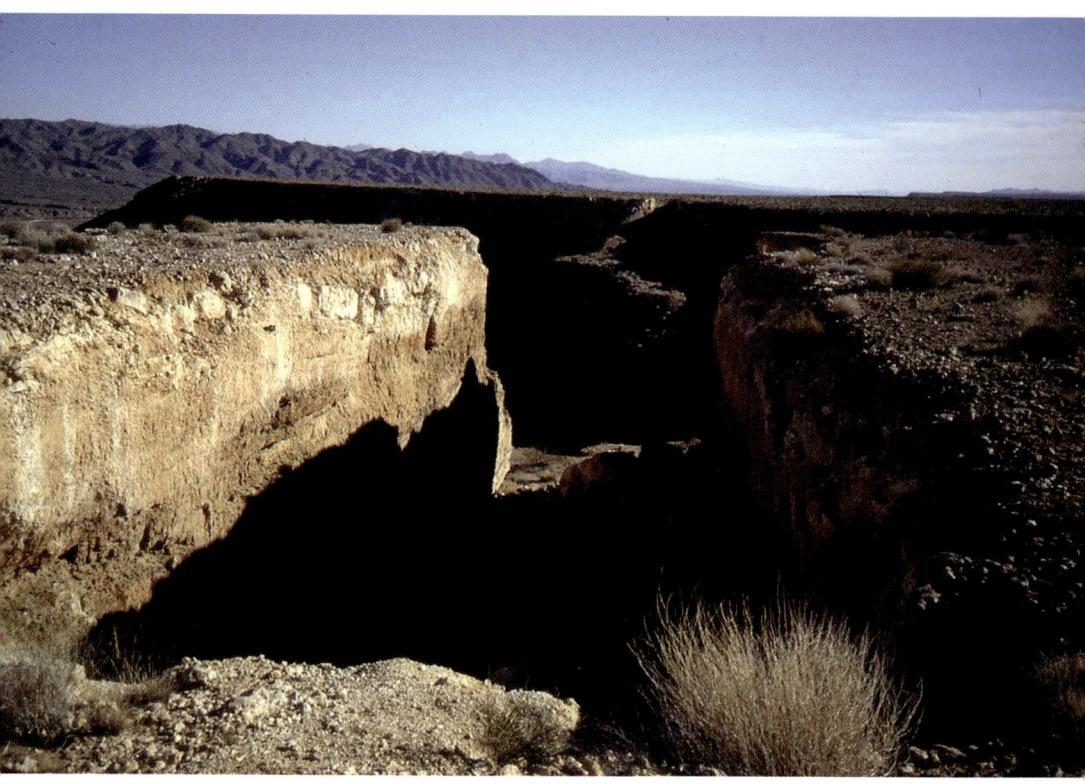

10 Michael Heizer, *Double Negative*, 1969–70, earthwork.

attends passionately to the *sui generis* of phenomena. In every volume of his writings, I have been struck by his local, particularizing perspective: not for him the writing of whole books, but rather that of individual essays that tackle specific places and ideas. That is not to say that he is without consistent tone and approach, even to the extent of a thread of conservative emphases that Helen Lefkowitz Horowitz confronts forthrightly in her recent book.[12] But the care and firmness of his looking are found wherever he visits.

This new book on Jackson explains how he developed his skill as a military observer in Hürtgen Forest, on the border between Germany and Belgium, after the D-Day landings in 1944. There he inspected landscapes, dwellings and environments, and learned to interpret photographs that the military needed to understand as they advanced; it was an ethology of 'landscape reconnaissance' that he would draw on later. He told an interviewer in 1988, 'I see things very clearly, and I rely on what I see . . . And I see things that other people don't see, and I call their attention to it.' It was, he wrote, 'History made visible' (*Traces*, p. 1).

Jackson's writings are invaluable and much admired, despite too much *artialisation* of place by other writers. Indeed, he could remark that 'perhaps we are too remote from nature' (*Traces*, p. 40), and refused to distance himself behind a language that was anything but precise and clear. It was his steady gaze that was essential. Wallace Stevens calls this instinct a 'vulgate of experience'. It was conveyed first in the journal, *Landscape*, that Jackson founded in 1951, in his drawings (illus. 9),[13] and in the clear, sometimes witty, dry essays gathered in a variety of collections that he published or were edited by others, including *Landscape in Sight: J. B. Jackson's America* (1997) by Helen Lefkowitz Horowitz.

What is needed here is to grasp how what Jackson saw helped him to discern and explain a *genius loci Americanus*. Not that he relied on the Latin phrase, except to note that a 'sense of place' was 'a much used expression . . . that seems to mean very little . . . an awkward and ambiguous modern translation of the Latin term *genius loci*'.[14] Yet he saw, rightly, that the Roman emphasis on spaces, structures or whole communities 'derived much of its unique quality from the presence or guardianship of a supernatural spirit. The visitor and the inhabitants were always aware of that benign presence and paid reverence to it on many occasions. The phrase implied celebration or ritual, and the location itself acquired a special status.'

But modern culture can reject any sense of supernatural or divine presence (*vide* Roger). Hence Jackson's insistence that place also had to be situated *in time*, which for much of his writings meant *today*. The majority of his essays are dedicated to details of place, and *Discovering the Vernacular Landscape* (1984) begins with such topics as roads, boundaries, forests, mobility, habitat and habit; a section on 'spaces sacred and profane' addresses such civil spaces as farming, where the farmer has been noble and independent since the days of Rome. Yet, while he cites Ruskin on the 'order, symmetry, and fruitfulness' of a garden, Jackson is quick to note how 'every society organizes space in political terms', and that the Southern farmer today does not conform to those ancient ideas: 'each age, each society develops its own unique kind of spatial organization.' What Jackson brought to places was indeed a deep yet secular awe for his own modern, more likely vernacular, forms of celebration and ritual.

In Jackson's collection *The Necessity for Ruins* (1980), a title that seems to invite our attention and need to revisit and revere fragments of the past, the title essay is sceptical of what such reverence would mean; he is puzzled by what the contemporary American scene offers by way of 'a historical object or a monument' and proceeds to survey and catalogue his own instinct for 'preservation'. Not everyone would assent, but the sureness of argument and the unflinching ordinariness of vision are remarkable.

Jackson contrasts two imagined monuments: on the one hand, a formal marble monument to 'President X', along with inscriptions, parades, singing of the national anthem and a model village that honours that president; on the other, the town of Centerville that decided to celebrate the arrival of the first locomotive, an Indian raid of 1847 and a new senior housing project, even encouraging the menfolk to grow beards. It becomes the 'Historical Pioneer Village'. The contrast is lovingly exaggerated, and some might find acceptable either mode of commemorating the past. But for Jackson, to re-enact the past, to reconstruct environments, to live in a 'historical, theatrical make-believe' will mean that history ceases to exist. So other essays in his volume take up 'The Discovery of the Street', 'The Domestication of the Garage' and a reconsideration of what a 'sacred grove' could be in America.

Jackson's concern was always landscape (see the collection *Landscapes*, 1979), yet these were composed of places, most often vernacular, whose beauty and fascination were derived from human presence and human intervention. A locality could establish a distinctive feel or meaning within a larger landscape – at once as large as America, as small as the suburb or the street. He is therefore a model, something of a beacon to shine on landscape places. Yet he risks being submerged in others' *'artialisation'*, rather than the naturalizing of nature. That will still require articulation – 'I gotta use words when I talk to ye.'

The following chapters, then, will take up some of the lessons that Jackson offers, by pursuing how painters, poets and travel writers have found different ways to identify what I still want to call – *pace* Jackson – *genius loci*. To lean once again on another distinguished French poet and writer, Yves Bonnefoy, his *Entretiens sur la poésie* (1990) proposes that *'le lieu est le miroir où la verité humaine peut . . . apparaître.'*[15] It is this 'appearing' that will be traced in the next chapters, before we finally embark on what landscape designers themselves have achieved, not only by doing a good job, but by making it easier for those who visit to grasp the secrets of the making of places that are not designed.

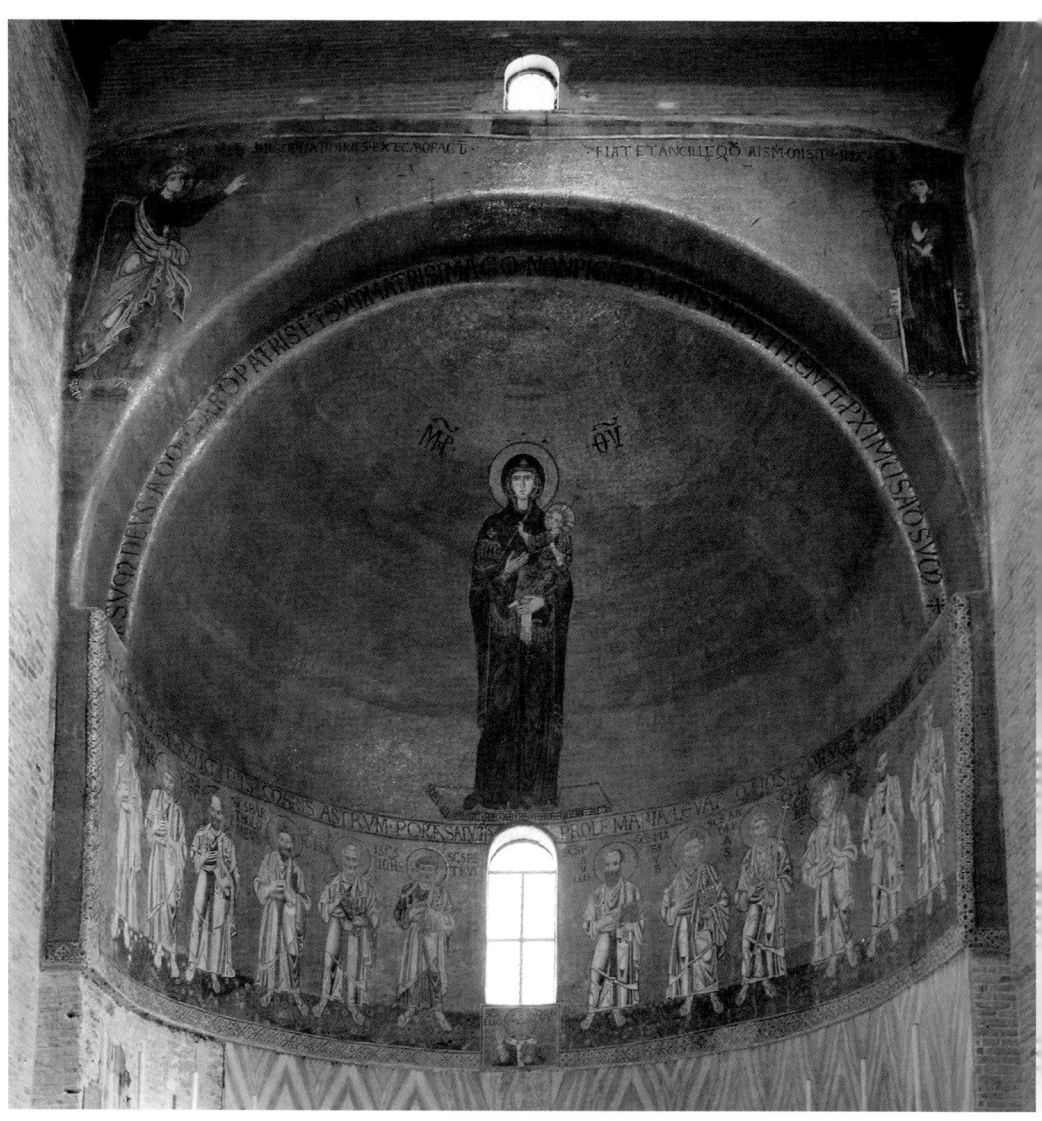

# THREE

# Torcello and the Expression of Place

If the stranger would learn in what spirit it was that the dominion of Venice was begun . . . let him ascend the tier of stern ledges that sweep around the altar of Torcello.

John Ruskin

John Ruskin wrote at great length (38 volumes in the Library Edition of his works), but he also drew, with skill and imagination, and he recognized how the paintings of Turner celebrated and conveyed a topography beyond words (beyond what that painter's titles or catalogue entries proposed for viewers of the paintings). But what Ruskin wrote about place falls short of some of his own graphic efforts to understand its significance for himself, and for our larger understanding of place. So when, maybe in 1858, he drew 'Grutli, Uri Rotstock from Lake Lucerne' (illus. 12), he allowed his understanding of Switzerland, its geology and its sublimity to be captured in an arresting image. He also knew how much Turner had painted in this area, and Ruskin had on several visits sought his own way of delineating spirit of place there. In a sketchbook that he later gave to the American writer and art historian Charles Eliot Norton, he made at least fifty drawings of Lucerne and its surroundings, each from the desire to capture the fresh essence of a place that he had learned – for

11 Apse mosaic of the Madonna and Child in the basilica of Santa Maria Assunta, Torcello.

himself and through Turner – to delight in: 'I am beginning to understand this lake for the first time, never before having been able to examine it bit by bit.'[1]

An earlier encounter with place, relying on both words and some images, came with Ruskin's interest in early Venetian sites, as he studied and drew materials for the three volumes of his *The Stones of Venice*. Among them is an early drawing made on the lagoon island of Torcello (illus. 13). This was where, it was said, during the fifth century refugees from barbarian invasions on the mainland (*terrafirma*) sought peace and the chance to flourish. Torcello eventually boasted dozens of churches, bridges and palaces. But its life and culture eventually shifted to sites with more scope to expand, such as the island of Murano and what is now Venice. On the latter's cluster of islands, steadily amplified with sandbanks and dredged infill, was established what Ruskin called the 'Glorious City in the Sea', admired throughout Europe and the Near East for its famed republic, although later

12 John Ruskin, 'Grutli, Uri Rotstock from Lake Lucerne', *c.* 1858, watercolour.

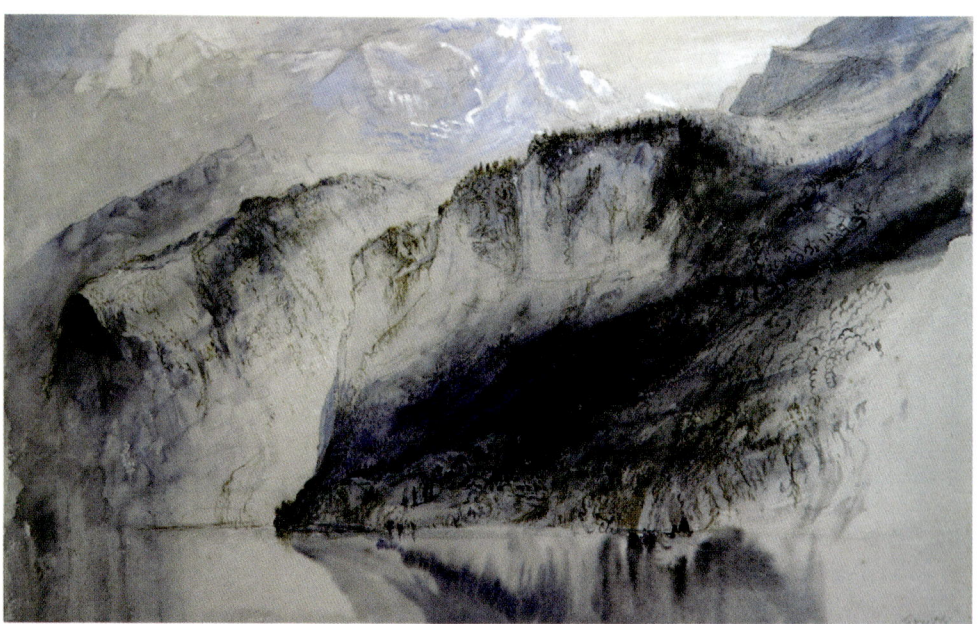

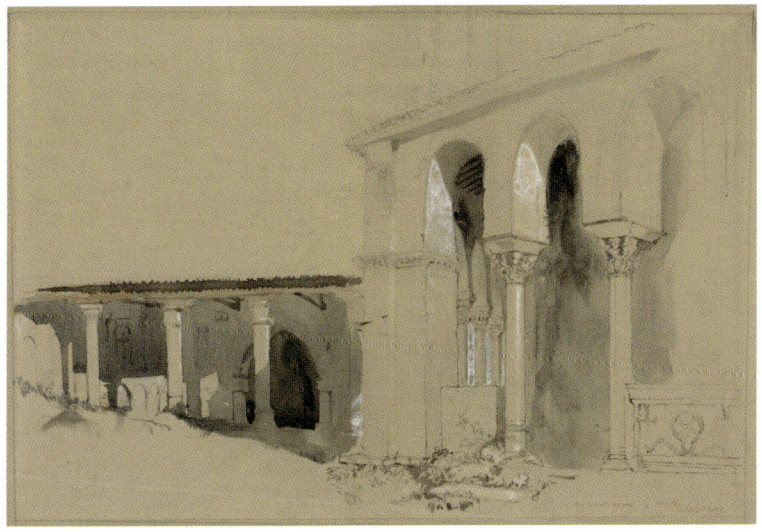

13 John Ruskin, drawing of the little campo with two churches on Torcello, 1850.

succumbing to invasion by Austrians, then the French, and today hordes of tourists.

Torcello itself remains relatively quiet and isolated, with some cultivated fields, sluggish canals, early palaces – elegant, if a touch forlorn – and two churches, with the *campanile* of its basilica (formerly cathedral) rising above the marshes. The island can be reached by public *vaporetto* for those clever enough to know that it is worth taking time to leave Venice (where too many spend but a day). But even for those visitors who stay longer, Torcello does not offer the plethora of information, descriptions and judgements that the guidebooks provide on Venice itself.

Once landed at Torcello, we follow a path beside a narrow canal towards a small square, with groups of buildings, including the basilica and a few palaces, and (since 1934) the Locanda Cipriani, where spending a night allows the chance of a combination of fine eating and the opportunity to be, as it were, alone in this old place of solitude and silence. Yet the cathedral and the adjacent church of Santa Fosca are rightly what first claim attention, and they were sketched by Ruskin in 1850. What he drew of them is wonderfully attentive to the ambience of these churches: their entrances, with steps down into the floor of the basilica; his careful attention to the capitals of Santa Fosca; the shadows; the weeds in the square; and the surrounding emptiness of the sheet of paper.

Ruskin had first been there five years earlier, in September, when he wrote to his father, 'I have been over to Torcello, a decent distance, but most interesting church, about the best preserved of its age – 8 or 900 – that I have seen, but in a horrible marsh . . . black & comfortless.'² He would write an extended chapter on it in the second volume of *The Stones of Venice*. It may be said to be one of the best, if personal, written responses to its *genius loci*, although the drawing of 1850 achieves the same with remarkable and suggestive ease.

Despite his Evangelical upbringing, the Catholic basilica moved Ruskin, for there he encountered a striking instance of Venetian purity and justice, the 'spirit' in which 'the dominion of Venice' was begun. There he found the nave's 'luminous shafts', and mosaics that have 'no artificial shadows . . . nor dark colours . . . all is fair and bright, and intended evidently to be regarded in hopefulness, and not with terror'. It was this ancient scene that he compared harshly with the modern worshippers and the building's messy, contemporary decorations ('dirty hangings' and 'dim pictures on warped and wasting canvas').

The chapter on Torcello comes early in the second volume, and, like his approach to Venice itself by gondola at the end of the first volume, the visitor will have arrived in Torcello after another journey across the lagoon, a supreme and carefully orchestrated movement towards an inevitable climax. Approaches often determine how we respond to places in retrospect, whether identified beforehand or stumbled on by chance. From a survey of the shapeless mounds amid the weeds and stagnant pools of the salt morass, Ruskin imagines ascending the tower of the former cathedral and surveying all points of the compass, at which he can behold the city to the west and begin to compare 'Mother and daughter . . . both in their widowhood, Torcello, and Venice'.[3]

A photograph by Carlo Naya, made some thirty years after Ruskin's first visit, shows the approach along the path beside the small canal that present-day visitors still use; a boat is being rowed towards the little square where the tower rises high. Another image, from about 1870, shows that small, grassy piazza, with the churches behind and a group of six inhabitants, one sitting on a chair, others pulling a cartload of hay (illus. 14).[4]

Having taken his reader to that 'rude brick campanile' of the basilica that rises over 'a waste of wild sea moor, of a lurid ashen grey', Ruskin turns to an arcade of delicate Greek marble, its capitals enriched with delicate sculpture, on the octagonal church of Santa Fosca, although it strikes the visitor, he says, as but a lowly cattle shed. The square where both churches are set is rendered as a pastoral scene, where 'cattle are feeding' and 'the mower's scythe' has swept the grass from the 'chief street' of this early city; the scent of mown grass is tellingly 'the only incense that fills the temple of

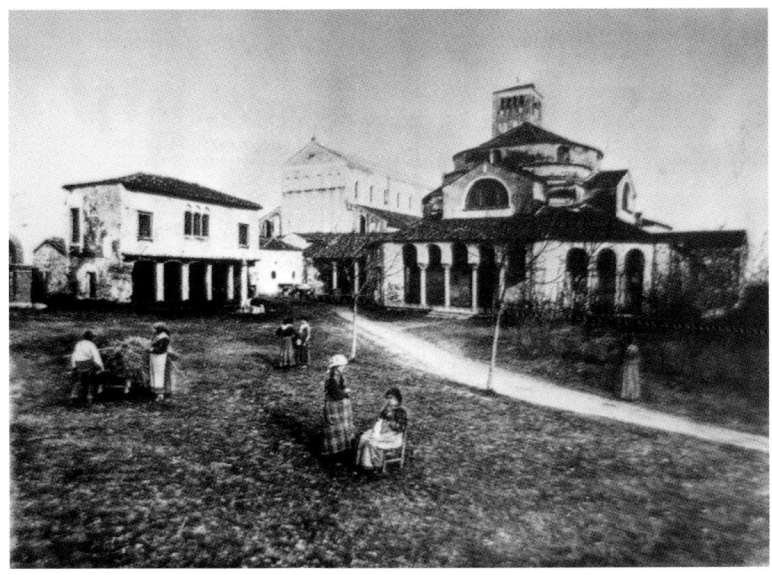

14  Naya Studio, gelatin print of churches in the square at Torcello, *c.* 1870.

55

their ancient virtue'. Otherwise: no people, just desolation, urban remains absorbed into nature, with 'scarcely [a] traceable footpath', silence and the smell of hay. The basilica itself is devoid of exterior ornamentation, save for carvings and some sculpture, and massive stone shutters with 'hung rings of stone, which answer the double purpose of stanchions and brackets'. It seems a 'refuge from Alpine storm [rather] than the cathedral of a [once] populous city'. Ruskin was beginning to learn for the first time something about this place that struck him as important.

Within, the shafts of white marble that line the nave of the basilica are 'among the best I have seen, as examples of perfectly calculated effect from every touch of the chisel'; each of them is different, and the various capitals 'graceful [and] fanciful'. What strikes him as well, as it does most visitors, is the pair of mosaics, one in the apse above the altar, the other on the west wall of the nave. In the golden apse behind the stepped circle of seats is a large, elongated image of a mourning Madonna holding her baby (illus. 11). A huge tear moves down her cheek as she points with the fingers of her right hand to Jesus in her arms, and gazes towards a huge, compartmentalized, intricate image of the Last Judgement that dominates the far end of the nave. She raises her hands to bless those who are saved or lost, the latter occupying only a small section at the bottom right of the image.

Ruskin writes that a Protestant might sorrow at the vain act of the Virgin's intercession, but that this 'ought not to blind him to the earnestness and singleness of the faith with which these men sought their sea solitudes'. This detailed and celebratory introit is then challenged by a reader who had not expected this 'mute language of early Christianity' in the architecture and mosaics, nor known how to 'read' the 'Gothic leafage springing into new life' on the capitals. Ruskin presents it as a challenge to his reader, but it was in essence the challenge that he felt himself and seems to have partly accepted.

In Torcello, Ruskin confronts a place where the austerity and simplicity of the basilica disarm what might have been a more hostile response to a Catholicism that he was brought up to suspect. He answers that challenge himself with a series of carefully detailed examinations of the church architecture, including plans and sketches of its capitals, from which he draws the conclusions that sustain his sense of the place's mystery and importance. He refuses to accept a description of the capitals as 'indifferently imitated from the Corinthian', and by exploring the shape and format of their acanthus leaves arrives at a more nuanced understanding of how the sculptor understood the true nature of their forms and drew each differently.

Ruskin's is undoubtedly a personal response to Torcello. That his writing declares more about himself, his own education and his thinking at the time of his visit than about the site is true, but it is hard to see how any complete and general response to it can be achieved without amalgamating or stockpiling a conspectus of other personal reactions. It is hard to achieve that consensus outside the covers of a considerable and authoritative guidebook that provides visitors with an arsenal of information and perhaps others' reactions – alternative understandings of this austere basilica and especially its striking mosaics.

For example, the Virgin Hodegetria, as she is rightly to be called, is not herself an intercessor, but by pointing to her son she acknowledges *his* role in saving souls. Christ's adult portrait at the summit of the Last Judgement fresco makes this clear, as he holds a Cross and helps those he has saved to clamber towards him. This interpretation, rather than Ruskin's more Protestant commentary, suggests a different approach to the way this basilica explains and asks its visitors to understand Christian ideas.

Attempts to probe how and why *genius loci* has been understood are, as Alain Roger argued, something that each of us brings to such an encounter. His explanation is that by a process of *artialisation* we seek to understand the meaning of places. We need to know how to read the frescoes, or be told how to do that – there in the nave, or because we already know the theology. If we grasp the large significance of the two images, we have entered into a far more nuanced understanding. But this is still wholly dependent on what individuals can bring to a place like this.

Ruskin's account of Torcello, as his lines in our epigraph make clear, was his way of helping a 'stranger' learn what the spirit was that inspired the early Venetian settlements. A later 'stranger', the American Henry James, was equally attentive to showing how a visitor might learn from Torcello, and he too saw the place as 'the mother-city of Venice'.[5] James is keenly aware of its decay (a 'case of unheeded collapse') and its urchins (the 'handsomest little brats in the world'). His main interest, however, is in the reminiscences of the great Venetian colourists, for he moves from Veronese to praising 'the perfect bath of light' in Torcello, so that 'I couldn't get rid of a fancy that we were cleaving the upper atmosphere on some hurrying cloud-skiff . . . there is nothing but the light to see.' And then the 'delicious stillness . . . I remember none so subtly audible save that of the Roman Campagna.' But what had taken Ruskin's eye in the cathedral was for James – although a building 'admirably primitive and curious', an interior 'rich in grimly mystical mosaics', with 'precious fragments in the pavement'– something to be puzzled by: the 'stony stare' of the Apostles in the apse seemingly 'wait vainly for some visible revival of primitive orthodoxy, and one may well wonder whether it finds much beguilement in the idly-gazing troops of Western heretics – passionless even in their heresy'. The contrast with Ruskin (whose interest in Venetian painting James notes elsewhere in his text) is acute and pointed. One wonders whether this American 'stranger' had read the chapter on Torcello in *The Stones of Venice* and signalled, ever so mildly and perhaps ironically, his distance from his English predecessor.

These days Torcello has survived with a little more life (and tourism) than Ruskin or James observed, and many in the basilica will doubtless be confronted with the same conflicts. But it is still powerful, the images of mosaic and architecture redolent of a belief that communicates itself, even if it is neither shared nor understood. What seems crucial here is how the aura of these two churches informs the whole site, whether the visitor climbs the tower, as Ruskin presumably did, or wanders into the fields and edges of the lagoon. Whether or not visitors know their Ruskin (probably not), the whole place is coloured in the way that Montaigne had seen as nature '*artialisée*', with the architecture, the mosaics and the explanations of them contributing a crucial influential commentary on the island itself. Above all, we recognize at Torcello many reasons for the expectations built up during the hour-long voyage across the lagoon, and the inevitable contrast between it and Venice itself.

Comparisons are frequently a key factor in grasping the significance of a specific place, as well as a sense of how to approach it, for the destination is often a place that we intuit as different from wherever we have come from. But what happens at Torcello, both in actuality and in imagination, is also important, as the close encounter with one element, the basilica, is transferred to a much larger understanding of its place in the landscape. This depends much on Ruskin's rhetorical skill, moving from examination of details – the pulpit in the basilica, for example – to a comparison of other such churches elsewhere and thence to a new appreciation of the simplicity and power of the place as he imagines it. The spirit of place at Torcello, he argues, is better understood by considering the architecture of the church and its landscape setting, 'the peculiar expression of the building', than by asking the 'stranger' to consider other aspects of Venetian culture – its wealth, arsenals, pageantry, palaces and senates' archives.

TORCELLO IS ALSO a suitable site in which to try and understand the significance of such encounters with its location in a larger landscape. Some eleven years after Ruskin's first visit, and six after he drew its churches, he composed the sixteen-page chapter on 'Turnerian Topography' in the fourth volume of *Modern Painters* (1856). And while the Turner paintings he was considering did not include any of Torcello (which in fact Turner never painted), the island is still a good example of how Ruskin proceeded with understanding place.

Like Turner, Ruskin was a dedicated topographer, concerned first with careful exploration, looking and description (written, drawn and eventually photographed, for he was an eager user of the new daguerreotype). He proceeds from discussing a 'Turnerian Picturesque' in the previous chapter to moving beyond 'the narrow enjoyment of outward forms'. While a Turnerian topography may sometimes be based on what a daguerreotype captures ('a mere copy of any given scene'), it requires not only the sympathy of an artist but care in finding a topic, or the 'character' of a site to work with, particularly 'some spot in itself notable by association'. This in its turn relies, most importantly, on memories both historical and personal. The latter include, obviously, direct contact with a site – exploring it, and doing so, if possible, on many occasions – but other responses in descriptions, images or archival references will shape what visitors find.

It was this that brought to a head Ruskin's understanding of a topographical imagination, when he sought out one of the sites on the alpine Pass of Faido that Turner had painted several times. He realized that Turner had not copied exactly what was there in front of him, 'giving not the actual facts . . . but the impression it made on his mind'; in this case, that memory was of the long descent through the mountains to the site, and indeed of the moment when the image was taken: 'the confused stones, which

15, 16 John Ruskin, sketches of the site of Faido as he found it and of how Turner drew it, from *Modern Painters*, vol. IV (1856).

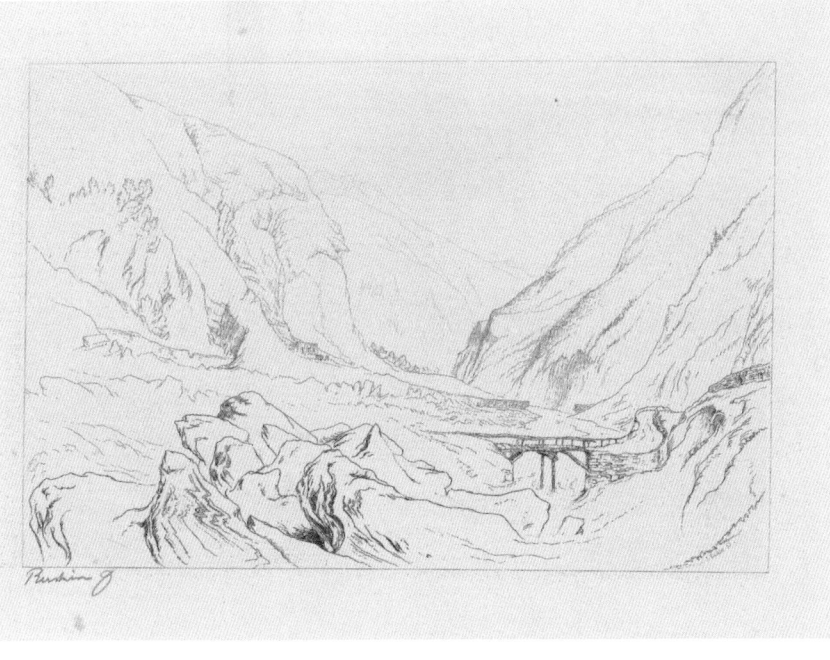

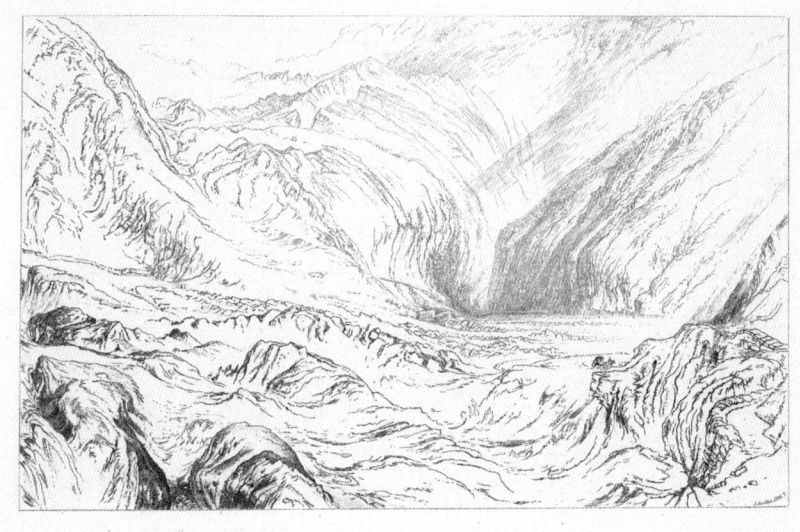

by themselves would be without any claim upon [the unprepared spectator], become exponents of the fury of the river by which he has journeyed all day long' (illus. 15, 16).

Returning from this later essay on topography in *Modern Painters* to the Torcello chapter in *The Stones of Venice*, a reader can see how actual physical sensations – walking, looking, hearing, smelling – contribute to what Ruskin calls a 'kind of mental chemistry', which is perhaps one of the more useful ways to describe how a place presents itself. *Genius loci* (a phrase Ruskin never uses, but that is an instinct throughout his explorations) requires steady looking and thence gives 'the far higher and deeper truth of mental vision'. It is selective of its elements, and maybe not what others would bring to bear on it, but it is always the personal reception of place that carries weight.

Whenever a place is described or drawn or photographed, it is this individual response that sustained it, and indeed would have sustained the experience before any attempt to record it. In the next three essays we explore accounts by painters, poets and travel writers in search of ways to articulate their encounters with specific places, some that mattered deeply to them, some encountered by chance, some the result of a determination to get the hang of a place that others had tried to explain.

# FOUR

# Places: J.M.W. Turner, Paul and John Nash

Turner . . . has an eye for that which, for want of a better name, we may call the mystery of a scene.

Henry James

There are places . . . whose relationship of parts creates a mystery, an enchantment, which cannot be analysed.

Paul Nash[1]

There are many artists whose work focuses on the spirit or expression of place. But these three painters – of landscape mainly – explored ways to make palpable what they saw in the world, not simply what the place itself declared, but what the artists saw at the moment (or moments) of their encounter, and also how it could be made available to their audiences. In a review of early English artists where Paul Nash sought to situate himself, he told the art historian Herbert Read how early landscapes had 'an imprisoned spirt':

this spirit is the source, the motive power which animates [English] art . . . if I were asked to describe this spirit I would say it is of the land; *genius loci* is indeed almost its conception. If its expression could be designated I would say it is almost entirely lyrical. Further, I dare not go except to recount history and to state my faith.[2]

John Nash shared much of his elder brother's conception of *genius loci*, but Paul's emphasis on the lyrical does not entirely address John's attention to what a place means. John was emphatically drawn to places in their own right (he drew widely within England and even Scotland), but he seems less concerned to stress their numinous qualities, instead valuing the very forms of landscapes, sometimes seeing topography a touch naively, but allowing that instinct to communicate the way he himself saw a site. He was undoubtedly influenced by Paul, but the poet Gordon Bottomley, during his long correspondence with the elder Nash, also noted how much he valued John's landscapes: he told his correspondent that the younger brother has 'taken to landscape seriously', but also thought that 'he does not feel the romance and poetry of land-scape as much as you'; yet his 'vivid actuality promises . . . an intense vein of poetry.'[3]

All three artists' emphasis on landscape is both personal and historical in the appeal to notions of *genius loci* in early landscape painters, but equally different in how that was announced. They steered viewers towards their own vision of place by painterly modes of presentation, but also, for Turner and Paul Nash, with words. Turner did this elaborately with titles and elaborate quota-tions from others (including Mark Akenside), or with his own verses about places and their meanings.[4] While John's titles seem predisposed to identify a place and time, Paul gave in his titles a clue to how the images might be understood. In 1936 he began a prose memoir entitled *Genius Loci*, which exactly suited his own fervent interest in how places spoke to him. In a long paragraph there he reflected that there are 'places . . . whose relationship of parts creates a mystery, an enchantment, which cannot be ana-lysed.'[5] He later changed the title of the memoir to *Outline* (the work was posthumously published by Faber in 1949, and reissued in 1988 and again in 2016). The new title hints perhaps at his own 'bounding line' (a phrase he took from William Blake); its sometimes quasi-surreal, or cubic, style aims to reveal how places are formed, then outlined, by this artist. The text of *Outline* contains many stabs at describing what his paintings wanted to achieve in respect of others' work, which is what his friend Gordon Bottomley admired: 'your Idea-Of-Landscape [is] a difficult thing to do, and you have netted its subtleties perfectly.'[6] Yet, however much words may direct their viewers towards the images themselves, it was still the painterly mode that must matter with visual artists, when each was concerned with his own understanding and representation of places.

ALTHOUGH TURNER'S WORK has been studied endlessly, what concerns my quest for his explorations of *genius loci* in how we use 'poetry' (see Nash's 'lyrical') as a resource and critical term – not simply verses as such, but beyond the prose of documentation or depiction – is a new version and vision of topography that is poetic. Turner and Nash are by no means alike, except that each discovered different, yet still painterly, ways to isolate and convey the poetry of landscape. That is my topic here.[7]

When Ruskin explained to Turner that 'the worst of his pictures was that one could never see enough of them,' the artist responded with 'That's part of their quality.' When Turner sold a painting to a New Yorker, the artist asked his buyer whether he liked it; the owner replied that he thought it 'indistinct', to which the artist said, 'indistinctness is my forte.' That term, as James wrote in our epigraph, has to serve 'for want of a better word'. But Nash would later achieve alternative painterly ways ('relationship of parts') for describing indistinctness, which Roger Cardinal has called the 'hidden qualities of natural things'.[8]

Turner, as Nash would do, had his roots in picturesque topography, Romantic poetry and the need or wish to attach literary glosses to his paintings through an often lengthy title or catalogue entry.[9] These were often taken by Turner from major poets such as John Milton or James Thomson, where, as Jack Lindsay writes, a new 'dynamic' emerged between 'an extreme point of comprehensive revelation and yet [one] . . . essentially transient', a dynamism where words express human emotions (*Sunset Ship*, p. 12). Turner's own verses, it must be admitted, were far less successful or even necessary in that verbal articulation of this 'comprehensive revelation'.

While words can provide some purchase on a comparison between the two artists, given Nash's titles and the extensive commentary on his images by himself and others, it is still the painterly emphasis of the way each artist presents his landscapes that is central. Turner's most intriguing picturesque device was to view landscape through architecture, a frame of branches or between the openings of a bridge.[10] The device sought to focus on what was meaningful in a specific place, and that it was a prominent motif is implied by his including a mezzotint of 'The Bridge in the Middle Distance' (illus. 17) in his *Liber studiorum*, a visual compendium of his major themes. There are the nymphs playing their instruments beside the water, but the eye is quickly taken past the thin stems of tree trunks into the landscape beyond, where the eight white openings in the eponymous bridge seem to fix our attention. But they deliver only emptiness, and the sense that beyond them is new territory, for ever to be explored. Turner's manuscript verses 'Fancy & Imagination' (*Sunset Ship*, p. 126) suggest that Turner's graphic and painterly imagination consist indeed in the fact that he similarly strove towards 'seats unknown':

What is imagination when its seats unknown
That lights the souls resource to soar beyond

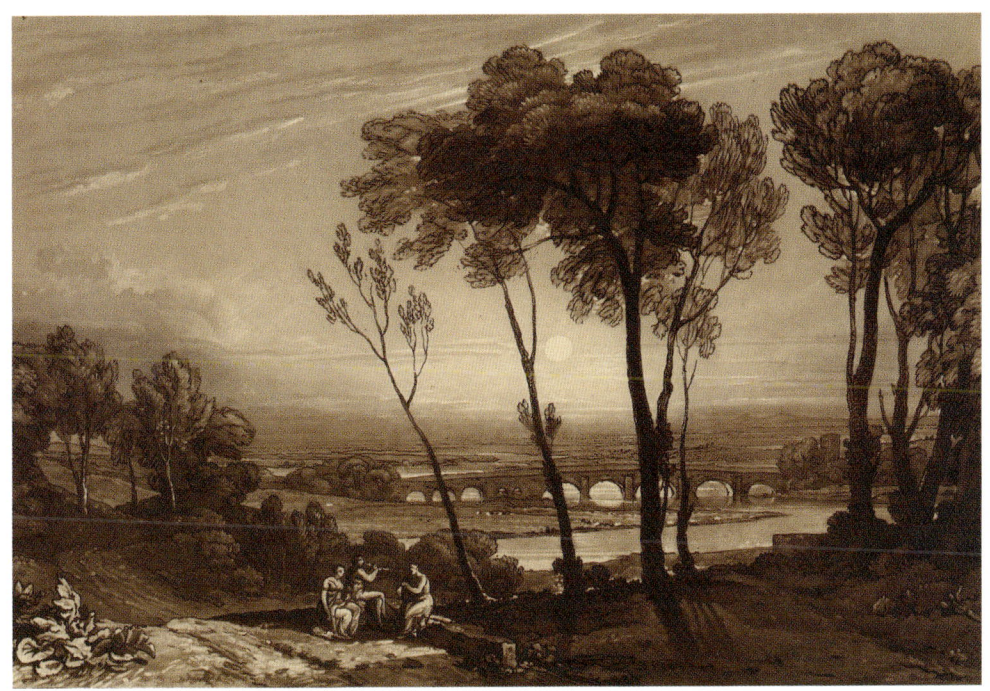

The powers of perception yet by knowledge
Of nature's forms and qualities feebly strong
To peruse the unknown force that urges all
Passions that mark the difference betwixt
The fool and he of sense the endowment
Given of our birth.

17 J.M.W. Turner, 'The Bridge in the Middle Distance', from *Liber studiorum* (1808).

Turner is too versatile and ambitious in the range of his subjects and motifs to be limited to one; it is, therefore, all the more fascinating to register his obsessive use of bridges to augment his sublime vocabulary, most obviously when they serve a purpose in his Turnerian topography. His fascination with bridges over the Moselle at Koblenz, the Walton Bridges, Kew Bridge, the Devil's Bridge on the St Gotthard Pass, that over the Arno in Florence, or over the enlarged river in Blenheim Park, Oxfordshire, among others, allows him to suggest the *quidditas*, or *haecceitas* ('thisness'[11]) of the scene that conjures a sense of the essence of that place. The emptiness, for want of a better word to describe the empty arches of his bridges, signals through its blankness, or luminosity, a world that viewers themselves may need to identify and explain. It throws them back on their own resources. Turner can give them the topographical context, often selecting or even naming a crucial and known historical or picturesque landmark, such as the Thames and Medway rivers, or Coniston Fells, but the viewer needs to know more. That is probably what the portraitist John Hoppner meant when he remarked to Joseph Farington that 'Turner left so much to be imagined';[12] the buck of response, its reception, passes to the alert and informed viewer.

Great landscapes, whether actual or painted, cannot be simply delightful, nor can they be just 'pretty landscape features', as Cardinal wrote of Paul Nash's imagery, or glimpses of a *locus amoenus* (which is a poetical term anyway).[13] They need at their best an intelligent and informed response to what is viewed, which requires patience, time and knowledge from both artist and viewer. Ruskin himself saw Turner's Italian paintings as 'perhaps universally an arrangement of remembrance': the melding of what the painter had seen, and his painterly arrangement of those memories, with the viewer's ability to recognize them.

Edmund Burke's *Enquiry into the Origin of our Ideas of the Sublime and Beautiful* (1757) had privileged the achievement of words over visual images, which were, in his conservative estimate of visual mimesis, 'exactly similar to those in nature'. Turner and others such as Joseph Wright of Derby, Henry Fuseli and Philip James de Loutherbourg called the bluff of that, but Turner excelled in finding *forms* for indistinctness. And he pushed his use of a mysterious quality of indistinctness beyond the emptiness of bridge openings. His *Passage of Mount St Gothard* (illus. 18) and his *Lonely Dell, Wharfedale* (illus. 19) lead the eye into an emptiness that is

18 J.M.W. Turner,
*Passage of Mount
St Gothard*, 1804,
watercolour.

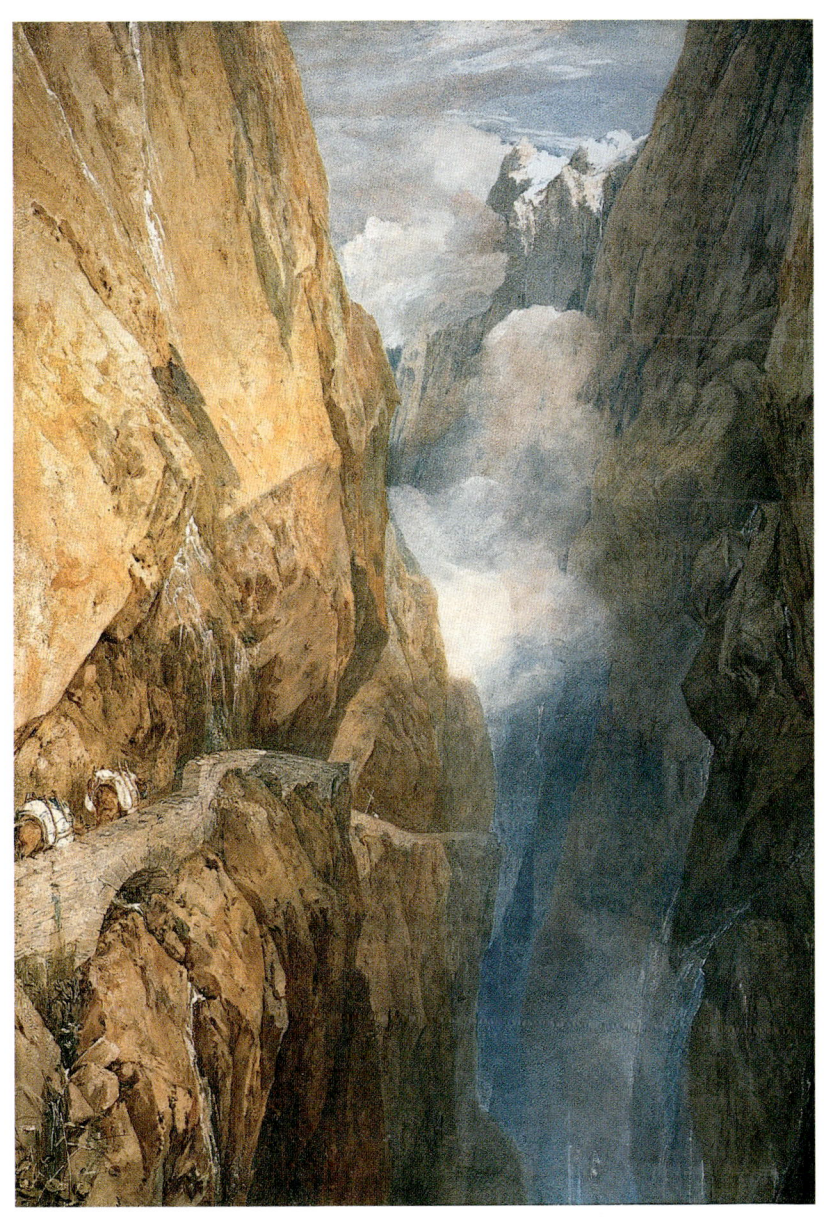

defined by its context: respectively rock, mist and a yawning chasm that are taken from the Gothard bridge itself, and the white rock and what animates the Yorkshire dell, such as the heron and kingfisher, which need some time to be spotted. This wonderful illumination of emptiness is central to Turner's most extraordinary paintings. He found it in his later return to paint the Falls of Clyde, where the nymphs are there to be sure, but absorbed, almost literally, into the painterly rendition (see illus. 5). Another extraordinary example is *High Street, Oxford* (illus. 20). The small figures imply presence, but the site itself is elusive, though the city church of St Mary is given more prominence, and locates where exactly we are in Oxford. By contrast, Nash is never interested in that kind of what James called 'mystery of scene', for he turns to precision and definiteness of forms (outlines), albeit rendered, if not unrealistically, where colour and shape declare a painterly mode of seeing. That a painter can use titles with powerful effect certainly helps, but as with *High Street, Oxford* or *Wharfedale*, a viewer's curiosity and visual patience will still yield more than words could offer.

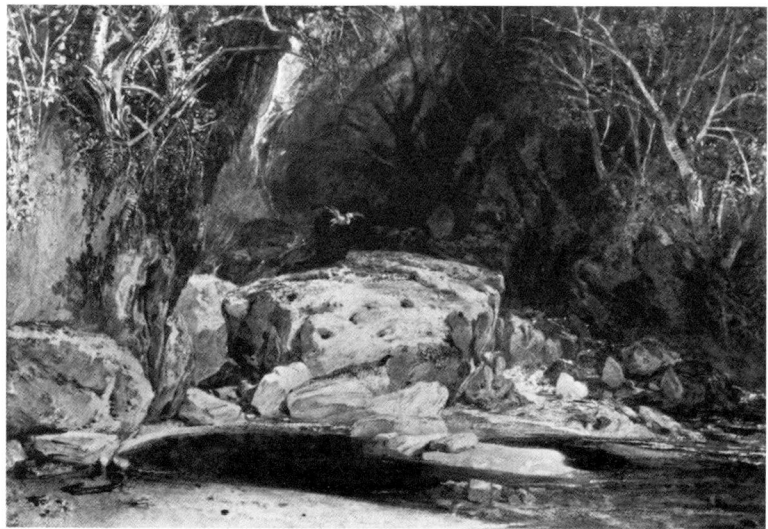

19  J.M.W. Turner,
*Lonely Dell,*
*Wharfedale, c.* 1818,
watercolour.

70

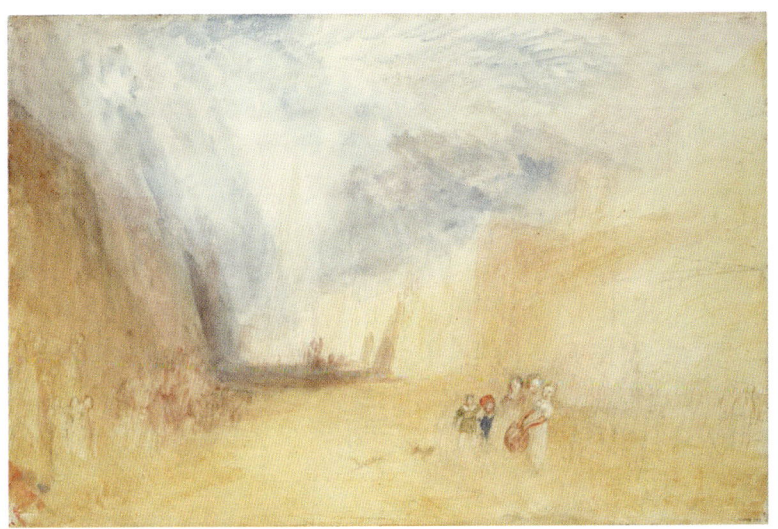

20 J.M.W. Turner, *High Street, Oxford, c.* 1837–9, graphite and watercolour on paper.

MARTIN PRICE saw in the late eighteenth-century sublime 'experiences whose power seemed incommensurate with a human scale or with formal elegance'.[14] Paul Nash accepted the claims of the sublime, but needed to couch it in human scale and formal means, (that is, forms that he could devise to represent what he saw); even if they can startle with their lack of verisimilitude, their abstractions still gesture to palpable objects, not luminous emptiness. When he quotes thirty lines from William Blake's 'To my friend Butts . . .' in *Outline*, Nash saw 'human' form in its vision of sunburst, and then realized how its meaning increased as he 'began to form a habit of visual expansion "into regions of air" [Blake's phrase] . . . an inward dilation of the eyes [whereby] I could increase my actual vision. I seemed to develop a power of interpenetration which disclosed strange phenomena' (*Outline*, pp. 63–4). He called this 'the mystery of clarity'. It was focused on local scenes that he knew intimately, and, unlike Turner, Nash did not need grand gestures to Roman history or to events in Byron's *Childe Harold's Pilgrimage*. In *Outline* he recognized the importance of his immediate environment: 'throughout my life, I was conscious always of the influence of the place at work upon my nerves – but never in any sinister degree, rather with a force gentle but insistent, charged with sweetness beyond physical experience, the promise of a joy utterly unreal' (pp. 27–8). He continued by explaining that whenever he was asked to describe exactly what was the 'place', he found it difficult to define: 'It has no fixed boundaries and, in element, is more like the sea whose tides determine its confines, now encroaching, now receding.'

For too long Paul Nash has been given prominence over his brother John, but a recent study of the latter's work elevates him, properly, into the same class.[15] While their images often seek out the same places, they also seem to exist in ways that are distinct, if hard to pin down; each seeks different ways to alert a viewer to the artist's sense of the mystery, the meaning of place, or whatever 'genius' resides in or haunts it. For John, what he sees and draws does not, unlike for Paul, 'work upon [his] nerves' so much as delight his eye.

Towards the end of his life Paul Nash wrote two articles for *Country Life*, 'Unseen Landscapes' and 'The Life of the Inanimate Object' (both May 1938).[16] Both articles declare much about his instinct to find words for landscapes or objects. They reveal his long-held interest in how still lifes find 'life' in his images, and how their newly discovered animation draws out what was invisible or unseen in the landscapes where they find themselves placed or imaged, and where they take command. Neither emphasis had the same claim on John's work, although, given his brother's *Country Life* titles, we can recognize a similar fascination with topographical forms and an artist's search for painterly equivalents. The watercolour *Trees in a Flood* (illus. 21) is at one level simply descriptive, but the tree shapes and the reflections stir the imagination. If John's *Trees in a Flood* is compared with Paul's *Trees Beside the Pond (The Pool)* sixteen years later, their common attention is clear; nonetheless, John's has both more sense of a specific place – although

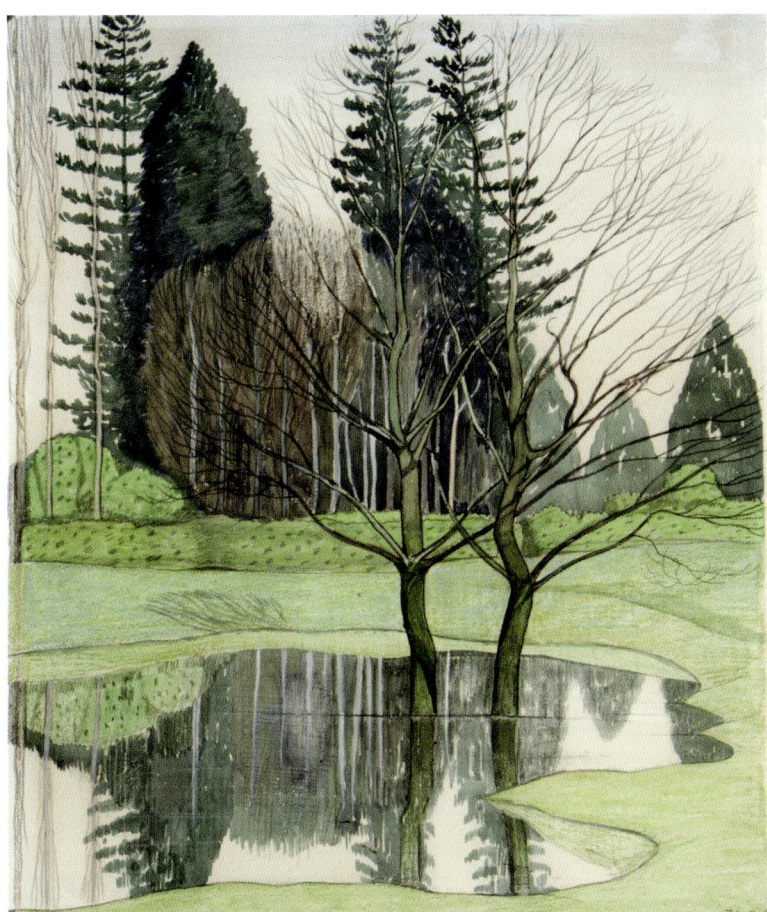

the trees are clearly stylized without losing their clarity; by contrast
Paul's trees are mute, the pond lifeless and the colours strangely
painterly – and the sense that this 'place' could be anywhere. John
offers what Bottomley in 1913, at the time John painted this watercolour, saw as his 'vein of poetry'.[17]

Similar terms can often be applied to both artists. But when
Bottomley writes of John's 'vivid actuality', it is different from Paul's
remark that he seemed to have developed 'a power of interpretation which discloses strange phenomena'. The strangeness for Paul

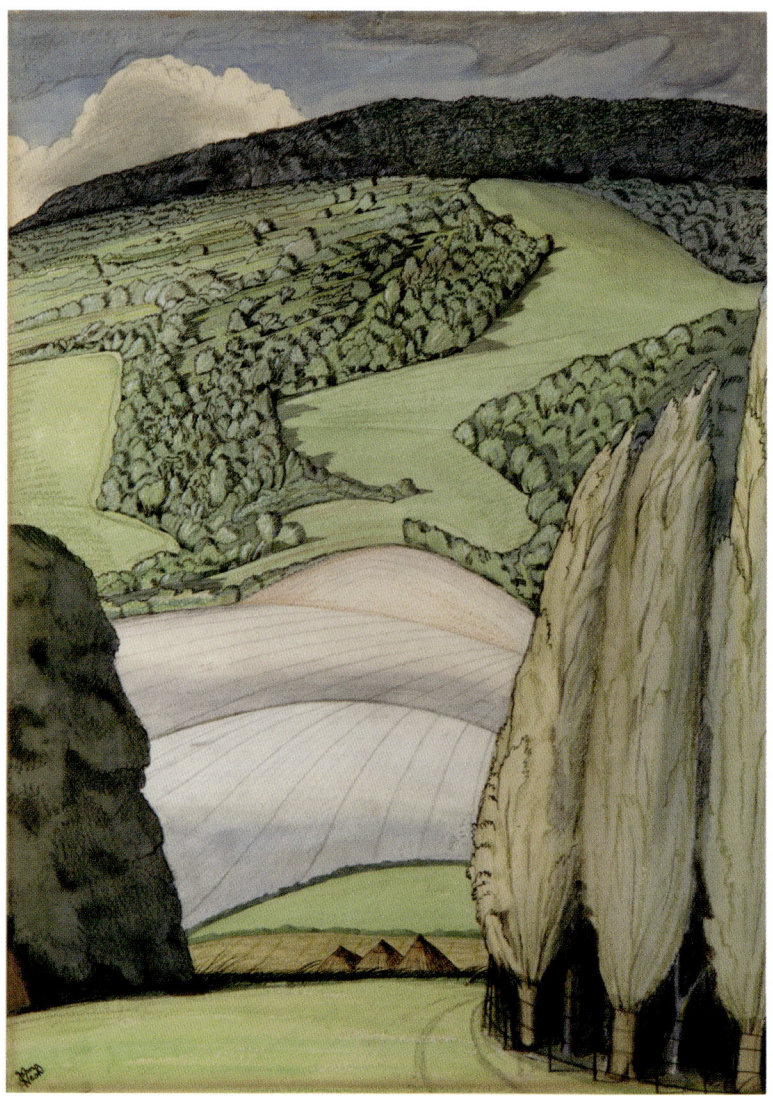

22 John Nash,
*Hillside, Whiteleaf,*
1922, watercolour
and ink on paper.

comes in various ways: through his titles and his verbal attempt
to explain his pictures, through his more conspicuous reliance on
moments of surrealism, and through his strong delight in the cubic
forms of his watercolours. John has an equal sense of and delight
in phenomena, but it is more personal – not least in his delight

with the countryside and the implied acknowledgement of human involvement in its management – and less eager to emphasize mystery, especially in his titles, which attend mostly to location and time or season. If he seeks to identify something in a landscape that is beyond what the eye can see, he opts to draw on a sense of the generality in the region or season, which are larger than the moment of looking.

If Paul Nash likes to create mystery in his images through a 'relationship of parts, an enchantment that cannot be analysed', John, while also quick to see geometry in topography, seems to cherish his attention to the natural or cultivated world. He wrote that he loved farmyards and saw them as the ideal 'natural' topic, and thought that 'cubism or anything else' was nothing in comparison with his representation of nature, and, given that agricultural emphasis, its implicit human presence.[18] His images attend to tractors, ploughed fields, stacked wheatsheaves, threshing, haymaking, roads and paths. That is not to deny his strong inclination that landscape and its representation needed 'design', but he was concerned that too many artists privileged 'the portrayal of *the anecdote* over its forms'. His *Hillside, Whiteleaf* of 1922 (illus. 22) is simple, eloquent of the topographical shapes he finds there and then transposes to the image, enjoying the somewhat abstracted shapes of trees, woodland and fields. Its achievement rests in how it invokes or suggests that landscape can be viewed rather than in an invitation to us to register any mystery in it. It was as if he were to revise Paul's aphorism, to find a 'clarity of mystery'.

Paul, in particular, has often been dubbed 'surreal' by critics.[19] If the term means something beyond the real or actual, beyond photographic verisimilitude, then truly we see more than what the ordinary eye, or the lens of the camera, might do. His *Winter Sea* of 1925–37 (illus. 23) is a vision of icy waves, crisp in their outlines; it is an eloquent interpretation of the subject that declares as much Nash's as the sea's wintry character. But it is not, to my eyes,

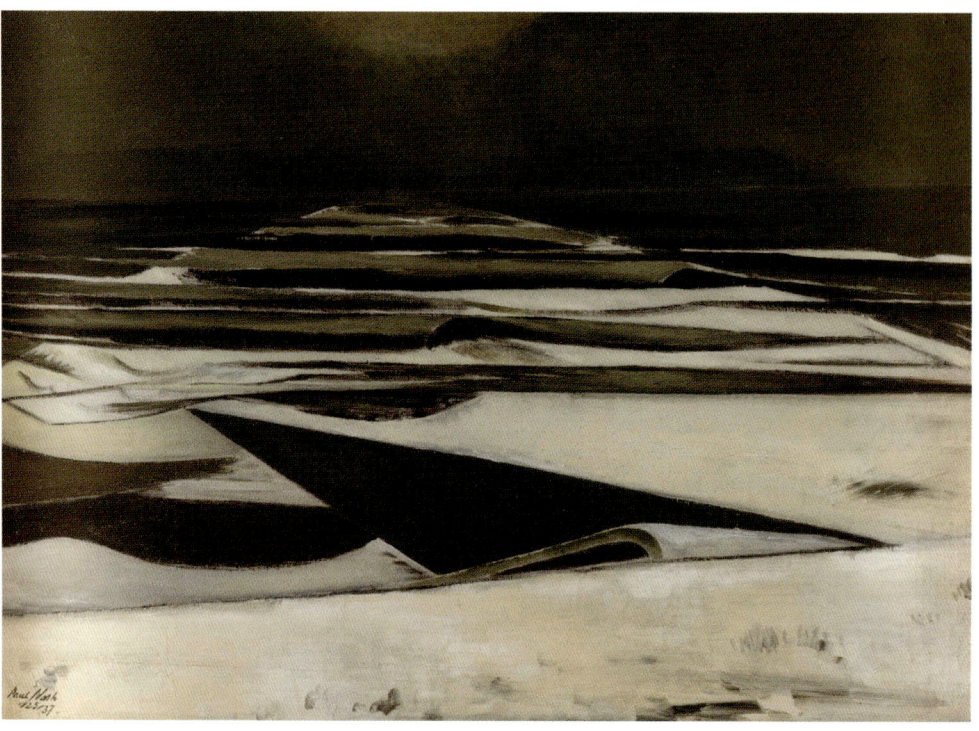

surrealist, although it has been seen as 'mechanical', compared to some of his photographs of ploughed fields, or to his watercolour *Earth Sea* (1937).[20] Where he can deliberately celebrate the mechanical is in his photographs of machinery or the superstructures of steamships, or in finding abstract items that serve as analogues to natural, or at least man-made, elements in landscape. His *Equivalents for the Megaliths* (illus. 24) uses a cluster of objects, an essay in still life, to draw out the mysteries of the landform pictured in the landscape background; the foreground cubes of the still life pull out and reveal similar shapes in the distant landscape, and that megalith at the top right was itself an ancient search for abstract forms that captured the mysteries of place. When in 1919 Paul started working with wood engravings, their technical format could combine a mechanical with a studied sense of distortion, all the while offering a firm relish of the subjects' form (illus. 25). John's woodcuts and book illustrations were also more abstract and more resolutely angular than his paintings and drawings.

But Paul in particular does not seem as surrealist as Giorgio di Chirico, about whom, along with other more general articles on surrealism, he wrote during the 1930s, and whom he occasionally came close to imitating, as in *Nostalgic Landscape* (1923 and 1938) or *Northern Adventure* (1929).[21] His best work seems far more committed to finding what he termed variously 'authentic place', or what was 'inexplicable' in a place, or its 'associative force'.[22] John, I suggest, found authentic places more readily explicable, although forceful, as in *Dorset Landscape* (illus. 26). Paul argued that his 'associative force' was *not* separable from the 'formal features' of place. He wrote about his early design of bookplates for a friend that they 'interpret[ed] the personal calamities of the owner' (*Outline*, p. 70),

24 Paul Nash, *Equivalents for the Megaliths*, 1935, oil on canvas.

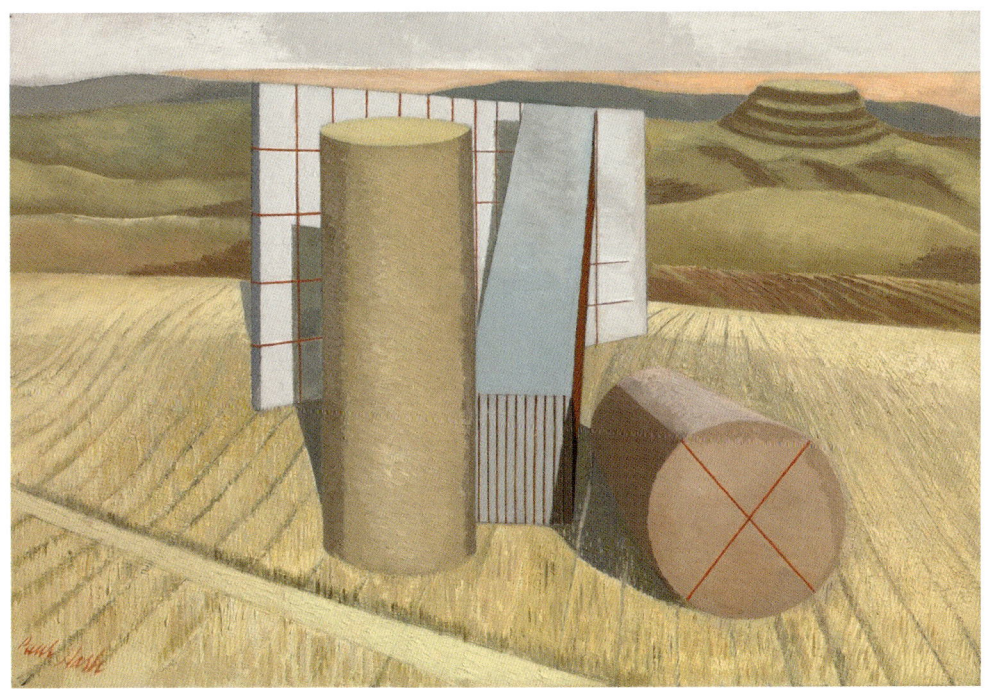

thus implying that the personality of a landscape is also disclosed. The epigraph to the conclusion to Lambirth's book on John Nash quotes Thomas Hardy's 'I want to see the deeper reality underlying the scenic, the expression of what are sometimes called abstract imaginings' (p. 313). That is true of John, yet the depth is, so to speak, revealed by his 'vivid actuality' and, what Bottomley also notices, his delight in his 'sense of contour'.[23]

25 Paul Nash, cover for *Places* (1923).

Paul's *Wittenham Clumps* (illus. 27) takes a familiar English topographical incident, with features of field, hill and clump clearly stated, yet coloured and shaped, with abstract outlines; even the cloud above echoes the rectangle of the ploughed field below.[24] A poster for a joint exhibition of the two Nash brothers in 1913 at the Dorien Gallery in Kensington showed two versions of Wittenham Clumps, as if each laid claim to this Iron Age fort with its copse of trees.[25] In Paul's picture a distant flock of birds hints at the life there and the movement of the air. He loved the hills' 'extraordinary prominence above the river . . . dome-like and each planted with a thick clump of trees whose mass had a curiously symmetrical and sculptured form . . . I felt their importance long before I knew their history.'[26] He thought this part of the country was 'marvellous' and saw it in mythical terms ('Pan-ish places down by the river . . . haunted by old gods long forgotten'[27]). Yet he also noted in *Outline* that what mattered most to him were 'their formal features' rather than 'any associative force'. Cardinal notes (p. 64) that sometimes Nash grasped this liaison of form and association 'intuitively' in his paintings, but that in contrast his verbal discussions 'are at times labored', and quotes Nash on how

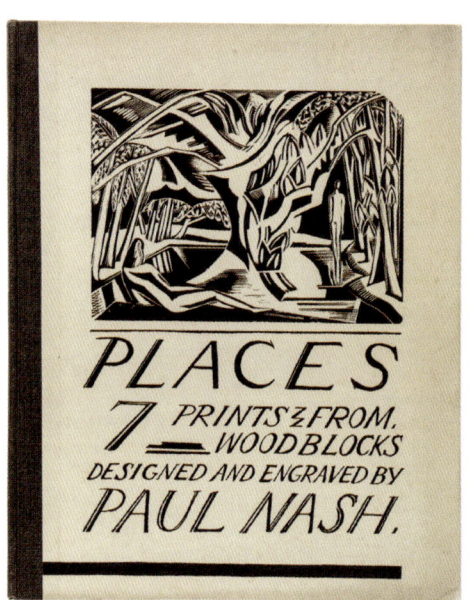

26 John Nash, *Dorset Landscape*, c. 1930, oil on canvas.

27 Paul Nash, *Wittenham Clumps*, 1912, watercolour, ink and chalk on paper.

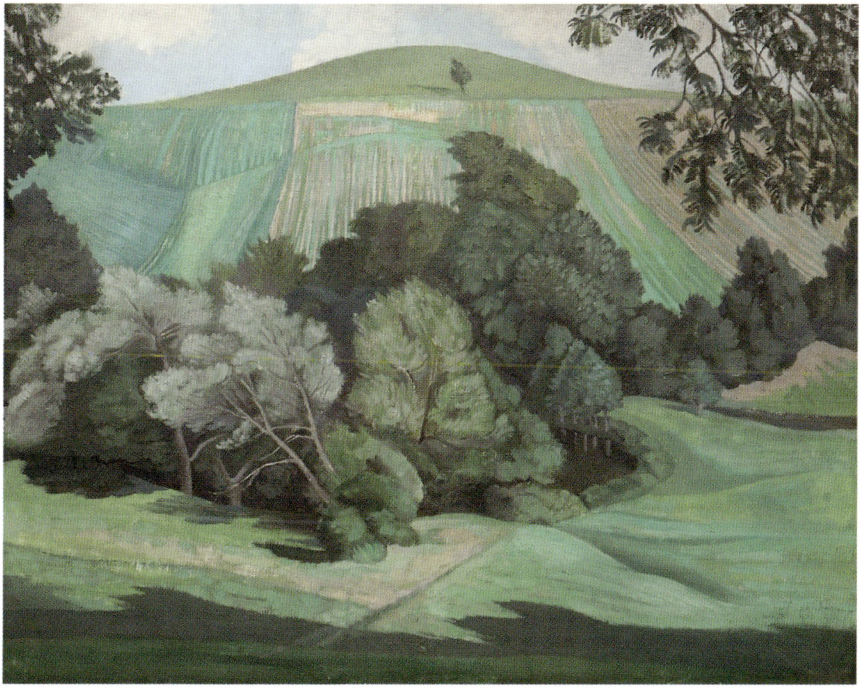

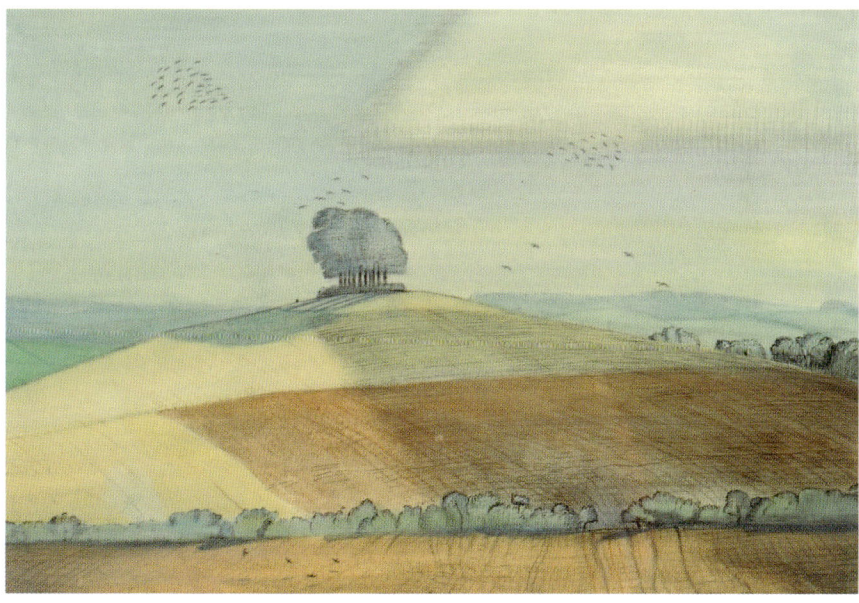

'as I grew up . . . [it was] the inner life of the subject, rather than its characteristic lineaments, which appealed to me.'

Nash's remarks about *Wittenham Clumps* are laboured to the extent that he alludes to Pan and 'old forgotten gods', which do load the pictures with extraneous meanings and associations; rather than searching for Pan, we should ourselves intuit how to read the watercolour's formal presence. That depends visually on its strange sense of shape and colour, and the birds that seem large compared to the rest of the landscape, and then perhaps, knowing other pictures, that we sense the modernity of its rendering, that it looks different and we wonder why. It suggests what Bottomley clearly identified in Nash as the 'secret places of your mind'.[28] When Paul entitled a watercolour 'The Hill' he thought that the hill 'could not belong to anyone in particular, but to an ancient people perhaps or to fairies even' (*Outline*, p. 128), another 'labouring' of his underlying perspective (he later found out that it belonged to a noble landowner). Verbal analysis may bring out the mystery of some physical scenery and thus point to some *genius loci*, but its 'characteristic lineaments' are reworked in colour and form to reveal their 'associative force'.

That inner life of the subject lends a distinctive tone or perspective to Paul's landscapes, but somewhat less than a wholly surrealist response. When criticized for the way the sun was depicted and made shadows, he argued that 'Nature . . . did not hold out against the needs of art,' and that 'in a picture they go the way you want them' (*Outline*, p. 193). Bottomley, with whom Nash maintained a detailed and lively correspondence over thirty years about painting, poetry, theatre and book design, did not 'see any need to be Surrealiste [*sic*], and you are the only Surrealist whom I care about.'[29] Yet he pointed out that what he called Nash's 'little puff-balls of colour in mysterious relationship' did not appeal to his 'angular Northern mind', which is perhaps why he used the French term. He might have meant a picture such as *Sunflower and Sun* (illus. 28): it sets the sunflower (a favourite theme for Nash) in front of a landscape composed of mysterious coloured blobs to the left, a sketchy field of trees and boulders on the right, and in the background some of the hillside clumps that Nash often sought out. Any surrealism surely offers to compare flower and sunshine and juxtapose them with a miscellany of landscape forms, yet everything here is in context: the landscape objects; the flower turning away from the viewer towards the sun, which sends its shaft of light from behind a cloud.

John Nash also painted *Wittenham Clumps from Sinodun House* in about 1913, when he was twenty (illus. 29).[30] The clump sits conspicuously on the hill, much smaller than the nearer house, of which John reported his fondness for the garden, although that is not what the watercolour presents. The solid block of the house and its chimneys and a dark slab of vegetation in front of it contrast with the landscape around it and on the far hillside; its geometry contrasts

28 Paul Nash, *Sunflower and Sun*, 1942, oil on canvas.

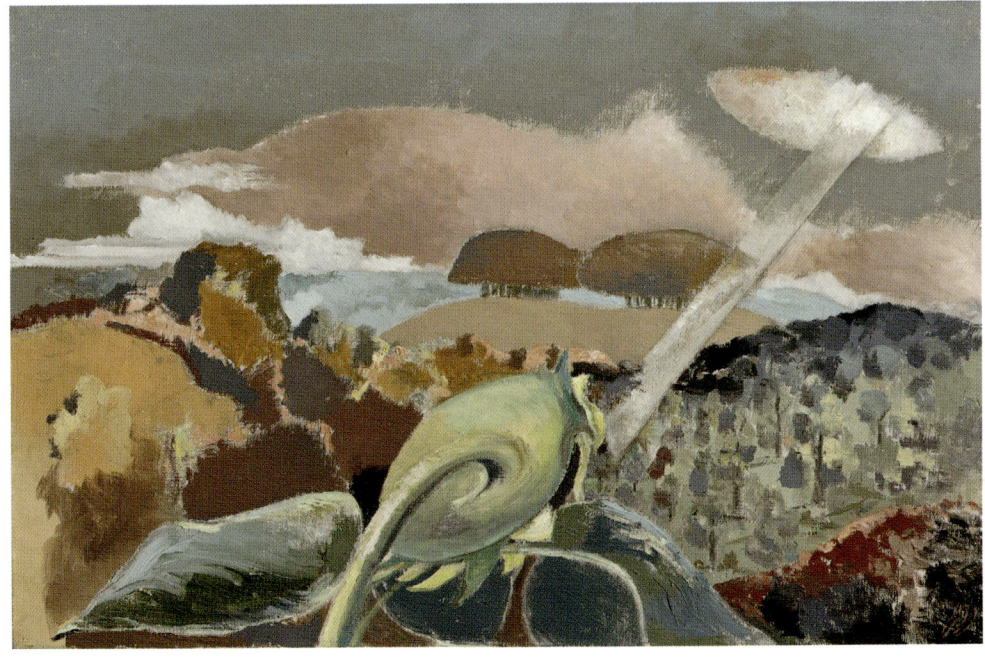

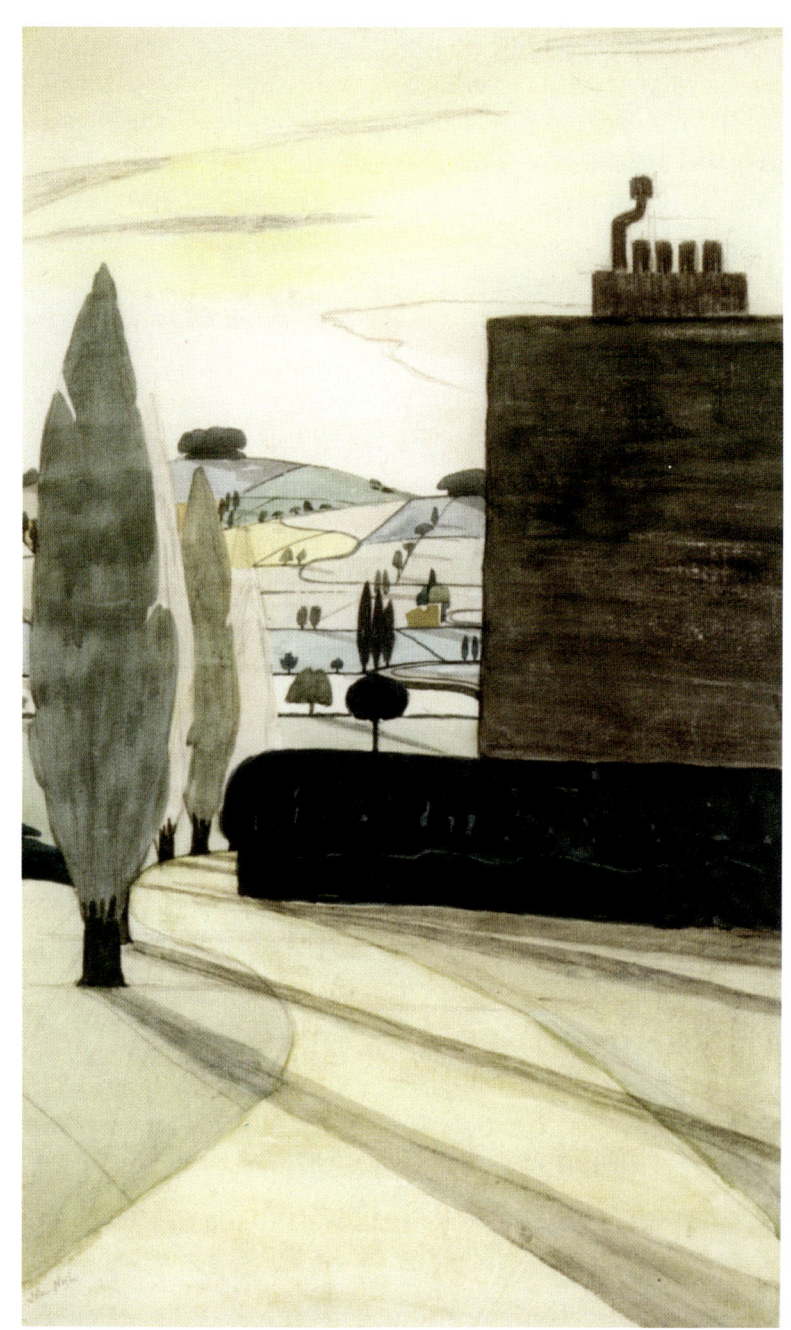

29  John Nash,
*Wittenham Clumps
from Sinodun House*,
*c.* 1913, watercolour
and pencil.

with the natural scenery, yet also somehow endorses the fact that the near garden with its poplar trees, the simple shapes of trees beyond and the pattern of fields below the clump are also conceived as somewhat abstracted. The poplars in the garden that send their shadows across the driveway and lawn are also simplified. This is a young work, but it feels confident in its handling, and in the way the forms represented tell, explain, what John was looking at. It lacks any sense of mystery about the place, while implying only how the artist wants to see it. It is highly attentive to the forms in land and image.

John uses buildings to set off the richness of landscape, and sometimes to contrast larger landscapes with the more social places of gardens and houses. Paul's gardens and orchards in *In a Garden* and *Summer Garden* (1914) are strangely diagrammatic, their trees and shrubs weird and dreamy, while the three robed girls in the former seem rightly at home; the picture was at one time entitled *Barbara in the Garden* (Barbara was their sister). John's *The Garden* (illus. 31) contrasts the lane as it winds across the fields with a hint

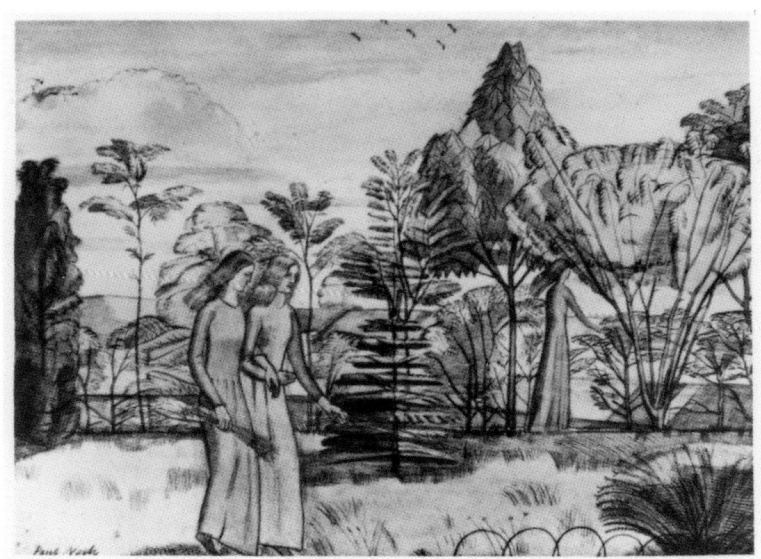

30  Paul Nash, *The Orchard*, 1914, watercolour, pencil and pen, collection of Stephen Stuart-Smith, painted in 1914 during Nash's first visit to meet Gordon Bottomley.

of garden railings in the foreground, and his *Landscape* (illus. 32) allows a hint of garden-ness in the foreground that contrasts, over its slight wire fence, with a wide panorama of ploughed fields, woodland and a striking, pale rainbow that arches over all. There are no figures in either, but nonetheless there is a sense of personal involvement in both the garden space and its relation with the landscape. He can sometimes be naive, as is shown by the pair of pigs searching in *Acorns*, or *The Storm*, *Deer Fence*, *Sky* or *Landscape with Windmill*, although they also imply the gaze of an innocent eye that records just what he sees.[31] *Cop Hill, Princes Risborough* (1919; illus. 33) is at first glance also naive, but plays wonderfully and delicately with the topography, shadows and tree shapes, and accords

31 John Nash,
*The Garden*, 1951,
oil on canvas.

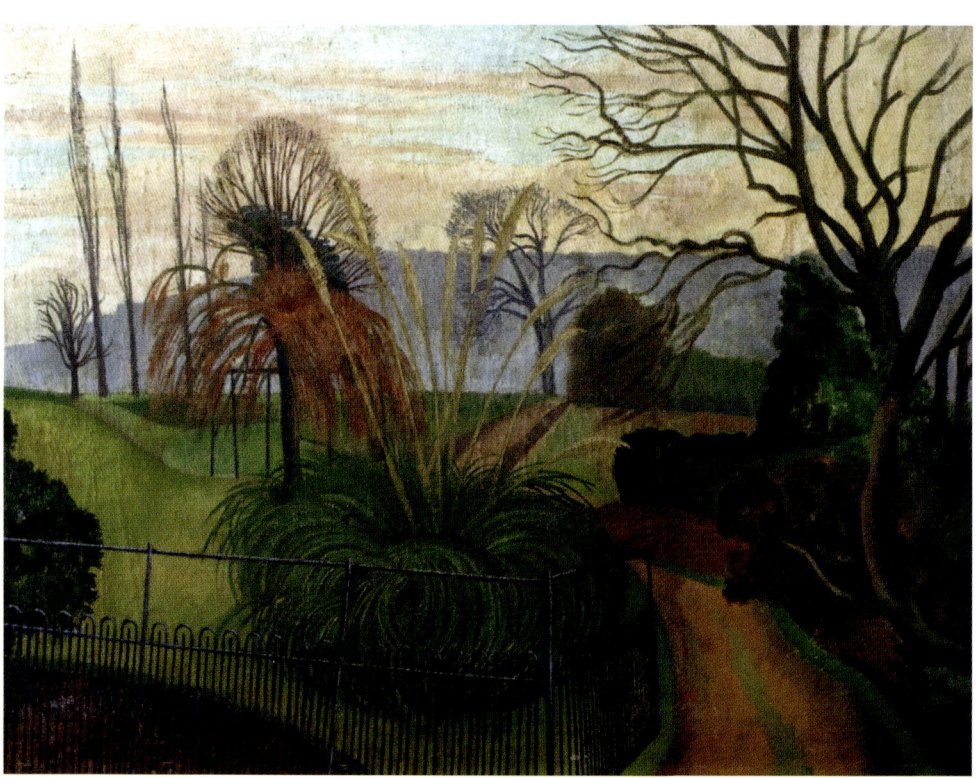

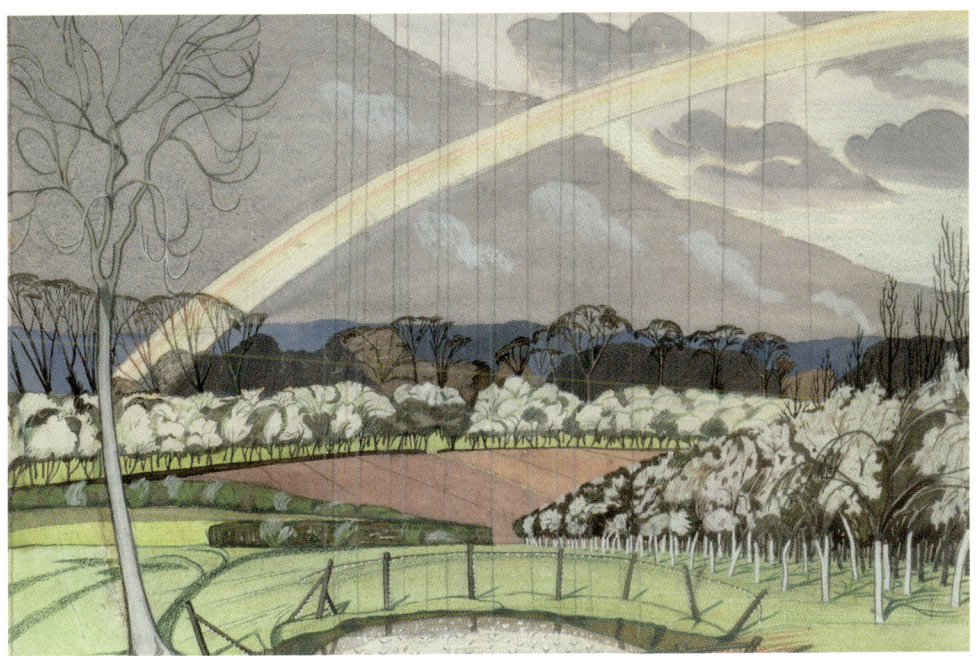

well with Lambirth's citation (p. 153) of Josef Albers's famous 'Art must do more than Nature. That's why it's art.'

Most of Paul's images hover on that edge between formal presence and implied association. A late painting, from 1936–8, entitled *Landscape from a Dream* does this unambiguously, and has been much interpreted: against a background of sea meeting the shore is placed a framed picture of red skies, depicting a flying bird and a series of globes; these also appear outside the picture in the landscape, alongside an open screen, where a hawk sits and grips its frame.[32] That the title is announced as a dream allows commentary to exploit its unconscious life, its very loaded associations. Nash's images of war are also powerful appeals to its devastations and the nightmares they bring, such as *Bomber in the Corn* (1940) or the ironic *We Are Making a New World* (1918), with its ruined trees and muddy humps of battle-scarred Ypres, the sun looming over a burnt tree stump.[33]

32 John Nash, *Landscape*, 1958, pencil and watercolour.

85

33 John Nash,
*Cop Hill, Princes Risborough*, 1919, pencil, watercolour, pastel, pen and ink.

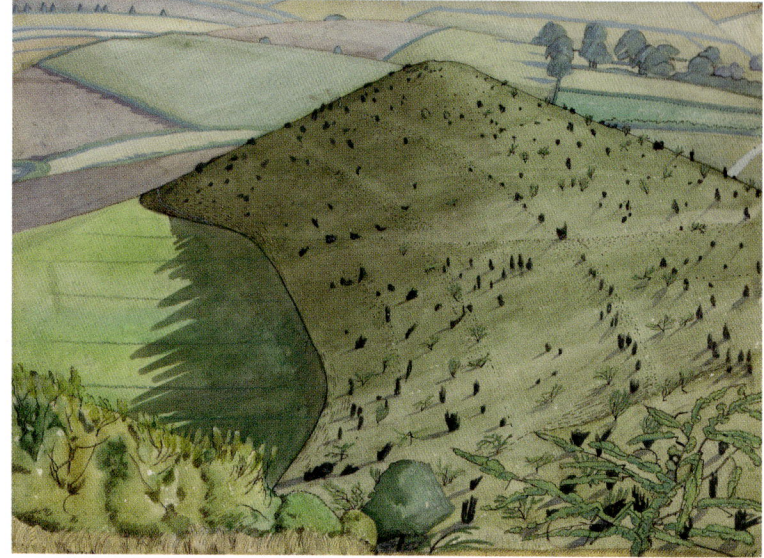

But when Paul noted, early in 1912, that he kept his 'imaginative invention drawings … separate from the Nature ones', it was at best a statement of what would eventually coalesce and collaborate. Later, in *Outline* (p. 62), he wrote, 'I began to turn to Nature for my scene, whilst the personages of that scene began to derive from my own imagination.' And that subsequent images which are not so 'separated' nor identified as 'dreams' suggest a dreamlike, even haunted, quality without underlining any collision of formal effect with dreams or 'visions'– this is, in truth, somewhat different from John's delight in nature.

Paul confessed to W. B. Yeats that, cycling home in the dark through the Colne Valley to Iver Heath, he had 'visions', and he annotated an original drawing of a hill rising above heaped trees and a chasm, where an angel is combating the Devil, with his verses that saw 'a dread place only seen in dreams' (*Elements*, cat. 5, and see *Outline*, pp. 61–4). More telling are paintings such as *The Wanderer* (illus. 34), which shows a tiny figure entering a distant wood, seen across the grassland, through which his tracks have cut

34 Paul Nash,
*The Wanderer*, 1911, watercolour, with blue chalk, heightened with graphite.

86

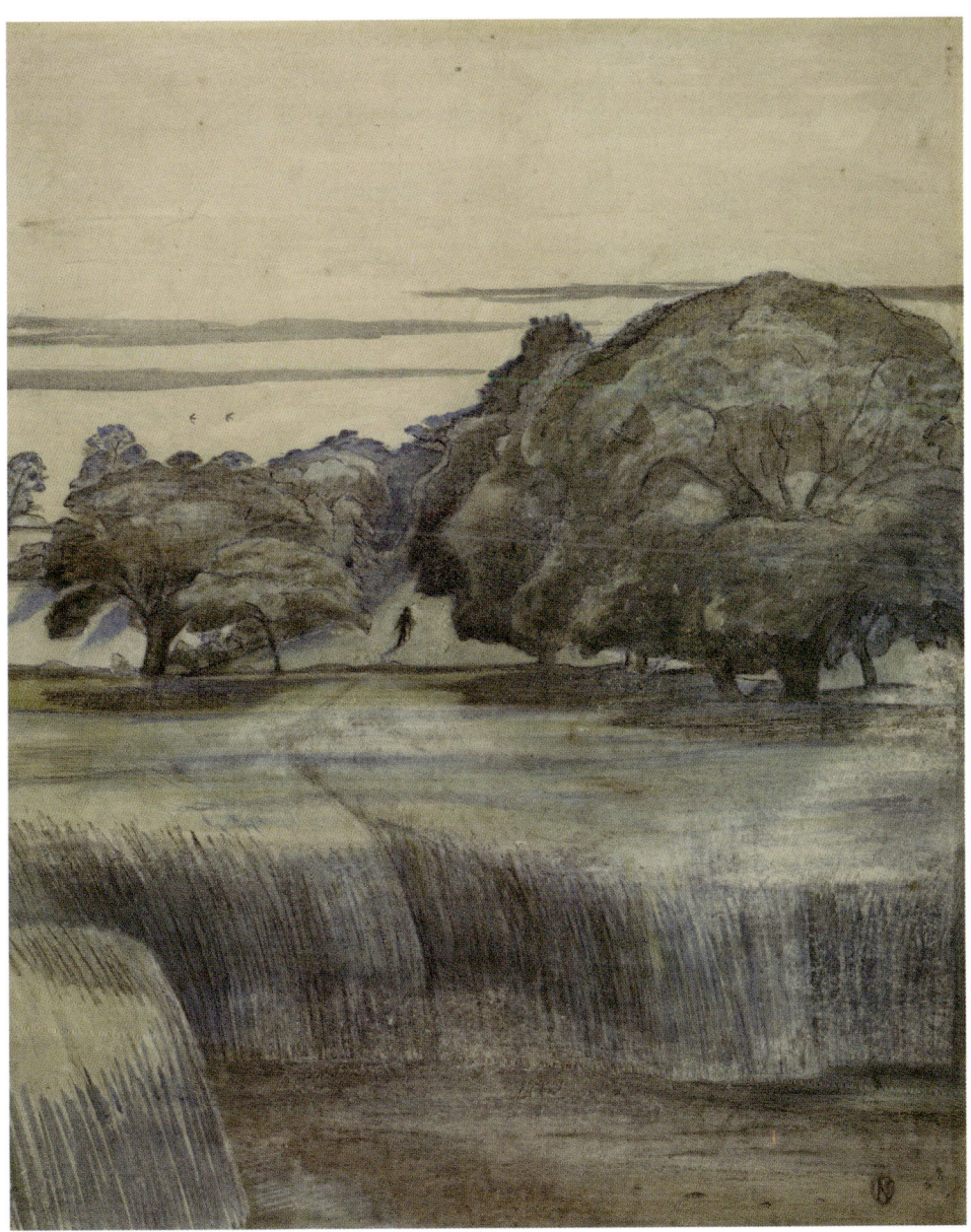

a path. Or *The Orchard*, where a small, naked intruder, his or her hands raised, is approaching the orchard, where branches spring into a pattern of globe-shaped foliage above a zigzag of cut paths. Those somewhat rare figures, which Nash is often accused of elim-inating in his images, are the surrogates for us, Nash's viewers, who wander into them and discover his places.[34] But even in *Wood on the Downs* (illus. 35), where there is no actual person, there are paths that invite; the woodland tempts us to enter, and on the hillside paths lead over and up the further slopes.

Indeed, paths either underscored or implied are a vital element in how we move through and encounter actual and numinous places, and this is key to the way a viewer of many Paul Nash paint-ings communicates and entices us into his understanding of place. Its genius is the landscape itself. In *Outline* he wrote that very early he delighted in paths and their 'purposeful' walks (p. 30), noting the different conditions of each part of the landscape through which he moved, watching its changing colours and the sights he took at certain points, its 'purposes'.

*The Orchard* was painted after Nash's visit to Bottomley in 1914, during which he made 26 drawings of his exploration of the Lake District and the poet's Silverdale. The two men would have engaged in a variety of discussions about how to conceive and represent *genius loci*, discussions they continued throughout their corre-spondence. Both were particularly enamoured of English landscape and its renderings, and both professed an affection for the work of Samuel Palmer and Edward Calvert.[35] Yet it is also crucial to note that poet and painter always work in different ways, however much these two sought a 'literary' colour, and despite their growing appre-ciation of each other's art – including Bottomley's encouragement of Nash's writing. While the resources of surrealism did sustain some of Nash's representation of place, it was his Englishness, and his sense of the objectivity of that native and ancient landscape, that anchored him. When he took up photography in 1931, it became

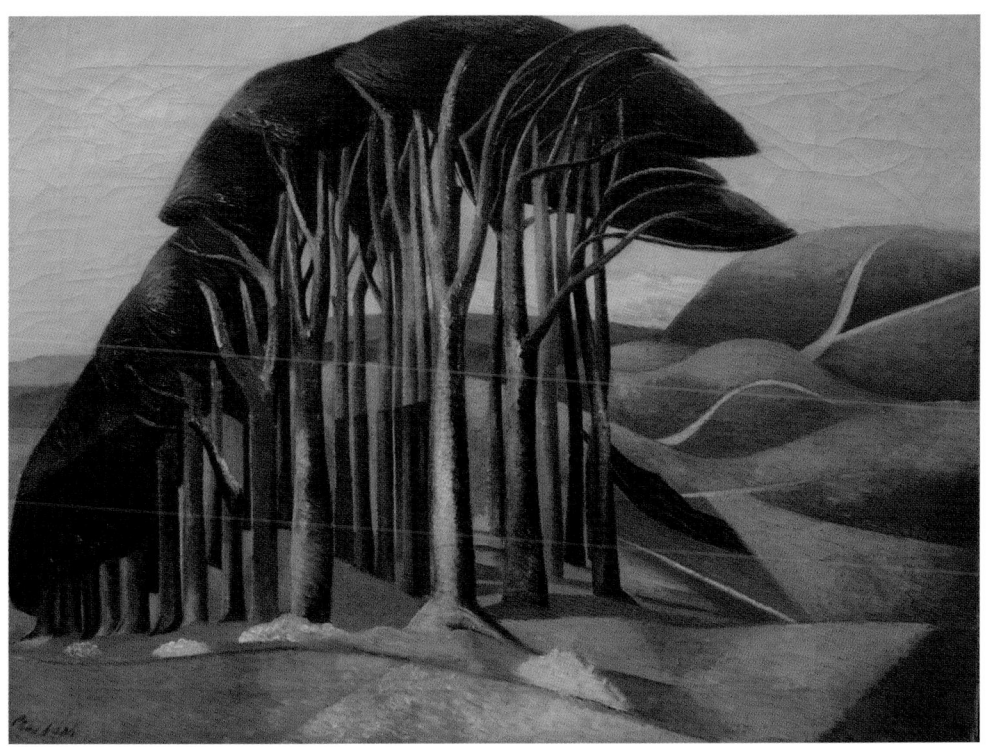

a central aspect of the way he viewed objects. *Stalking Horse* (1941) was essentially a photo of an upturned tree, but, taken from an angle, along with its title, it finds an unexpected poetry in the inanimate object.[36] The selection of his photographs in the Dulwich exhibition (*Elements*, pp. 120–45) attests to his fascination with palpable objects – derelict piers, close-ups of broken windows, edges of concrete, still-life assemblages – that are sometimes disconcerting in their selection of new possibilities, such as the uprooted tree that rears up in *Monster Field* (ibid., cat. 61).

35 Paul Nash, *Wood on the Downs*, 1929, oil on canvas.

The issue of 'poetry' (i.e. not verse, but a move beyond 'prose') is clear in the long correspondence between the two artists. Early in their exchange Bottomley advised that 'Workers *in all the arts* need to watch and wait to understand the *nature of things*' (p. 2; my italics). He added that the 'real thing is to get using to saying with a pencil what you want to say, until you instinctively think in lines and masses' (p. 2); he might have said the same thing of a camera as of the pen. Nash replied immediately: 'thinking in lines and masses – never really thought of it before now' (p. 4). The phrasing, its latent recognition of *ut pictura poesis*, is apt for both of them: a need to show or say something *instinctively* in image, photograph or word. Bottomley once told Nash that 'the greatest mystery is obtained by the greatest definity' (p. 86), and later sent him a piece from *The Times* where the writer urged painters (he was writing about the Royal Academy) 'to apply this sharpness of accent to the forms of nature', whereby they would 'express the artist's own individual interest in the objects which he paints'. Bottomley would complain on at least one occasion that some Nash drawings 'were not those with the most You in them' (p. 87).

Nash continued to turn to landscape, not for the sake of the landscape itself, but for the '"things behind", the dweller in the innermost: whose light shines thro' sometimes' (ibid., p. 42; also quoted in *Outline*, p. 83). Bottomley, too, seemed to agree that mere 'literary' references were not needed, although 'a vital picture' might eventually elicit them. But it was his 'firm belief that it is impossible, to construct a picture that, *au fond*, does not make references (conscious or unconscious, intentional or instinctive) to the eye's experiences of external nature'.[37]

While Bottomley, quoted above, thought John had an instinct for 'poetry', it was the poetry of topographical forms that inspired him, and Bottomley himself in 1941 remarked on John's compositional skill, 'his sense of contour – rather than of a technical likeness'.[38] 'Contour' may seem close to Paul's 'outlines', but the latter suggests the enclosure of something to be elucidated and explained, whereas 'contour' is far more topographical in its attention to the way the land is shaped, as in John's *Hillside, Whiteleaf* (see illus. 22). And Bottomley's remark is more astute and generous than when, in 1912, he saw only John's 'good sense of decorative disposition of his masses'.[39]

Paul Nash himself said of his painted '"visions", [that] some of [them] were supplemented by "poems"' (ibid., p. 75). Yet a few years earlier he saw 'a deep inner necessity upon us to express our sense of the rhythms and cadences of immortality *in terms of the earth*' (p. 165; my italics). And Nash himself, after one of his rare visits to the Bottomleys' home near Carnforth, recalled how 'Silverdale [was] a mysterious place that enchanted me.' Poet and painter are alert to multiple aspects of landscape and its places – Nash was fascinated by sound and smell (see *Outline*, pp. 33, 36). Even as he enjoyed London, he confessed that the impressions of the countryside were vital to his inspiration; but sounds and smells, which are just feasible for a poet to grasp, cannot declare themselves in a painter – another art, garden-making, is also different in that respect.[40]

Nash's interest in designing sets and costumes for Bottomley's verse plays was an intricate part of his sense of *genius loci*.[41] A writer in *Elements* notes that Nash used 'landscape as if it were a stage of a theatre' (p. 12). That is acute, for a stage set will help to locate the action in a setting that is appropriate or even symbolic. Nash's landscapes too are drawn where we may sense an action, but unlike with a Bottomley play, where actors' speech, gestures and the plot all speak to an audience, viewers of Nash images have to invent or intuit that action or story from what he paints or draws. Nash himself in 1927 volunteered that he shared with Bottomley a passion with 'the Theatre', for there 'we can always meet and "deny Nature"' (p. 190) – by which, I assume, he meant that a theatrical experience (notably in poetic drama, Bottomley's

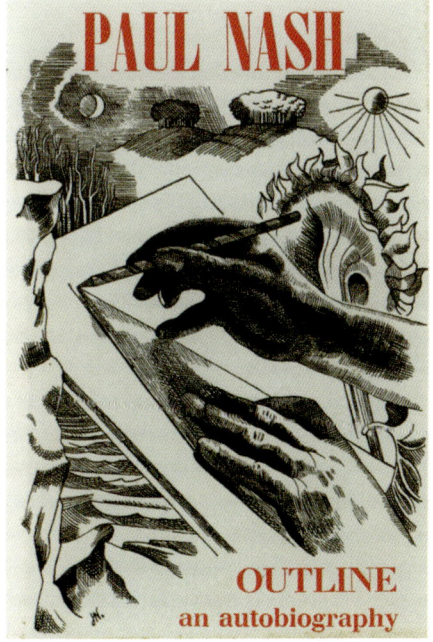

36 John Nash, cover design for Paul Nash's *Outline* (1949).

preferred medium) allowed a measure of what human nature could be, while offering it in ways that privileged its poetry. Certainly the titles of his paintings help, but in the end, sometimes taking the hint of the title and sometimes not, individuals find their own way into the pictures, like those solitary folk in his woods and orchards that also seek a path of their own.

When Paul Nash began his autobiography in 1936 under the title *Genius Loci*, that term, or even obsession, guided a great deal of his painting about which Bottomley enthused; that he later changed the title to *Outline* implied a similar attention to the formal play of shapes and some of his more surrealist work. Both titles are implied in John's cover (illus. 36) for Faber & Faber's posthumous edition of *Outline* (1949). A pair of hands draws a pencil outline of a triangle on a sheet of paper that seems to be propped against a landscape of waves (or maybe a ploughed field), with a sunflower, a sun, a half moon, a woodland and two clumps of trees on a hill. It was an elegant tribute to a brother painter whose presence inhabited the very landscapes that he was in the act of drawing. It recalls Pope's sense that a topography, its genius of place, could itself be brought into being by the rival aegis of another genius, the designer, as here the artist. So for Nash the topography of 'garden, hill, copse, bird, stone, gate, ladder, window, moon, sun, clouds, sea' (Cardinal, p. 7) became the zones and forms of his imagination.

# FIVE

# Poets on *Genius Loci*:
# *Ut natura poesis*

Forms that are or seem
When sleepers wake and yet still dream,
And when it's vanished still declare,
With only bed and bedstead there
That heavens had opened.
W. B. Yeats

I wanted to write a poem
That you would understand.
For what good is it to me
If you can't understand it?
But you got to try hard.
William Carlos Williams, from 'January Morning'

Writers and painters may choose the same subjects and topics, but the results and how we read them are necessarily different. Words serve writers, well or poorly. Poets provide illuminating ways into our understanding of *genius loci*. This and the following chapter – which address those who write about travel, where a central concern is obviously that of place – suggest alternative kinds of resource that writers can bring to bear when understanding and maybe explaining the meanings of places.

A painting by Joseph Wright of Derby in 1781 shows Sir Brooke Boothby reclining in the forest of his Derbyshire estate (illus. 37). The gesture of a hand at the chin relies on the long-established way to indicate thoughtfulness, so it is an eloquent display of an individual meditating, perhaps even dreaming. But he also holds a closed book, on the spine of which we may read the word 'Rousseau'. Its title is not disclosed.

Now Jean-Jacques Rousseau had spent a year and a half in Staffordshire in 1776–7, and Boothby was delighted by his work; he even paid for the publication of Rousseau's *Dialogues* two years after the philosopher's death. The book Boothby holds may be that publication, *Juge de Jean-Jacques*, but the author's name on the spine hints at a more general appreciation and, given the way Wright poses his subject, suggests the book might well be Rousseau's

37 Joseph Wright of Derby, *Sir Brooke Boothby*, 1781, oil on canvas.

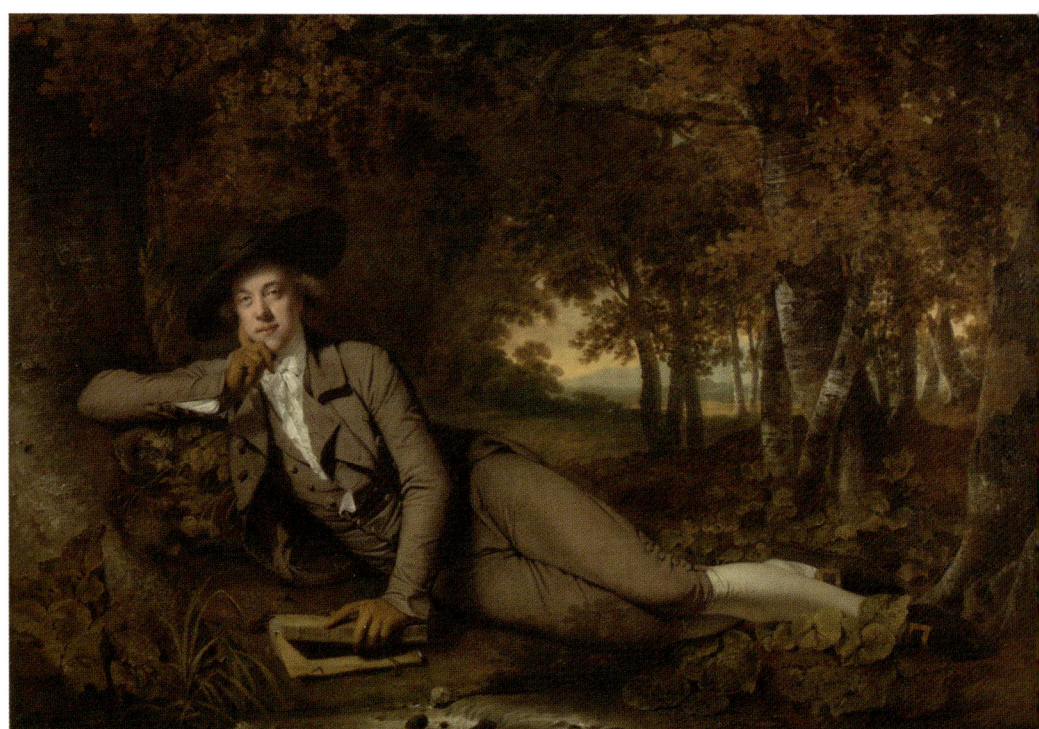

*Rêveries du promeneur solitaire*; this sorts with the image of the walker resting and dreaming on the floor of his own woodland. It is for the viewer of the painting, not Rousseau's words (whatever they might be), to intuit what reveries Boothby may be enjoying. The painting and its book may work together, but they point in different directions.

Roman poets had found landscape phenomena a potent topic and signifier for noumena, and there are some fascinating moments of a similar habit in much later cultures, as explored in Bruce Chatwin's *The Songlines*, where Australian Aboriginals who own a particular stretch of territory sing about it as they walk. A similar activity comes with many poets who, without resource to specific beliefs about Rome's *genius loci*, take possession of a special locality and announce its significance for them, or even for a wider readership. Landscape could often serve in this way as metaphor, as does one of the most famous English prospect poems, *Cooper's Hill*, by John Denham in 1642.[1] Many topographies besides that particular English landmark found their voice in a poet's verbal disclosure of their significance, moments of *prosopopoeia*. The late Brian Morris explores his Welshness in many poems about its landscape: the dying river valley of 'Ffair Rhod' or his meditations on water in 'He Praises the Virtues of Liquidity' are directly about the way he sees a locality and how it 'speaks' to him and so to his readers.

One of the rarest attempts to identify and explain *placefulness* comes in the work and life of Gerard Manley Hopkins. In his dedication to the writings of Duns Scotus (*c.* 1266–1308), he found ways to isolate and celebrate the individuality of any person, music or event, but (for my purposes) specifically place. Hopkins called this 'inscape', the unique quality and character of something, and he explained it as 'the essential and only lasting thing . . . [an] individually-distinctive beauty'. This was a particular mark of that poet's mind, and one that his poems constantly explored; yet he is not a unique figure in modern arts in the quest to capture the essential shape and meanings of objects in the world. A potent example, besides Cubism or the work of Paul and John Nash, is the painterly equivalent of Clive Bell's desire for 'significant form'.[2] But Hopkins is a powerful voice in identifying inscape, and his sonnet on 'The Windhover' is an astonishing tour de force that captures the significant form of the bird's flight: 'Brute beauty and valour and act'. For some readers, since he dedicated his poem 'To Christ the Lord', it will be a metaphor for Christ, but it is in the first place an inventive way to find words for the phenomenon of the hawk's flight.[3]

The world around the Jesuit Hopkins, its events and persons, is explored in his search for faith, but some emerge for their own sakes, like that on the Windhover, and in some writings and diary entries on other objects (including some of his own sketches). Thus in his sonnet 'Duns Scotus' Oxford' he hails Scotus, who is supposed to have worked there towards the end of his life, as 'Of realty the rarest-veinèd unraveller' (that is to say, he saw in Scotus a rare attention to explaining and celebrating real places, and from Scotus he took the Latin term *haecceitas*, 'thisness', from the Latin *haec*). In the octet Hopkins lists the elements of the city that mean most to him, and describes how from out of its surroundings of 'rural keeping – folk, flocks, and flowers' had grown the 'Towery city and branchy between towers;/ Cuckoo-echoing, bell-swarmèd, lark-charmèd, rook-racked, river-rounded'. Contrast is so often the essence in understanding place, for Oxford achieves its *inscape* as distinct from the city's 'base and brickest skirt' that has grown up around the once 'rural keeping'. It lets the poet praise and follow Scotus in what has been called 'the outward reflection of the inner nature of a thing'.[4] What is instructive in Hopkins's poetry is that he can make clear the way a place or event is less described than informed by the reader's awareness of his effort.

Hopkins is an important presence in modernist poetry in his search for moments of inscape. But earlier Romantic poets also alighted on their own sense of place or 'thisness'. If painters such as Turner and Nash relied on what they and their critics termed 'poetry', then poets saw the situation in reverse. From the English Lakeland to Italy, or to Grecian urns, they looked, if not before they wrote, then at least in a way that sustained their writing. They saw what can be called picturesque possibilities, although that is a lazy term these days. Their *land*scapes seem to anticipate Hopkins's in-scape, as they envisage places recognized and defined through their writing. Nash indeed has been called a neo-Romantic painter, so it is useful to see *genius loci* from a different, verbal perspective. Turner gave to the sublime a distinct and highly personal sense of place; Romantic poets and their descendants equally saw that location was essential to their sense of *genius loci*, and their responses to it had a basis in seen objects and particular places. This dual response to landscape lies at the centre of works by a later poet, Wallace Stevens, whose 'An Ordinary Evening in New Haven' (of which more below) calls for both the 'poem of pure reality, untouched/ By trope or deviation' *and* the inclusion of 'the spirit's alchemicana'.

WILLIAM WORDSWORTH's lines in 'A Poet's Epitaph' speak of views and their associations, of a place's physical form and what introspection delivers:

> The outward shows of sky and earth
> Of hill and valley, he has viewed;
> And impulses of deeper birth
> Have come to him in solitude.

Hill and vales are 'shows', or theatres, which reveal themselves as places of performance, and in need of response, which includes involvement more than spectatorship. It is those 'deeper' reactions that mark and define the Romantic understanding of place. With the Romantics, this was hugely important, but imagery depended much on an individual identification of what a place meant (sometimes experienced 'in solitude'), even if the original impulse had been visual or concerned with the seen. The landscape of 'Kubla Khan' (published 1816) was derived from Samuel Taylor Coleridge's encyclopaedic readings, but was coloured as much by what he wanted his readers to see.

More relevant is not Coleridge's poetic alchemy, but his philosophical ideas of the imagination. In *Biographia literaria* (1817), a somewhat rambling and discursive sequence of chapters is stopped by his need to establish in almost note-like sentences where he is going.[5] He then posits two imaginations. The first, derived clearly from eighteenth-century empiricism, is what keen and alert minds *see* and so understand in the world around them, and is bound to be individually assessed, even if much is shared between people of similar tastes and education. This, Coleridge explains, is 'the living power and prime agent of all human perception . . . a repetition in the finite [human] mind of the eternal act of creation'. It is a huge claim, but a potent one. The second is what an imagination makes of that original stimulus and response. In the sense that the secondary imagination is not primary, but rather what Coleridge calls an 'echo of the former, co-existing with the conscious will, yet still as identical with the primary in the agency, differing only in degree, and in the mode of its operation', it seems ambiguous.

Yet that ambiguity is crucial. Is the sense of place primary, and its mimesis in word, or image, only secondary? Does the secondary imagination diminish the power and virtues of the primary experience, or does the 'conscious will' of the artist, which marks the 'degree and mode' of the observer, triumph? If it does, is it his or her ability, in Coleridge's words, 'to unify and to unite'? The secondary imagination 'is essentially vital, even as all objects (*as* objects) are essentially fixed and dead'. That is precisely the fashion in which Augustin Berque sought to anchor a spirit of place in both the real world of nature and the real world of the individual's imagination, as we saw in Chapter Two. Phenomenology (Berque's specific emphasis) consists in large part in the finding of words (*logos*) to articulate the external world (*phenomena*).

That slippage is wonderfully captured in Wordsworth's account of the boy on Windermere in *The Prelude*, mimicking the hooting of owls among the crags, only to have the 'responsive' vale return both his imitations and the owls' own answering calls. The real hoots and the boy's imitations arrive as echoes, which the poet then remakes in his own lines, along with his new sense of the mystery of that place and moment:

> At evening, when the earliest stars began
> To move along the edges of the hills,
> Rising or setting, would he stand alone
> Beneath the trees or by the glimmering lake,
> And there, with fingers interwoven, both hands
> Pressed closely palm to palm, and to his mouth
> Uplifted, he, as through an instrument,
> Blew mimic hootings to the silent owls
> That they might answer them. – And they would shout
> Across the watery Vale, and shout again,
> Responsive to his call, with quivering peals,
> And long halloes, and screams, and echoes loud
> Redoubled and redoubled; concourse wild
> Of mirth and jocund din! And when it chanced
> That pauses of deep silence mock'd his skill,
> Then sometimes, in that silence, while he hung
> Listening, a gentle shock of mild surprize
> Has carried far into his heart the voice
> Of mountain torrents; or the visible scene
> Would enter unawares into his mind
> With all its solemn imagery, its rocks,

Its woods, and that uncertain Heaven, received
Into the bosom of the steady lake.[6]

A visible scene can enter unawares into his mind. That is one of the most active ways of articulating how we register a place – it is both a scenery and an instinctive or unconscious mental recognition. Actual echoes of both real owls and the boy's imitations – a primary and also secondary experience in Coleridge's terms – surprise the poet into a mental vision of the scene; what was visible and of course audible affects both mind and thus the secondary imagination of *The Prelude*.

Echoes, both actual and mimetic, can be eloquent yet also ambiguous forms of *genius loci*, since they emerge from a site when circumstances allow and inform a listener's sense of it, not least because they may add an aural as well as a visual notion of a site. Early scientists connected with the Royal Society were fascinated by echoes and how they intimated place. Robert Plot's histories of Oxfordshire (1677) and Staffordshire (1686) contain entries on actual echoes, while John Evelyn enjoyed a similar acoustical effect on a bridge over the River Marne in France, 'where the renowned echo returns the voice 9 or 10 times being provoked by a good singer'. But Evelyn was also interested in artificial echoes, having seen and drawn an example in the Tuileries in Paris, and even argued in his manuscript 'Elysium Britannicum' (begun in the 1650s) that an ideal garden ought always to include one (illus. 38). Whether that was ever achieved is unclear, although in the eighteenth century one was apparently contrived in a Kentucky garden for David Meade.[7] But the vogue for real echoes in landscape became a part more of romantic experience than of practical design. Alfred, Lord Tennyson, added one lyric in 1850 to *The Princess* (1847) on the dying echoes of a bugle that mingled with the sunset on castle walls, inspired by echoes at Killarney in 1848 (the lyric was beautifully set to music by Benjamin Britten in 1943 in his

38 John Evelyn, sketch describing the artificial echo created in the Tuileries, in his *Elysium Britannicum; or, The Royal Gardens* (1700).

But we will conclude what we haue sayd with a
Diagram of that Artificiall Echo (to giue ŏ Gardner
a Garden Instance) which we find erected at the ends
of the long walks of the Thuilleries in Paris; which
without much stresse of the voice maintaines an
Heroick Verse very well; for which it rarely suites
with the Serenades of those beautifull Ladys that
frequent it such Evenings as they present that
Elysium spardes with the beauties of yͤ illustrious
Court, And by this, such as are affected wͭh
Musiq e Solitude, may euen in flat e leuell places
(like this) where nature affords no assistance, Erect
an Artificiall Echo.

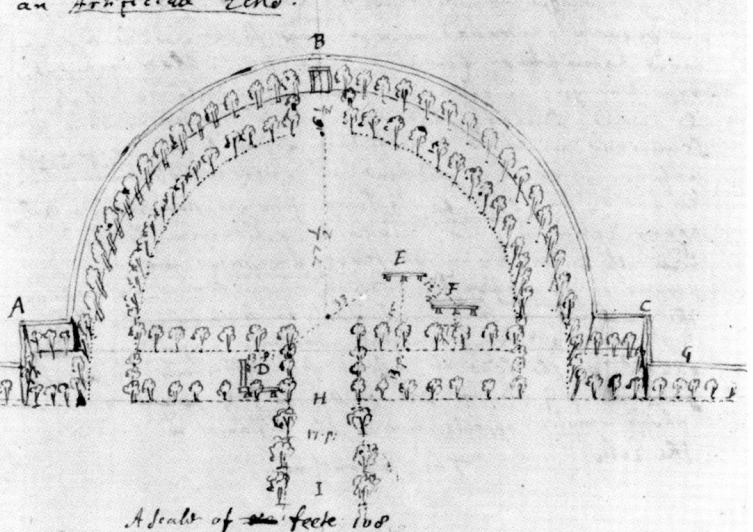

A scale of feete 108

A·B·C the wall of 15 foote high with his angles. D·E·F·
the Focuses where they speake or sing: EF for the
Singers e D for the Auditors being benches: g·g· part of
the Wall wͨh enclose the Thuilleries Garden. H the Entrance
into the Echo planted with double ranges of lime trees,
round the Circle: I the long walke of the Garden planted
wͭh elmes described cap: 6. &ͨ:

*Serenade for Tenor, Horn and Strings*). Echoes contribute a powerful sense of place, even when they are initiated by a visitor hooting like an owl.

But beyond a new recognition of place come (again in *The Prelude*) mental forms that no longer mirror familiar shapes, yet which inhabit the imagination thereafter:

> No familiar shapes
> Remained, no pleasant images of trees,
> Of sea or sky, no colours of green fields;
> But huge and mighty forms, that do not live
> Like living men, moved slowly through the mind.

For Wordsworth and his friends, the Lake District was a precious site in both life and imagination, and that area become a destination for many in the years that followed his and others' writings and drawings about it. It was a 'place', whether a source of the picturesque or of the sublime, which elicited a range of ideas and associations, a veritable field of, and the search for, a new and personal Romantic spirit of place.[8] Wordsworth's friend and co-contributor to the *Lyrical Ballads*, Coleridge, came to the Lakes first as a visitor; his records of those encounters, drawing at first on what he learned from Wordsworth, were recorded in his extensive notebooks. These have been re-published, and are also discussed by Keir Davidson under a title that conveys Coleridge's excitement: *O Joy for Me! Samuel Taylor Coleridge and the Origins of Fellwalking in the Lake District, 1790–1802.*[9]

What is important about Coleridge's sense of a Lakeland *genius loci* is that it was focused more and more on the act of walking and exploring, and less and less on any stationary moments of picturesque reaction or recollections of what others had witnessed. His notes show him in the process of seeing, assessing and formalizing what to record of Lakeland fells in a series of excursions:

some alone, some in the company of Wordsworth and his sister Dorothy in 1799 and 1800, and some with Robert Southey and William Hazlitt in 1803. He invoked these contributions of raw material later for the primary and secondary imaginations. Davidson finds in his writing 'some meaningful, direct connection' with the landscape (p. 30), in contrast to some of the earlier eighteenth-century accounts by residents or early visitors who documented, drew or mapped (as did George Smith in 1747) what was called an 'enchanted ground'. John Dalton used that phrase in 1755 in a descriptive poem narrating the visits of two ladies to the Vale of Keswick after they had visited the coal mines at Whitehaven – geology and its attendant industry provoking some of the interesting early responses to the area. The remainder of Davidson's account moves from more familiar ways in John Brown and Thomas Gray to Thomas West and William Gilpin. In great part they espoused less any empirical response than the process of registering the natural world through the Claude glass used by Gray, or the prose and illustrations in the work of other writers, especially Gilpin's *Observation*. It was also gradually accepted that visitors would find the expected 'stations' from which to take their stationary views of key moments and prospects. As John Brown had written, what was wanted was to 'give you [the reader] a complete idea', which would require 'the united powers of Claude [Lorrain], Salvator [Rosa] and [Nicolas] Poussin'.

It was the experience of fell-walking that initiated a different, more immediate sense of places between the customary 'stations' that 'broke the mould of the Picturesque' (Davidson, p. 45). It started, Davidson argues, with Joseph Palmer's *A Fortnight's Ramble to the Lakes by a Rambler in 1792*.[10] Less interested in making something of a guidebook, although reacting often in a picturesque mode, Palmer sought to respond to both local economy and inhabitants, for his 'mind was actively employed', and it may well be that Coleridge knew of him when he wrote his own observations.

Coleridge was a newcomer to the Lakes. He was drawn there in part by knowing Dorothy and William Wordsworth, the latter of whom had written

Therefore am I still
A lover of the meadows and the woods,
And mountains; and of all that we behold
From this green earth; of all the mighty world
Of eye, and ear, – both what they half create,
And what perceive.'
('Lines Composed a Few Miles above Tintern Abbey', ll. 102–7)

But Coleridge gradually developed his own keen and unmediated sense of what he saw. His explorations were lengthy and adventurous, relying on local instruction, local histories and guides, and, above all, his own curiosity and energy – of which we have evidence from the length of his walks, the often risky descents (not following what have today become known and well-marked routes) and his ability to put up with rain, mist and disorientation (for some of his excursions were undertaken in little-frequented areas).

Davidson's book intersperses his commentary with quotations from Coleridge, his own detailed maps of Coleridge's routes (as far as can be determined), one sketch by Coleridge himself (illus. 39) of a route based on a map in William Hutchinson's *History of the County of Cumberland* (1794), photographs of the lakes today, and a range of other writings. The undertaking is useful, but it masks what a direct reading of letters and the notebooks (which were wonderfully edited between 1957 and 1990 by Kathleen Coburn) can yield, and Davidson tends, sometimes awkwardly, to speculate on what Coleridge would have felt. In fact, the poet disclosed much himself.

Unsurprisingly, Coleridge is well aware of what he encounters and experiences; 'everyman his own path-maker', he notes in 1802. His annotations gradually move away from conventional responses

39 Coleridge's map of a nine-day walk in 1802, from his *Notebooks*.

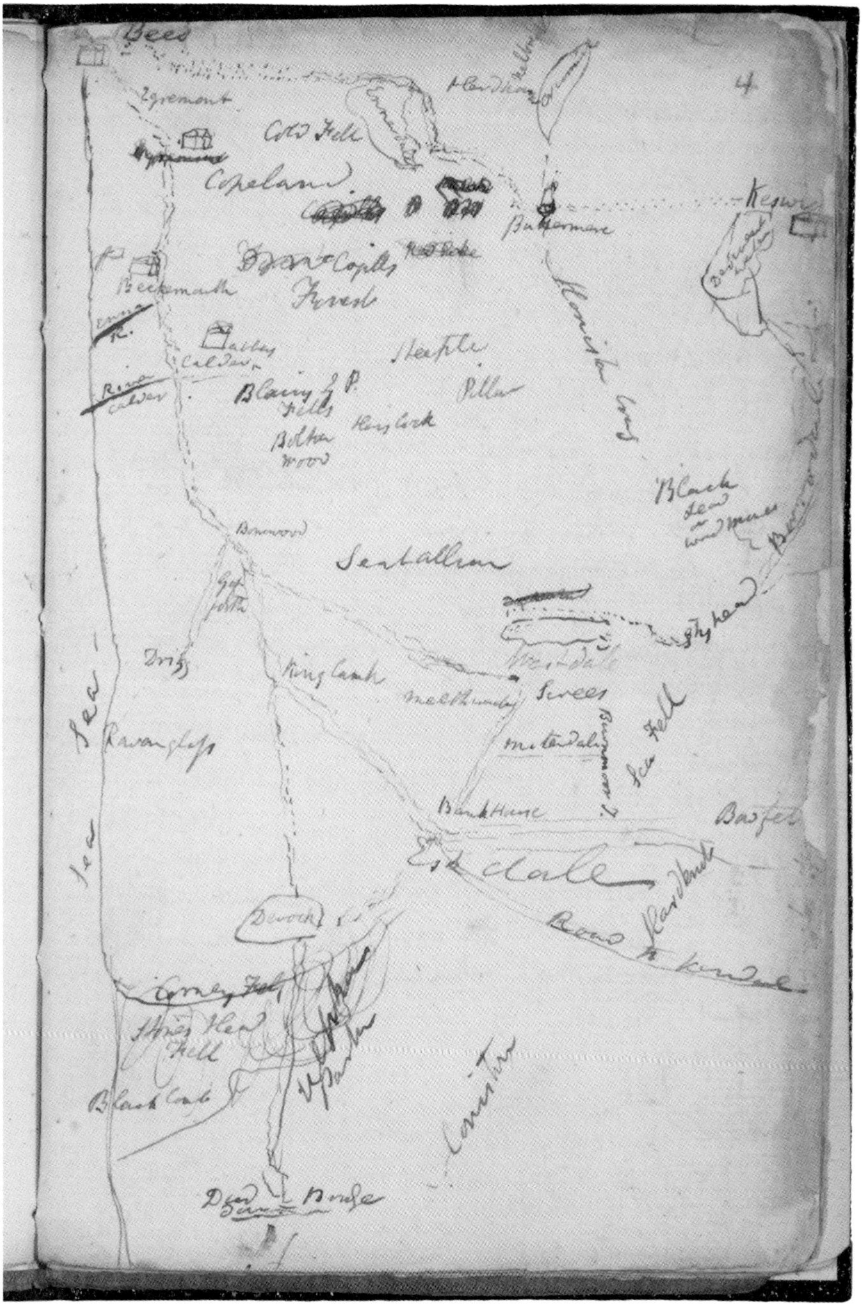

Bees

Egremont

Cold Fell

Copeland

4

Handborough

Buttermere

Keswick

Copills

Forest

Beckermouth

Calder

Steeple

Blaing J P

Pillar

River Calder

Bolton Wood

Haycock

Black
Sew
Wood moss

Brownwood

Seatallron

Gosforth

Drigg

Kinglank

Wastdale

melthwaite

Screes

mitardalam...

Sca Fell

Ravenglass

Sea

Sea

Black Horne

Bowfell

Eskdale

Hardknott

Road to Kendal

Devoch

Corney Fell

Hinds Head Fell

Black Cole

Canister

Dead Bridge

to try out his own emphases. He once noticed 'ladies reading Gilpin', or found a ruin less interesting than convention or Gilpin required of him. He learned the geography of the lakes, got to know the people who gave him shelter and a bed for the night, and gathered information from shepherds and casual encounters on the fells. He moves restlessly between wider views and small details ('little liquid icicles'). On Helvellyn he grappled with how to articulate his experiences:

> No words can convey any idea of this prodigious wilderness, that precipice fine on this side was but a ridge, sharp as a jagged knife [perhaps what is now called Striding Edge], level so long, and then ascending boldly . . . [another crag to his right] plunges down, like a waterfall, reaches a level steepness, and again plunges! (Davidson, p. 104)

> between the Mountains & the clouds, & slanting adown the clouds, and adown the Mountains, are columns or arches of misty light. (pp. 111ff)

This same interest in the way atmosphere prompts the memory and feeling is narrated in Coleridge's wonderful poem 'This Lime-Tree Bower my Prison'. Confined because of an injury, he thinks of the walks that his departed friends are presumably enjoying, while his own imagination dilates on sites he has known, their experiences and his vicarious grasp of meanings for both his friends and him: they

> gazing round
> On the wide landscape, gaze till all doth seem
> Less gross than bodily; and of such hues
> As veil the Almighty Spirits, when yet He makes
> Spirits perceive His presence.

Another great meditation, 'The Aeolian Harp', transcribes what the harp placed in the casement window declares: that

> all of animated nature
> Be but organic harps diversely framed,
> That tremble into thought, as o'er them sweeps
> Plastic and vast, one intellectual breeze,
> At once the Soul of each, and God of all.

These poems are poetic versions of how in Lakeland Coleridge would grasp the essence of physical places and then their potential significance for him, and for the reader. For poets and prose writers bridge the gap between themselves and the location, and then, in what they write, extend that bridge towards the reader. Thus in the Lakes Coleridge connects 'the purple lights of the scattered Clouds above' with his intimation that 'now I am enjoying the Godlikeness of the Place.' He does hope to find a 'oneness, there being infinite Perceptions – yet there must be a oneness, not an intense Unity but an Absolute Unity', lines that hint perhaps at what in *Biographia literaria* he would later see as the poet's desire to unify and unite the primary imagination's recollection of creation. Overall, much of his notebooks and some of the subsequent letters to friends about his wanderings in Lakeland do describe, but move beyond keen observations of forms, details and even sounds to see a larger (if not absolute) unity in place.

A more straightforward account of the Lakes comes from Wordsworth himself, published variously from 1822 and in a fifth edition as *A Guide Through the District of the Lakes in the North of England* in 1835.[11] It drew on his own explorations and on earlier tours and commentaries. It also drew on Dorothy Wordsworth's own writing, notably her account of climbing Scafell Pike, the highest peak in England, in 1818, which was absorbed into her brother's *Description of the Scenery of the Lakes in Northern England* (1822).

The text, whether his or Dorothy's, carefully notes the different shapes and heights of the fells, the silence on the summit, the qualities of different moments and the sequence of impressions.

Poets do have a special role in attempting discussion of place, for, as Stevens wrote, they allow both realities 'untouched/ By trope' and the mysteries of the spirit of place. Stevens's own poetry is strangely apt for managing how noumena are concealed and can be made manifest in what we see around us, 'the vulgate of experience'. There is, for example, the jar that he places on a round hilltop in Tennessee that took dominion over all the sprawling and 'slovenly wilderness'. His title for this poem is that it is an 'Anecdote of the Jar', but it is more. The poem as anecdote is more than the giving of a story of that deliberate insertion of the jar into the landscape, for it asks of the reader what the gesture – of the jar and of the poem – means.[12]

The richer and more magical poem 'The Idea of Order at Key West' allows both the 'genius of the sea' and the poet's 'rage to order words of the sea'. It directs us towards grasping 'Whose spirit is this? we said, because we knew/ It was the spirit that we sought and knew/ That we should ask this often as she sang.' Stevens's fascination with what the sea – particularly that of Florida – says to him is taken up in a variety of poems: its colour and atmosphere in 'Fabliau of Florida', for example, or as a place where a 'scholar of darkness' can understand how the elements of the 'Venereal Soil' of Florida ('Convolvulus and coral,/ Buzzards and live-moss') will disclose mysteries. His 'Farewell to Florida' contrasts the south of Key West with a cold north where he will be content, yet nostalgic that he had known 'that that land is forever gone/ And that she will not follow in any word/ Or look, nor ever again in thought, except/ That I loved her once.' That distinction and contrast between north and south mark Stevens's own idea of the distance between what a place itself vouchsafed and the elements of it that survive in the poet's mind.

It is unfair, for sure, to see Stevens as simply a poet of place, but he is nonetheless a poet of places and things imagined and grasped, and his 'Thirteen Ways of Looking at a Blackbird' plays engagingly with similar contrasts between the bird and the 'noble accents/ And lucid, inescapable rhythms' by which he can discern the genius of the bird in its shades of inscape. Where he does focus on real places – New England, the Alps – he is endlessly challenged about 'the Adequacy of Landscape'.

This becomes the central and much-explored concern in 'An Ordinary Evening in New Haven'. Reality is a potent container, but what is contained therein is also crucial ('the spirit that goes roundabout/ And through included, not merely the visible/ The solid'). New Haven is certainly concerned with the real, but it is a 'Reality as a thing seen by the mind,/ Not that which is but that which is apprehended'. Stevens is willing and admires what is seen, but the apprehension and its poetry are the centre of his vision. The reality of New Haven is, however, 'the beginning. Not the end./ Naked Alpha, not the hierophant Omega', yet the 'dense investiture' of the latter becomes a significant mode of explaining *genius loci*. From the Romans to the Aboriginals, from John Dennis to Hopkins, it is the realities of place that accommodate and proclaim whatever secrets and meanings individuals, or sometimes communities, discover in them. The poet's role is to probe the 'Reality as a thing seen by the mind', and this must needs come back to a view of place, 'A view of New Haven, say, through the certain eye'.

Although poets will find their subjects anywhere – as Stevens says, New Haven is just an example – they can draw out a skill in describing (their 'certain eye'), while at the same time drawing out the meaning of place. This is achieved in many ways: by the acknowledgement of the Almighty – the Creator of the universe – in Coleridge; or the more Platonic gift of poetry for Stevens and his interlocuter, Ramon Fernandez, who stands for all alert readers of the sea in 'The Idea of Order at Key West'; and the poets themselves who proved the 'less legible meanings' of sound, colour and 'the motions of the sea'. In those cases, the emphasis is on the disclosure of *thisness* by the poet, which the reader (and by implication a visitor to that place) must discover.

Another very different fund of verse that addresses location was collected by John Holloway in *The Oxford Book of Local Verses* (1987). Holloway is quick to point out that his anthology 'does not mean verses about places or the specific events that happened in them.'[13] Indeed, what this rich and unexpected gathering does is to highlight what people thought about a place or a particular object (such as silverware or ceramics), and then, more forcibly, whatever events might be associated with things or places. The verses – many of which are anonymous – are reflections, inscriptions, epitaphs, even versified graffiti, that alert visitors to local meanings. Among them are Milton's Well in Gloucestershire, where each aspect of the landscape 'raises the poet's thoughts on high'; a tree trunk split in two in Yorkshire that – in a vernacular mode of *prosopopoeia* – the visitor asks to 'Speak, if thy knotted trunk has a got a tongue,/ And tell us how things looked when thou wast young'; and a chapel of ease, complete with vault, animated by some rural wit by acknowledging that there are spirits above and spirits below.

Another approach to *genius loci* is focused on a specific landscape object, ruins, whose initial emptiness or desolation can be filled with words. In *Ruins* (2011), Margaret Randall combines her photographs of these architectural remains, usually taken from an unusual or vertiginous angle, with her poems. There are here two different perspectives that trigger poems, rival artefactual modes of grasping ruined places: the specific (Kiet Siel, Pueblo Bonito, Machu Picchu, Hovenweep); and the unspecified, 'liminal spaces', where Hermes, the god of travellers and boundaries,

> slips between tectonic plates,
> balancing a present that disappears

and a future never quite brought to focus,
pulls us
between one last burst of rage
and the perfect halves
of this geode opening to our touch.[14]

Some of the best and most intriguing place poems are those
that leave it to the reader, once he or she is carefully inserted into
the scene that the poem describes, to determine any larger significance. Such a task is bestowed in William Carlos Williams's
eight-line poem 'The Red Wheelbarrow': for, as its first line makes
clear, 'so much depends' – but what exactly? – on the fact that the
redness of the wheelbarrow, glazed with rainwater, is 'beside the
white/ chickens'. The phenomena are as it were painted, just as we
see them, so that we must deduce their significance. It is at once an
examination of colours and what rain brings out in them, and a
more mystical invitation to see more.

It is curiously the prose poem that can draw us closer to perspectives on the spirit of place, for it allows both the objectivity of
prose and the tropes of verse; at its best, prose will not distinguish
between them. Stevens saw that what could be 'apprehended' was
found in 'A mirror, a lake of reflections . . ./ A glassy ocean', and
the French poet Yves Bonnefoy, cited earlier, also saw *lieu* as the
mirror where some 'true humanity may emerge'. Yet unlike the
Claude glass, which reflects scenery for the artist to draw, or even
Narcissus gazing at his own reflection in the waters, this mirror is
the direct apprehension of how poets enable and understand the
place that they confront.

Michel Collot's fascination with literary geography, explored
in his discussion of others' writings in Chapter Two, has a counter-
part in his own collection of poems in prose, *Le parti pris des lieux*
(2018). The word *parti* contains a multitude of meanings in French,
but here it suggests choice, resolution or even bonus taken from a

place.[15] He is also surely thinking here of another writer, Francis Ponge, whose equivalent title – *Le parti pris des choses* (1942/9) – and argument speak to the same point: that language is the medium of our direct involvement with things, as with place. The epigraphs of Collot's collection include one that argues that '*La parole poétique est celle qui se porte vers l'autre rive, comme un pont. C'est dans le proche qu'elle découvre un lointain*' (Poetic words carry one to the other bank, like a bridge; it is the near that discovers the distant). It continues by saying that such a discovery increases endlessly – '*profondeur qui s'accroît sans cesse*'.

Collot's poems are personal and autobiographical at first but become more impersonal, although the poet is clearly moved by his own presence in specific places. There are poems that engage with history, with travel, with topography. Poetry is for Collot forever linked to space and time, or rather 'two types of temporality'. The summits of mountains emerge from the shadows, phosphorescent in the moonlight, a glimmer colours the page blue, a deaf voice emerges from silence, snow grates its teeth in the writing.[16] Squeezed between mountains and the sea, a small hill reveals '*une oasis de verdure entre deux déserts*'. A rocky path beside the Levron dialogues with the water of that stream – '*la voix des eaux nous accompagne . . . Je l'écoute et j'essaie de capter le message*'. Athens, Montmartre, Sissinghurst, Constable country, the paintings of Pierre Tal-Coat or Patrick Le Corf, the drawings of places (*Lieux*) by Michèle Iznardo, the geologies of Yves Noblet – all speak of what they describe and yet articulate Collot's own perceptions of their subjects. The poem on Constable country is a good example of how what one sees is nevertheless transformed into something larger, the contrast between *pays* (country) and *paysage* (landscape). The rural environs of Flatford (*pays*), owing to their modest dimensions, do not make a landscape (*paysage*), and it is their '*muséification*' that renders them a true landscape, '*une œuvre d'art en puissance*'. This also makes sense of Alain Roger's notion that we inevitably

bring to places what we have acquired beforehand in our imagination. Yet it complicates our sense of 'Constable's country' by
collapsing our visits there and our recollections of it into a location
represented elsewhere and in our mind.

This collapsing, or palimpsestic thinking, of places is always at
work for poets and artists. It also inevitably colours how we concern
ourselves with a larger range of cultural and political meanings.
The twentieth-century Palestinian poet Mahmoud Darwish wrote
'On this Earth There Is What Deserves Life', and his lines move
among various life-giving moments; yet it is the incident of place
that seems to recur endlessly:

> April's hesitancy,
> the smell of bread
> at dawn . . . grass on a stone . . . the hour of sun in the prison
>     yards, clouds
> imitating a herd of creatures . . . mother of beginnings
> and mother of ends.[17]

That his poem ends by calling the place 'Palestine' makes his work
clearly and convincingly political. Politics inflected Lampedusa's
novel *The Leopard*, and it plays out more emphatically even in some
travel writings that confront places where current conflict emerges
from a longer history.

SIX

# Travel Writers on Place

My books are always about living in places, not just rushing through
them.

Lawrence Durrell[1]

Stay longer, travel deeper.

Paul Theroux, *On the Plain of Snakes* (2019)

One might think that travel books would allow access to
different notions of *genius loci*. Yet many are concerned
simply with informing travellers about where to lodge,
which sites to visit and which restaurants to find, and offering
language tips. These are of course important, and may be useful in
directing visitors to some sense of a plausible *genius loci* that involves
ideas of gastronomy or language, but they otherwise leave to the
individual the opportunity to probe the significance (or otherwise)
of place. Guidebooks attest to phenomena far less to noumena. The
excellent TCI guide to Venice, cited in Chapter Three, is a mine
of crucial and useful information, but makes little of the aura of
that strange location of Torcello.

The significance of place is found more often in books where
writers have different approaches, not avoiding useful directions
and insights that they themselves have acquired, but rather seeking

to isolate whatever is distinctive for them as they travel: writers such as Henry James in *A Little Tour in France* (first published in serial form in 1883, then in toto in 1884), D. H. Lawrence's *Mornings in Mexico* (1927), Ford Madox Ford's *Provence* (1933), Lawrence Durrell's *Bitter Lemons* (1957) or Paul Theroux's *On the Plain of Snakes* (2019).[2] And it is certainly easier to isolate such attributes when the places are, for one reason or another, deemed exotic. It is through the imaginations of all these writers – for all were novelists or poets – that we find intimations of significance. Or sometimes not: at the very end of James's French tour, when he arrives in Dijon, he 'found, rather to my chagrin, that there was not a great deal, from the pictorial point of view, to be done with Dijon' (p. 250)! It is interesting that James relies here on a picturesque standard, an Anglo-American bias that affects all these writers – as with Durrell seeing the road near his house in Bellapais as 'a favourite painting' (p. 159). It is as if recourse to painting allows the writer to signal, without explaining, a more profound experience; it failed to work at Dijon for James, but did better in Cyprus for Durrell.

James ends his book with 'the thing that pleased me best at Dijon was the little old Parc, a charming public garden' (p. 251), although this was obviously not a *lieu* that permitted of being thought as an *haut lieu*. What the traveller brings can also be significant: James at the end of his travels is simply not sufficiently impressed. Personally, I have found much to admire and cherish about Dijon, but mainly because I have good friends there, enjoy Burgundy wine, know its university and, with my professional interest in gardens, found James's 'charming public garden' interesting at the very least. But that last stopping point did give James something to be achieved, because it helped him to see all France as 'more distinct' (p. 250). He could distinguish some larger and diffused *genius loci* from a more ordinary, local encounter.

All those books provide an interesting route into what notions of *genius loci* have been determined by a variety of distinctive and significant writers, as well as what fails to appeal. There are other writers whose genre could be allied to travel writing, such as John McPhee, whose journeys in *Encounters with the Archdruid* (1971) are used to situate intellectually and geographically the four real people he meets in different wildernesses, and whose journeys in *Pieces of the Frame* (1975) describe his encounters between nature and humans. These will also provide a fruitful perspective on how *genius loci* is envisaged and/or constructed.

## Provence

Henry James is no ordinary travel writer, to be sure. *A Little Tour in France*, describing a six-week tour in 1882, was his first in that genre, and he would much later continue with what he called 'scenes' or 'hours', such as *English Hours*, essays collected in 1905, *The American Scene* in 1907 and *Italian Hours* in 1909. Although he describes *A Little Tour* as 'an idle journey' (p. 133), recounted in 'these light pages' (p. 7), it was as calculated an art as were his great novels, and he was as fascinated by his encounter with place as he was when exploring the nuances and subtleties of personal stories in the novels.

James was 'essentially painterly and documentary', wrote Leon Edel in his introduction to *English Hours* in 1981. That is also true of James's time in France. But, while he is eager to note that there can be picturesque spots that are 'the most sketchable' (pp. 137–8), the texture of those chapters derives from his extremely careful observations, from what he brings from his readings and from paintings he has seen, his attention to history, to continuity and its preservation. So Toulouse 'has an air of a vignette of Gustave Doré, a couplet of Victor Hugo' (p. 144). He is bored by a custodian's interest in a 'scientific' display of treasures in the Capitol of Toulouse, for he wanted 'simply the spectacle, the pictures, and I didn't care in the least for the classifications'; instead, he liked the southern light in its garden with the artefacts displayed there, which 'the soil of the very place has yielded'. His varying concern for both 'bits' (p. 141) and, alternatively, 'taking complete possession of place', obtaining 'a rounded felicity' and 'a general impression' of Carcassonne, suggests that the former allows a picturesque response, the latter more consideration.

James notices picturesqueness at Les Baux, for he has, of course, 'read as much in the handbook of Murray' (a reference to the classic Victorian series of utterly reliable guides). He has also read Alphonse Daudet, for the love of whom he has spent three hours at Tarascon, where he purchases a local pamphlet but cannot find all that the writer points him to. He reads 'a luminous description' by Eugène-Emmanuel Viollet-le-Duc of Carcassonne, where he observes that the French architect's 'recondite' pamphlet provides an extensive history of the fortifications, yet notes that he is 'not one of those [who] have a head for such things, and having extracted these facts, he had made all the use of M. Viollet-le-Duc's pamphlet of which I was capable' (p. 150). Indeed, the 'perfect details [of] the fortifications of Carcassonne', newly conserved by Viollet-le-Duc, were 'no doubt . . . more affecting' forty years ago, when they were still ruins. James is attentive to things that dismay him but is politely merciless when he writes of them; unsurprisingly sceptical, even mildly ironic, at the spectacle of Viollet-le-Duc's wonderful evocations of the past's 'complete restorations', he approves of just one crumbling section, 'in order that the spirit of M. Viollet-le-Duc alone may pervade it' elsewhere by comparison.

James writes, as do many who seek to clarify some *genius loci*, that the Pont du Gard 'speaks [of the Romans] . . . in a manner with which they might have been satisfied' (p. 171). But this is sleight of hand, a *prosopopoeia*, for it is James who speaks and finds words there. His is a perfect instance of Alain Roger's contention that *genius loci* simply does not exist, but must be placed there by the visitor. Yet, as Augustin Berque responds, that emphasis is insufficient, even if utterly rational; it will inevitably exist in what a visitor – in this case one who is learned, alert and a touch ironic – brings to it, and that contribution now informs the Pont du Gard. I must have had my copy of James with me when I visited it years ago, and his descriptive precision in the 1870s is as much his own intimate style as it is, now, inseparable from the reactions of many later visitors. Huge, solid, unexpected, with 'at the same time a certain stupidity, a vague brutality', its exaggeration is typical of all Roman rigour, 'for I suppose a race which could do nothing small is as defective as a race that can do nothing great' (pp. 170–71); one might query whether Catullus or even Horace did not display small skills. He is more careful when he hears voices from the past that are not there, but which emerge in his memories, as when in moonlight at the ancient theatre of Arles he leans on the parapet and notes that 'it was not impossible to listen to the murmurs and shudders, the thick voice of the circus, that died away fifteen years ago.' The double negative allows an understanding of place that clearly involves his, not the theatre's murmurs.

James relies heavily on the notebooks he filled during his visits to many cities and towns (for 'France may be Paris, but Paris is not France'), and these yield observations particularly on buildings that 'tell' him much. Nîmes is 'a town of three or four fine features rather than a town with, as I may say, a general figure', he writes, yet he surrenders himself to its 'certain contagion of antiquity' and 'to contemplation and reveries', for he had indeed 'touched for a moment the ancient world'. He also relishes learned societies where poems in the 'fine old *langue d'orc* are declaimed' (p. 135). He can stop and talk to a cripple who had campaigned in Mexico and who was leaning against Carcassonne's 'romantic walls', gazing at the Pyrenees, and James is 'struck [by] so great a deal of history for so modest a figure' (p. 147).

What characterizes James's whole approach, in Provence especially, is his dedicated attention to each place, to what he might derive from its perusal and its frequent comparison with other towns and cities and, above all, with Italy, although he defends himself against such comparisons. His conduct in towns has moments of good travel business – good hotels, where he can find food ('I was obliged to cultivate relations with its cuisine') – but he goes at length into how he himself sees and values what he discovers.

I began with James for reasons of chronology, and in Provence because it seems to be James who hovers over Ford Madox Ford's later book on that region. Ford makes fun of James's 'endless sentences', his 'exact phrases with the air of savouring them, like a bull-finch cracking hemp-seed' (pp. 193 and 140). Compared to Ford's *Provence*, this section of James's *Little Tour* allows serious excursions into what was beginning by the mid-nineteenth century to be a notable 'place' that solicited some deeper research. James was 'a votary, always, in the first instance', he confessed, 'of a general impression' (p. 145), into which he then introduced measured descriptions and judgements. By contrast, Ford was 'a most engaging charlatan', as Graham Greene called him, and his Provence is less a question of accuracy or objectivity than an imaginary fabrication that owes equal parts to fact and to his own invention of its place in the cultural history of France. Ford's biographer, Max Saunders, believes that it is not a question of whether Ford is truthful, because the better question is 'What does it mean?' Indeed, *how* does it mean for him and for his readers? What *was* its 'frame of mind' (pp. 50 and 69)? Habit of mind prompts many travellers, but in Ford's case he rather enjoys shifting or inventing the frame.[3]

Years later William Carlos Williams wrote a poem about Ford, an affectionate yet ironic response that begins by asking Ford whether he now found Heaven better than Provence, and believing the answer would have to be no. It will 'never be the same/ Provence to us/ now you are gone': these lines capture the eccentricity of Ford's response to the region, its warm acknowledgement of 'your sacred garlic' and the cafe chairs that strained as he lowered his bulk on to them.[4]

Ford saw Provence from many viewpoints – some geographical, some literary, some amusing, ironic and teasing. His sense of
what constituted the physical area was flexible. Sometimes Provence
began at Lyons, sometimes further south, and sometimes it was only
the land east of the Rhône, with its cluster of towns including
Arles, Avignon and Aix and his beloved Tarascon; he drew a diagram to make that point (illus. 40). James by contrast approaches
Provence from the west; he liked Daudet, who was born in Nîmes
but who Ford said was not a 'true Provençal' because, for 'all its
charms and the *mises à mort* and the Maison Carrée and one
memorable eating place, Nîmes is not true Provence' (p. 25).

If it is 'difficult to explain the fine shades of London to an alien',
then it might be grasped for Ford's readers by seeing Provence from
and through the lens of London. There are starlings in London and
nightingales in Provence, where he acquired the 'habit of writing
in that bird's strains' (p. 26). There are no cafes in London, but many
good examples in Provence. Ford's sentences jump mischievously
from place to place, from one perspective to another, and his tone
both is engaging and yet makes it hard to ascertain how we should

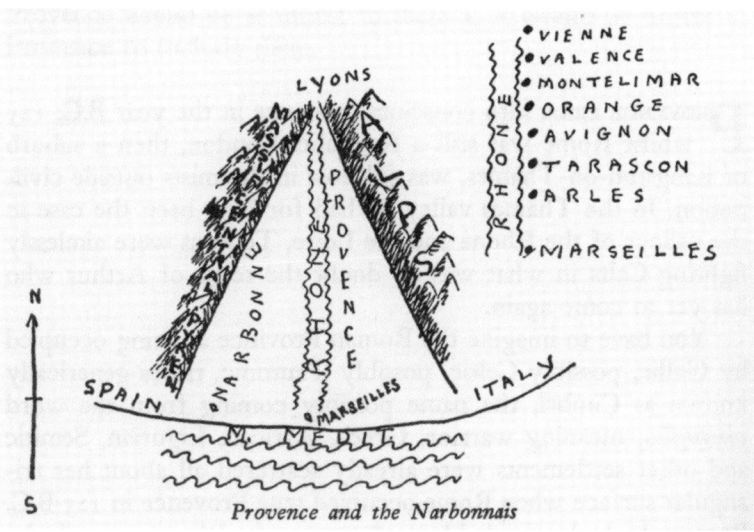

40 Ford Madox
Ford's sketch of 'his'
Provence, 1933.

applaud a self-confessed con artist. He recognizes that Provence was on the Grand Trade Route of the Silk Road from Cathay (China) to Western Europe, but then somehow envisages that the route makes a stop at Ottery St Mary in Devon, from where he meets a businessman he encounters in Provence. This traveller, though, has no idea that a famous poet lived in that Devon town (that is, Coleridge), and predictably behaves like any boorish Brit who hates to travel. Provence, by contrast, Ford says, 'is a book of travel'. Yet Ford's travels are as much actual as imaginary. Provence's characteristics of place can be its shrewdness, its frugality and little sense of the 'vicissitudes' that bedevil other places (p. 41). It has sun, white walls, orange rocks and the 'perfume of rosemary, lavender, thyme and orange blossoms'. He loves its gastronomy, above all its garlic, but – 'though it would be unkind to say so' – we have to 'do the best we can with Provence food'. Yet he is thankful that in Provence 'the apple will not flourish and the Brussels sprout will not grow at all' (p. 78).

But Ford found much in Provence beyond food and drink. His father, the music critic Francis Hueffer, had written on the troubadours and knew Frédéric Mistral, the poet who revived the Provencal language, and these literary associations colour his son's prose and his quotations there from the troubadours. Ford has confidence in what writers have taught him about Provence, for it has been 'my fate in life to be brought constantly into contact with the great, to which fact I attribute at once my modesty and what I have of a sense of humor' (p. 40). The book is indeed filled with gestures towards those famous others, including Henry James.

## Mexico

Two 'greats' have visited and written about Mexico. D. H. Lawrence in the 1920s and Paul Theroux in 2019 are eloquent about how they might discern its *genius loci*: as a whole, at specific places and at different times of the day or month, and more obviously at very different cultural moments in our growing (mis)understanding of Mexico, especially for a reader who has never visited. Theroux comes upon the house in Oaxaca where Lawrence and his wife, Frieda, lived while the former was writing *Mornings in Mexico* and his Mexican novel, *The Plumed Serpent* (1926), but then notes how much has changed, transforming the region from a rurality of farms and farmlands to an improvised urban settlement of ill-supervised zoning (p. 261). While Lawrence, Theroux thinks, is somewhat sentimental about that countryside, he himself is open to a very mixed, impressionistic appraisal of the whole nation.

These two books – *Mornings in Mexico* and *On the Plain of Snakes* (2019) – are intriguing examples of *géographie littéraire*, being by good writers and more than usually focused on the actual geography, physical as well as cultural in all its local manifestations. Both writers were travellers; Theroux astonishingly so, as his publications reveal, while Lawrence produced three other travel books, *Twilight in Italy* (1916), *Sea and Sardinia* (1923) and *Etruscan Places* (1932). Both found that travel allowed them to recognize in themselves a version of otherness, as 'outsider' or *gringo*. At the same time each was strikingly aware of his own being, with its accumulated understanding of ways that he could bring to bear on place. Theroux, towards the end of his lengthy journey, asks, 'What did I reveal of myself?' (p. 246), and his answer is considerably more mixed as well as much more sustained and lengthy than Lawrence's response to the same question. In particular, Theroux spends much of his opening section rehearsing the many writers and visitors who had visited and written of Mexico, comparing them with his earlier and extensive excursions elsewhere in the world, thus laying out a fund of perspectives against which he could test his own in Mexico.

Theroux seizes on snakes as an example of 'thatness'. *That* is the Mexico flag, where an eagle gnaws at a rearing rattler, which is what he thinks about as he meets his first snake on p. 4 (harmless, he later realizes). But there are 26 species of rattlesnake, 'not to mention . . . milk snakes, blind snakes, rat snakes, pit vipers, worm-sized garden snakes, and ten-foot-long boa constrictors'. There is also the cock-and-bull story of a local legend about 'an elusive snake with the rose on its head' (p. 350). As Lawrence takes his first morning walk, he also sees an eagle looking for snakes. Yet snakes have an emblematic and metaphorical life on the flag and also in the language the writers use. Lawrence invokes 'reptilian gloom'; slow oxen sway their great horns 'as a snake sways itself'; his last chapter, being now in Arizona, is about the 'Hopi Snake Dance', at the end of which 'the aboriginal Americans [are] riding into their shut-in reservations. While the white Americans hurry back to their motor cars' (p. 90).[5]

Lawrence originally drafted eight essays for *Mornings in Mexico*; more were added later. The book's tone, at least from a hundred years on, is somewhat uncertain. Its opening sees Mexico, 'when all is said and done', as having 'a faint, physical scent of its own, as each human being has'; this is 'inexplicable', but consists of 'resin and perspiration and sunburned earth and urine among other things' (p. 9). Smells are vital elements of anyone's response to a specific place, although they are hard to verbalize, as are sounds. Lawrence reveals clearly a reverence for, and a curiosity and delight in, the local colours, costumes, dialects and people he encounters, the dramatis personae of his wanderings. His text is punctured with Spanish, as he signals what *tepache* or *panteón* means (respectively a fermented drink and a cemetery), and he lingers lovingly at the start over how the parrots are mimicking the barking and the name of a *perro* (dog). Yet there is also a clear sense that he is 'other', but what that otherness means for his readers is, and was probably meant to be, unsettling.

Lawrence does not believe in evolution, 'a long string hooked on to a First Cause, and being slowly twisted in unbroken continuity through the ages' (pp. 12–13). Instead he opts for what the Aztecs called 'the Suns . . . worlds successively created and destroyed', which seem thenceforth to sustain his keen consideration of how this Mexican visit confronts the mysterious light of one such 'sun' before its extinction; his essays seek to identify these suns before they are blown out like candles.

Lawrence wants to render 'the Indian in his own terms' (p. 55), even though this writer happens to be English. For example, he contrasts the Indians' sense of entertainment with the conventional European appetite for theatrical dramas that please with their confidence in any depiction of 'the Universal Mind' (p. 53). It is, he says, 'almost impossible for the white people to approach the Indian without either sentimentality or dislike'; the opportunity to explain one person's consciousness from another's requires 'a little Ghost inside you which sees both ways, or even many ways' (p. 34). But that is impossible, so you must push aside one mode while understanding the other. This dialogue is what sustains Lawrence's essays: eager to value both modes, yet wary of conde-scending. In Indigenous songs and dances there is no actor or audience, and above all no judgement, as would pertain in the European theatrical experience. So he proceeds to explain the 'Dance of the Sprouting Corn' and the 'Hopi Snake Dance'.

Both are wonderful, detailed chapters, but the two are very different. The first admits of little distance between Lawrence and his subjects, and the second presents the dance as being performed for tourists who arrive in hordes of black automobiles, 'like a funeral cortège?' (p. 71). In the first, the mystery of 'germination . . . *putting forth*, resurrection, life springing within the seed' (p. 70) are (as he puts it elsewhere) what penetrate 'straight to at the dia-phragm' (p. 11). That this ritual is accomplished during the week 'after Easter, after Christ Risen' is a tellingly, if only slightly, subtle hint of the collision and merger of two traditions.

Lawrence sees the rituals of the snake dance as being delib-erately opposed to the cultural preferences of its audience, 'who can hardly wait for the mummery to cease' (p. 82). He observes its celebration of 'the great convulsive powers' (p. 78), for 'Man, little man, with his consciousness and his will, must both submit to the great origin-powers of his life, and conquer them' (p. 87). It is a tour de force, balanced between the innate religion of the dancers and snake-handlers and the distance that Lawrence senses for his reader and, perhaps, for himself: 'the gulf of mutual negation between us'.

Both Lawrence and Theroux seek a proper identification of the 'real' Mexico as a clue to the apprehension of its *genius loci*. In the 1920s Lawrence was interested in what and exactly where Mexico was: one little town speaks of the whole, because 'there is a resinous smell of ocoye wood . . . and of Morning, and even of Mexico' (p. 9). Almost a hundred years later, in *On the Plain of Snakes*, Theroux muses that 'even in the grip of NAFTA newfangledness, the eternal Mexico persists' (p. 107). He uses that same word 'eternal' in the caption for a photograph of a mounted herder shepherding his flock of sheep below the sixteenth-century Padre Tembleque aqueduct northeast of Mexico City. Yet there are eternities *and* eternities: once, Aztec and Spanish conquistadores; now, the gangs of cartels, the constant flow of migrants northwards or those deported south back to Mexico, and those who live and work on both sides of the border (the anticipated 'Murus Hadrianus Trumpus'; p. 32), including those who swim the river, work for a while in the United States, then swim back 'home' safely. Theroux confesses earlier that he has not found any other traveller 'who has been able to sum up Mexico' (p. 9), and neither the border guard nor the immigration officer with whom he tries to talk declares they have ever been across the border.

By the end Theroux realizes that the 31 states of Mexico may be 'summed up' as being in three parts (p. 230): the 'north of the country lies in America's cruel, teasing, overwhelming shadow – a shadow that contains factory towns, industrial areas, smuggler enclaves and drug routes'. Mexico City in the middle is 'like an entire nation of twenty-million people – much larger than any Central American republic'. The south is the 'poorest region . . . a place apart, rooted in the distant past, some of its people so innocent of Spanish, they still speak the language of the 2,500-year-old civilization'. And he recalls the British writer and critic V. S. Pritchett (writing about Spain), 'The past of a place survives in its poor' (p. 109).

Theroux's most intriguing section is 'Borderlands', a 'jaunt' from one end of Mexico to the other, undertaken because he wishes 'to have a notion of the whole border' (p. 24). It opens the rich, paradoxical exploration of his Mexico in the following chapters, for 'just across the street Mexico began,' wrote Jack Kerouac (p. 6), upon whom, among many other writers, Theroux relies in his book.[6] While the Mexican landscape can look just like Texas, it is nevertheless divided, for a treaty of 1836 turned the river valley at Reynosa into 'two countries' (p. 98). This stark contrast is sometimes extreme, as when he meets and is stopped by police and gives them a bribe to allow him to continue, and sometimes wonderfully negotiated, or when, by arrangement, he teaches a creative-writing class in Mexico City. In Nogales (Heroica Nogales), another border town, he discovers how much is hidden in its downtown: factories, restaurants, residences, malls, migrants, sad and happy stories. Theroux's skill is not only that he stays longer, probing more deeply, but that he makes friends and contacts Mexican writers and foreigners who have settled there.

Towards the end of his travels Theroux registers for a class to improve his Spanish, and this is a long section of the book in which (besides allowing his readers to improve their own Spanish) he makes friends with other, much younger students, learns about culture and acquires the use of the subjective tense – just as earlier, while teaching in Mexico City, he made new friends and contacts. His students there were a fund of information and helped him to explore (they were at times nervous about where he wanted to be taken, but were truly inventive in enabling his excursions). At the very end, in 'The

Way Back', he realizes that he is 'a different person now, because I knew where I had been. I had made friends on the road through the plain of snakes, and that had lifted my spirits' (p. 432).

This is a book full of stories, revealed occasionally from what Theroux derives from his notes, and occasionally from narratives supplied by those he met and quotes in full, or by those who had visited the United States and returned to their villages (the inhabitants of one of which seem mostly to have gone at one time or another to Poughkeepsie, New York). He interviews Indigenous Mexicans whose first language was Zapote and who are barely able to communicate through their own poor grasp of Spanish. But in the course of a dozen such interviews he gets to hear those who have landed in El Comedar, the Eating Place, run by the Jesuits ('BIENVENIDOS MIGRANTES DEPORTADOS Y EN TRANSITO'). Stories, snapshots and anecdotes obtained through both chance encounters and organized rendezvous are his principal mode of enquiry and writing. However, Mexico is not a world that is '*wholly graspable*' (p. 3), for its graspability is illusive, although perpetually sought for. He can also hope to capture 'the texture of Mexican life in general', what he terms '*el mundo* Mexico' (p. 13). This need for generalities haunts not only his endless collection of particulars, but also all those who seek a *genius loci* among the impressionist suggestions of foreign places. Theroux may be occasionally 'beguiled' by picturesque townscapes – 'its handsome church and friendly shop owners, its good restaurant and taco stands' (p. 15) – but 'as a time-killing tourist' (p. 211) he cannot be satisfied for long. He searches 'the underworld, the *inframundo* of Mexican traditional belief' (pp. 338–9).

Theroux is diligent, enquiring, nervous, but bold in the face of discovery, taking both directions for the safest routes through the land of cartels and warring gangs, and suggestions of places to eat (for its 'Culture is cuisine'; p. 109), from people he trusts. He is endless (and has to be) in observing the country's stark contrasts:

the 'dark side of Mexico, the Mexico that everyone whispers about' (p. 113), which gives rise to another Mexican mantra, 'there is no business without terror' (p. 124), a sinister Mexico that lurks behind the 'fussily picturesque, tastefully restored in parts' (p. 123). Yet he admires the courtesy of the people, their avoidance of confrontation (p. 115), the successful Technical University at Monterrey, and marvels 'at this desert landscape, its stark beauty and unexpected wildness' (p. 432). In 'Mexico's Detroit', Saltillo, he finds good museums, venerable buildings, bad housing and five car plants. There is little traffic as he goes south, but there are lines of trucks with cars heading north for Texas.

*On the Plain of Snakes* is a big book; not for nothing does Theroux advise visitors to stay longer and travel deeper. Yet it is also, inevitably, impressionistic, since however deep you delve, fitting the pieces of this jigsaw together is challenging. As someone who has never been to Mexico, I find the scope of Theroux's detailed attention and curiosity both impressive and, often, too much to hang on to (an index as well as a map would have been a boon). It is a book that constantly confronts what Mexico – all the different Mexicos – mean, and how he (and the reader) must sort the trivial (or the seemingly trivial) from the tough and unpalatable.

An academic and writer living in Oaxaca guides Theroux through the events of the Day of the Dead. This is an event that features substantially in Malcolm Lowry's famous novel *Under the Volcano* (1947), an immense and gruelling tragedy (in some sense autobiographical) that traces how Geoffrey Firmin, a British ex-consul, drowning himself in mescal and unable to be saved by his ex-wife and half-brother, dies in a ravine under the two volcanos Popocatépetl and Iztaccihuatl. Theroux finds Lowry's writing 'florid and hyperbolic', and quotes Firmin's view of Oaxaca 'as a breaking heart, a sudden peal of stifled bells in a gale, the last syllables of one dying of thirst in the desert' (p. 227). That novel and *On the Plain of Snakes* differ in their tones and representations of the Day of the Dead. Theroux's searches are more anthropological, although he is deeply involved in understanding how the cacophony and masquerades of that event can be explained as 'forms of protest, the daily routine turned upside down' (p. 252). Here are two very different perspectives on *genius loci*, yet each is necessary to grasp what Theroux calls that 'underworld, the *inframundo* of Mexican traditional belief'.

## Cyprus

Language, history, landscape, food, rituals, friends and chance encounters all contribute to, and sustain, memories. A spirit of one place or the spirits of various places can be communicated through the mind, via print or imagery, and on the ground. Lawrence Durrell explores and recounts Cyprus's varied and still complicated history, and traces how that allure was increasingly tarnished by the island's struggle for independence from Britain. *Bitter Lemons*, unlike his earlier books on other Greek islands, *Prospero's Cell* (1945) on Corfu and *Reflections on a Marine Venus* (1953) on Rhodes, gradually changes its focus and tone as he becomes involved in the politics of Enosis, the Cypriot movement to disengage from British oversight and align with Greece. That political narrative gradually grows throughout the book until it becomes the counterweight to Durrell's earlier affection for the island: thus a newer *genius loci* to confront, and at least temporarily to overwhelm his pleasure and residence there.

As with Lampedusa in Sicily, for Durrell in Cyprus politics are central to a sense of place, although *Bitter Lemons* and a thirteen-line poem with the same title take different routes. The poem, published in *Private Lines, Nicosia 1955*, does not mention Cyprus by name (although the island is named when the poem is reprinted at the end of the book *Bitter Lemons*). It takes one moment of equipoise upon which the book obviously expands: a balancing between, on the one hand, acts of bitterness, memory tortured and things best left 'unsaid', and on the other, 'beauty, darkness, vehemence' and the 'sea-nurses' keeping the sea calm like 'tears unshed'. It may hint, in the light of the book, at bitterness, but the poem does not seek to test the writer's relish of the island against the raw, bitter politics that would later erupt.

Durrell's delight in and appreciation of what Cyprus means is sustained by his historical sense and his knowledge of Greek ('perhaps language was the key'; p. 37). Language and the past of place are crucial indices of *genius loci*, although they require skill in finding ways to use them. Durrell had always been taken by exotic places; his *The Alexandria Quartet* (1957–60; a tetralogy that I found fascinating initially, but later thought overwrought) displayed his zest for unfamiliar and foreign places as well as for the mundane and pragmatic. In Cyprus, he not only speaks Greek but enjoys the way that allows him more intimacy with place and with the Greek population, as well as with Turks and Armenians, for he experiences Cyprus through 'its people rather than its landscape' (p. 53). And he is alert to the need to accumulate impressions; one chapter, 'The Swallows Gather', collects isolated remarks and encounters recorded in his notebook, while another ('A Telling of Omens'), recounting his teaching in Nicosia, explores the fierce and complex reactions of his students, some of them being the earliest protesters against Britain's Commonwealth rule.

Durrell went to Cyprus in the first place to live (finding and building a house, constructed by Greek workmen with a Turkish overseer), and then as a civil servant involved with Enosis, serving as information officer for this British outpost, a place known far better by specialists there than by any politician or civil servant in Westminster. At first he was 'full of optimism' (p. 140), happy and able, as he seemed to be able to live and function in two worlds. For himself, at least, he seems to have achieved a measure of success, but what he called the 'stock-market of world affairs' (p. 101) destroyed that good fellowship.

The last section of the book follows a brief account of the killing at point-blank range of a schoolmaster, whom Durrell knew well, by a student. But then, to counter that horrible moment, he recounts at length a whole day spent with that schoolmaster, Panos, in the days before he was killed: they walked, picked flowers and visited places that each knew well, and they avoided politics for the most part, except when Panos says unhappily that he thinks 'Enosis is right and must one day come,' yet regrets that it is violence that would 'bring Enosis sooner than polite talk will' (p. 233). Even the taxi driver who drove Durrell by night to the heavily guarded airport, for his final departure from the island, explained: 'You see, the trouble with the Greeks is that we are really so pro-British' (p. 250), something that Durrell was told constantly during his last year on the island. While 'so many of our [the British] national characteristics are misinterpreted' (p. 35), 'belief in our fair-mindedness and political honesty was unshakable' (p. 120). Yet shaken it was, and Durrell discovered that he could not find his 'way forward among all these mutually contradictory propositions' (p. 194), including Turkish opposition to Cyprus's alliance with Greece. The island remains divided.

So what constitutes Durrell's identification of Cyprus as a special place? How does its *genius loci* manifest? He is attentive to landscape despite his preference for its people, and intimate in a Cypriot way with his neighbours, who are courteous even when the crisis looms and he is known to be returning to England. His learning curve is impressive, and he has read widely, as his bibliography attests. Yet that confidence and security are imperilled by his appointment as information officer to the governor of the island during the civil wars with Enosis, and by the baffling ineptitude of Britain's colonial mentality, which refuses to espouse a European vision. As he leaves Cyprus, he realized that he was 'very tired after this two years' spell as a servant of the Crown; and I had achieved nothing. It was good to be leaving' (p. 246).

*Bitter Lemons* as a whole shows that Durrell had achieved a sense of the complexity of place. Islands are, perhaps, 'places where different destinies can meet and intersect in the full isolation of time' (p. 20). Other regimes had enjoyed very different occupations of the island: the Lusignans were in Cyprus for 300 years, Venice for just 82; the Turks stayed for 300, and the British for 78; 'What does it all mean?' asks one of Durrell's students (p. 149). His house below the Gothic Abbey of Bellapais and the village's 'Tree of Idleness', where he loved to meet neighbours, became a place to which even those same neighbours thought he was foolish to return; an Enosis slogan arguing for LIBERTY OR DEATH (p. 187) was daubed in blue paint under the tree.

*Genius loci* is determined in large part by history's fact and by the fictions that emerge from that (with fiction often being more compelling). Durrell leans on both aspects of Cyprus's history. Indeed, to please his new neighbours he invents the whopping lie that his brother died at Thermopylae in the First World War. Throughout his three years in Cyprus (1953–7) he absorbs fictions and legends and reformulates them into his own understanding of the island. Soon after he arrives, his driver tells him, under 'the coarse net of the carob tree – a stranger to me', that Richard Coeur de Lion landed on this bit of coast; yet a footnote observes that 'he was wrong'. The crazy, drunken Frangos 'made up everything out of his own head' (p. 87). But there are moments when facts emerge from the mysteries of narrative, and coalesce into a plausible history. The role of Byzantium was 'the true source', Durrell is told by an Israeli journalist, 'of Greek thinking, Greek *moeurs*' (p. 121). Cyprus, Durrell realizes, 'was more Eastern than its landscape would suggest, and like a good Levantine I must wait and see' (p. 32). He soon came to see, in a chapter entitled 'The Feast of Unreason', that British and Cypriot 'offered one a gallery of humours which could only be fully enjoyed by one who, like myself, had a stake in neither' (p. 36). In a sense he did have a stake, although that constituted a house he had to leave and a lost confidence that based 'everything upon Anglo-Greek amity' (p. 153), none of which he would recover.

Those four writers are concerned with what they found personally in various places, none invoking or relying on the phrase *genius loci*, but surely all seeking to find it for themselves, and for others (hence writing and being published). All five books would be required reading if one were to visit any of these places. For most of them the search must explore how a specific culture was formed and then shaped their own awareness and its own; this was most palpable in Mexico and Cyprus, but nonetheless what lingered behind Provence was an ancient sense of lost and rediscovered languages both literal and topographical, and then what James and Ford brought to its disclosure. They were all focused on the past and the modes by which earlier places had been understood and also the life of those in later times.

It is that same emphasis that is explored in Bruce Chatwin's extraordinary book *The Songlines* of 1987.[7] This rich, multifaceted narrative has two foci that are relevant here. It asks how places were understood and, above all, used as a means of knowing where they were in the world. The Australian Aboriginal 'could not believe the country existed until they could see and sing it': '"To exist" is "to be perceived"' (p. 14). The songlines were ritualistic, a 'spaghetti of Iliad and Odysseys . . . in which every "episode" was readable in terms of geology' (p. 13) and topography. But a song was also a means of distinguishing its singers from others outside the clan, as they sang out the 'name of everything that crossed their path – birds, animals, plants, rocks, waterholes – and so [sang] the world into existence' (p. 2). Chatwin also saw that these Australian rituals were 'universal . . . the means by which men organized social life' (p. 73).

The arguments about how to 'organize social life' in its broadest sense are the stuff of John McPhee's book *Encounters with the Archdruid*, for it is essentially about geology: both the literal stuff beneath the earth and the ground on which we can feel secure and happy as we move above and through it. Three essays take McPhee with David Brower, a militant conservationist, member of the Sierra Club and promotor of its publications, to travel with others committed in their turn to very opposite concerns: a mineral engineer, a builder of huge dams and a developer of resorts, who thinks all conservationists are druids who 'sacrifice people and worship trees'. At issue for McPhee, for whom conservation is a central concern, is what makes a place a place, what makes a there here (to reverse Gertrude Stein). The dialogues on their excursions are obviously re-created by McPhee (he hardly carried a tape recorder with him), but that fictionist mode of reportage is able to make their disagreements more conspicuous and thoughtful. The places they visit – Glacier Peak Wilderness, the Sea Plantation on Cumberland Island, the river through Cascade Canyon – are the places whose essence, importance and happiness are disclosed through description and conversations; in these dialogues the reader must be alert to where the emphasis lies, without the author doing much obviously to tip the scales of the debate.

*Encounters with the Archdruid* is similar to another volume by McPhee, *Pieces of the Frame*, where frames limit and focus an enclosed image, but we are left without being able to be precise about what it signifies or where the author wishes to put his foot down; the image is just there to be studied (or, in this case, read). It is a bit like the poem by William Carlos Williams quoted in Chapter Five, in that *we* must decide what something amounts to. For Williams 'so much depends upon' a red wheelbarrow, glazed with rain, and the white chickens – depends, that is to say, on how readers of those austere eight lines deduce for themselves what that image might mean or imply. So McPhee frames the places that he visits and discusses with others in such a way that we ourselves must recognize, value and debate what exactly that *genius ipsus loci* really is. We must decide how McPhee has 'put together' his own wheelbarrow and its contexts, although in his case there are infinitely more detailed and intricate objects within his frames.

It is at once hard and easy to see where McPhee is taking us, even if one is firmly on the side of the druid. Dialogues are tricky in that they allow each speaker his or her own voice, and although McPhee himself enters with queries and narrative biographies of the leading discussants, the task becomes trickier when we need to identify how McPhee, giving due weight to Brower's interlocutors, delivers his own perspective.

We return, once again, to the idea that *genius loci* does not exist in itself, and that individuals craft for themselves the meanings and spirit of place. The conflict between a preservationist such as Brower and someone who wants to see copper mining thrive will be clear to those who agree with the former, although the latter's arguments about the likely impermanence of such intrusion and the importance of copper are not negligible; each wants to live within cultures that we seem unable to change easily. What animates these debates is that collectively we assemble – some of us more than others, by virtue of education and experience of places – an inherent concern to understand the place or places that we frequent or meet for the first time. It is a thumping platitude, as well as doubtless an awkward confession to have to make, that such collectivity emerges from complex societies.

One of the means in which we can confront complexity is through the professional works of landscape architects, at least those who dedicate themselves to specific sites, however large, where such complexity may be resolved in some practical form. It always seems to me that landscape design is in essence a paradoxical activity. Some think nature and design are completely in conflict, while others hint at that paradox, such as Alexander Pope when he brings together a good designer and somebody who respects the genius of place.

# SEVEN

# Landscape Architecture and the Fabrication of Place

What would it mean for a culture to give up on its past?
Stephen Greenblatt[1]

The declaration and 'visibility' of *genius loci* are, or can be, most obvious in the work of landscape architects. Whether or not they understand any historical identity or meaning in the site, whatever they do there should make that place more visible, more focused, more enthralling, as well as a place people might want to visit and to spend time. In doing so the landscape architect could provide meaning for that particular place.

It is obvious that most landscape architects are capable of making clear, or clearer, what a place means, whether or not they choose to invoke the Latin *genius loci*. It is even, these days, plausible that many people acquire their ability to read other, non-designed spaces in the light of what they have acquired in public parks, famous gardens and landscapes, whether those of the past or more recent ones. At the very least, designed places can instruct our awareness of other sites, because they teach us to grasp the differences between them.

When in 1955 Kathryn Gustafson created Les Jardins de l'Imaginaire in the town of Terrasson in the Perigord, France, she envisaged a variety of different kinds or types of garden (hence the plural in Jardin*s*). There was an outdoor amphitheatre with a range of benches for an audience, a series of hydraulic effects in the *chemin des fontaines*, a rose garden with arbours, a sacred wood, a topiary garden and a tunnel of trees. Collectively, they suggest the range of design types that a public park – and indeed any garden project – could invoke.[2]

Despite having originally been conducted through this famous garden by a not very accomplished guide, I realized that beyond the remarkable vocabulary of garden forms was the sense – although the term is not used by the designer, nor was it by my guide on that occasion – that each offered a different impression of that designed space, a distinct *genius loci*. There was only one suggestion that the Jardins de l'Imaginaire could be appealing to that long-established sense of meaning in a place, and that was its entrance. Visitors walk through a woodland, and above them, winding through the branches, is a silver thread, Ariadne's thread. Now in Greek myth Ariadne's thread constituted a means of mastering a complex lab-yrinth. In Terrasson the initial walkway leads one into the series of different garden types, where the visitor gets a distinct sense that beyond the materials and effects there lurks a different experience.

Ariadne is there a means of recalling an older garden story. History and myth have a compelling role to play in landscape architecture, a topic that I explored in *Historical Ground*, although in that book I scarcely mentioned the term *genius loci*.[3] But its argu-ment was nonetheless that contemporary landscapes might be able to achieve two relevant things: to recall the past of some site or culture; or to invent a 'history' for that location. For this second option I borrowed, from Touchstone in Shakespeare's *As You Like It*, the term 'feigned history' – as in 'the truest poetry is the most feigning'. Yet, as Shakespeare may imply, feigning need not be only Elizabethan or Jacobean, for it can work too as a contemporary mode of landscape poetry (and sometimes prose). Its presence in contemporary landscape is interesting because many people, even commentators on landscape history, are less attuned to whether a site has been invented or 'feigned'. Modern design, sometimes inconspicuously but endlessly, reuses formal elements of past designs, so that an echo of past practical design is technically visible in the works we see today – in terracing, parterres, statuary, pools, fountains, planting patterns and so on. In current work we can thus appreciate how history seeps out in its repertoire of established elements. But it can do more than that, as we see with Ariadne's thread.

History is essentially narrative ('Once upon a time . . .'),[4] and Ariadne's thread in the treetops is a form of visual narrative, talking us into the gardens. But landscape projects rarely involve words; indeed, several designers I know are opposed to any verbal additive in their work, I suppose because it muddles the language of the genre. A few do, however, rely on verbal supplements. The architect Robert Venturi does so often, and the entrance to his new library at Dumbarton Oaks in Washington, DC, explains the founders' vision in words (aptly enough for a library) and addresses visitors as they enter the courtyard. Several projects by Lawrence Halprin also find that the addition of readable text clarifies and directs viewers

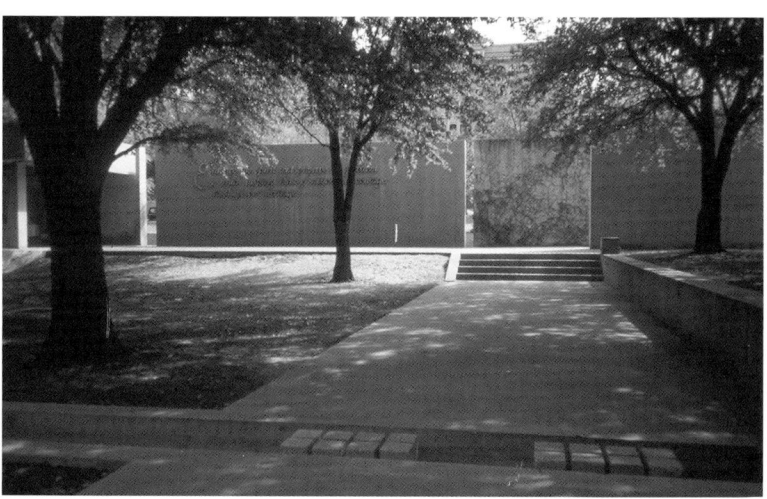

41 Lawrence Halprin, Heritage Park in Fort Worth, Texas, 1976.

towards the historical importance of the design and its location, as at Heritage Park in Fort Worth, Texas (illus. 41). In the FDR Memorial in Washington, DC, not only are quotations engraved on the walls but FDR's terms as president are narrated or spelled out in a succession of four rooms where each term is announced. That depends obviously on how one enters that sequence, which can be explored from two directions, although one can always backtrack, or grasp mentally the narrative of his four terms once the sequence of rooms has been negotiated and understood. Indeed, it is likely that for most designs sequence is not necessary for a narrative, and some history that requires a certain narrative can be adduced in retrospect. At Stowe the historical and cultural contrasts of a Temple of Ancient Virtue with, across the 'River Styx', a Temple of Modern Worthies, each with statues and inscriptions, can be eventually understood in whatever order they are visited.

Another key aspect of historical narrative, whether fashioned by original witnesses or by those who write about them later, is that it is not always objective. History is shaped and coloured by the fact that it is told by someone to somebody else, hence the words of Robert Woods Bliss and Mildred Barnes Bliss, the founders of Dumbarton Oaks, addressed to the estate's visitors, and hence the various reactions to visitors to the Jardins de l'Imaginaire. Furthermore, later 'readers' will find different interpretations of events. That is perhaps especially true of landscape architecture, which – with or without words – must anticipate the responses of a variety of visitors, even those who are there at the same time. That complicates how best to appreciate the sense of place that a designer has drawn out or devised there. Indeed, the usual lack of words within landscape design – absent inscriptions or verbal prompts – leaves visitors with considerable freedom to devise their own understanding.

THREE CONTEMPORARY LANDSCAPE designs in New York City can make clear the different approaches to history, found or feigned. One exploits the history of a specific site and makes clear how through modern rethinking derelict and abandoned infrastructure can be brought alive, while acknowledging its past. A second invents a history for an empty ground.[5] A third physically changes the design to imply or invite the manipulation of a public square in a busy downtown business area. Each offers a different response to Stephen Greenblatt's query about how a contemporary culture would look if the past were not forgotten but rethought.

The High Line (2009; illus. 42) remakes a disused railway line as both a place where one is aware of the former route and its reasons for having been there, and a destination with new vibrancy and a clear sense of dialogue between past and future. It was originally installed in 1934 to bring freight trains into a busy industrial neighbourhood of New York, but the last train ran through it in 1980, by which time the surrounding area had dissolved into a sea of car parks and bases for the trucking industry that had superseded the railway. The High Line follows that route, passing between and beneath old and new buildings, some of which are apartments with views of the line from their windows. Original rails and railway sleepers were left in place, now supplemented with concrete facsimiles. Abundant weeds, overgrown bushes and wildlife flourished on the line once it was abandoned. But these were refashioned by the distinguished Dutch horticulturist Piet Oudolf into an exciting but still plausible re-creation of wasteland overgrowth. This was exactly what the project's lead designer, James Corner of Field Operations, had observed in his native England, where the many small rural railway lines abandoned during the 1960s were left to sprout weeds and sometimes rare wild flowers, becoming traffic-free places where people could walk, cycle and exercise their dogs.

These days the High Line is crowded and metropolitan, giving great views of the city below and around it, so that old and new coexist. Visitors can appreciate that the High Line is the result of inspired transformation; they might also learn what the railway track was previously used for, and so begin to understand the gradual evolution of this area of Manhattan. But they can also enjoy a traffic-free elevated promenade, an American version of the Parisian Promenade Plantée, one of the very early attempts to refurbish a disused urban railway line.

This very French example starts near the Gare de Lyon and runs northwards for several kilometres. It is enhanced from time to time with trelliswork, flower beds and pools, and includes a small grass park that marks the site of the former chateau of Reuilly. The excitement and huge success of the High Line undoubtedly eclipsed much recollection of this plausible predecessor, and the two have rarely been compared. But in both design and use, they are radically different. In contrast to the Promenade Plantée, the High Line's feigning of wasteland planting is more in keeping with the narrative, more reminiscent of what had been there during the line's abandonment. And, in my experience, it is infinitely more used

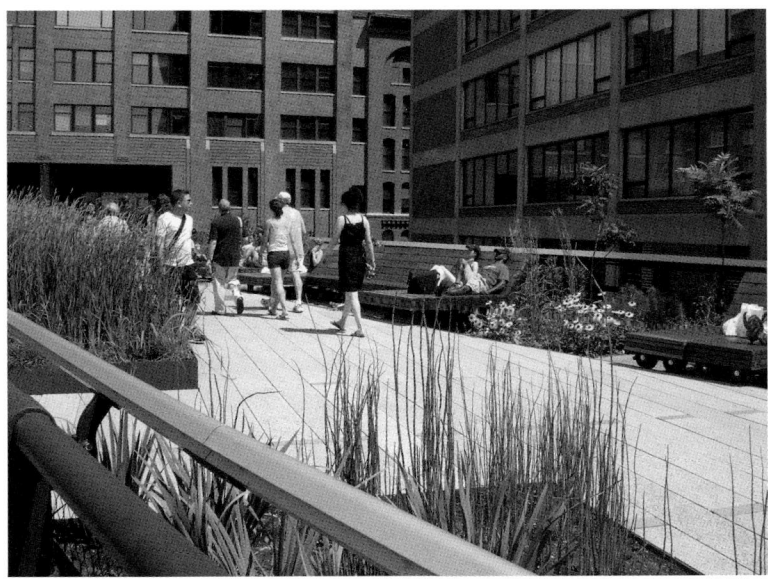

42 High Line, Manhattan.

and visited than the Parisian one. Furthermore, the American example traverses a central and exciting part of New York, while the French takes the walker through a much less iconic section of Paris.

Teardrop Park, a rectangular block of 0.7 hectares (1¾ ac) east of the Hudson River, has also been transformed (2006; illus. 43). On a site of rubble formed from the remains of the nearby Twin Towers rise four apartment buildings, and in their midst are paths, small segments of lawn, benches, a children's play area and a 3.6-metre-tall (12 ft) bluestone wall that cuts through the park, with an opening inserted at its midpoint (illus. 44). The wall's tilted slabs are like a geological section or slice of landscape, and that topographical feature in this relatively small site is striking. The wall itself is unavoidable, at first sight somewhat puzzling – since the site could not yield, nor would it have retained such a geology – but nonetheless compelling, especially in winter, when the rain creates miniature frozen waterfalls down its slabs. Those who know New York State may well recognize the wall as a re-creation of the geological cuts made through the landscape on the throughways that lead north from the city, such as the Taconic State Parkway. The wall was created off-site as a full-scale mock-up before being reassembled in Manhattan.

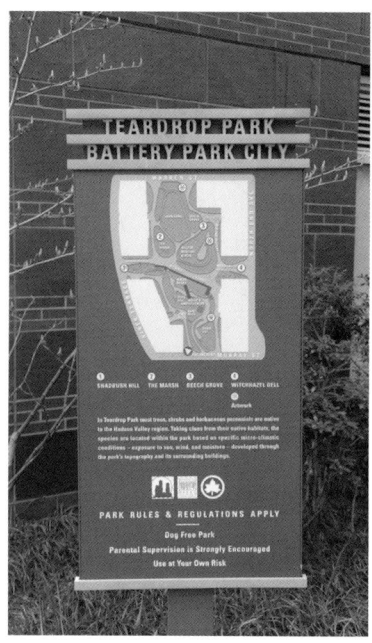

43 Plan of Teardrop Park, Manhattan.

The character of place, as defined in the eighteenth century by Samuel Johnson and practised by designers such as Humphry Repton, directed those designers' thinking, at once pragmatic and even poetic, at least as it elicited some more than phenomenal pleasure in its clients and visitors. Of course, a sense of meaning for a specific place may well change, and Repton himself was well aware of that. A recent example are the changes that have taken

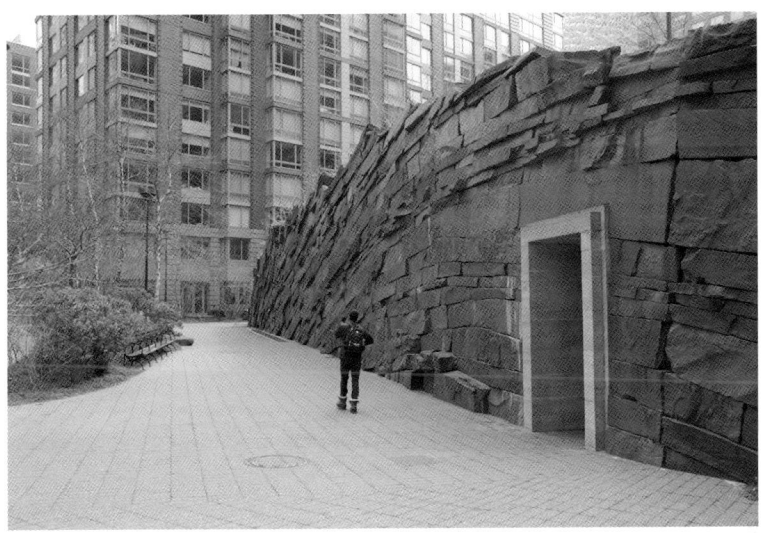

place in Jacob Javits Plaza, New York (illus. 45, 46). This square was originally dominated by Richard Serra's *Tilted Arc* (1981), but the piece loomed unnervingly over the workers who used the park, so it was removed and replaced in 1997 with Martha Schwartz's happy, curving green benches on a purple ground, snaking around grassy mounds. Yet those sitting on the benches had the strange sense of talking to people seated slightly behind them, and perhaps the somewhat crazy colours and curvaceous forms were not what this very public area needed. Schwartz's design was replaced in 2013 with a design by Michael Van Valkenburgh that, with its emphasis on garden materials, regular benches and scattered stools, made a more usable and social space. *De gustibus non est disputandum.*

These sites offer distinct ways in which a *genius loci* can be drawn out, whether emerging from the materials of a site or being fabricated on it. A commentator on Teardrop Park, Erik de Jong, thinks that a 'traditional concept like genius loci obviously would not suffice as a starting point to design here'. But a modernist understanding that a spirit of place can be feigned or invented for a site that is empty of such a concept is nonetheless the way to begin,

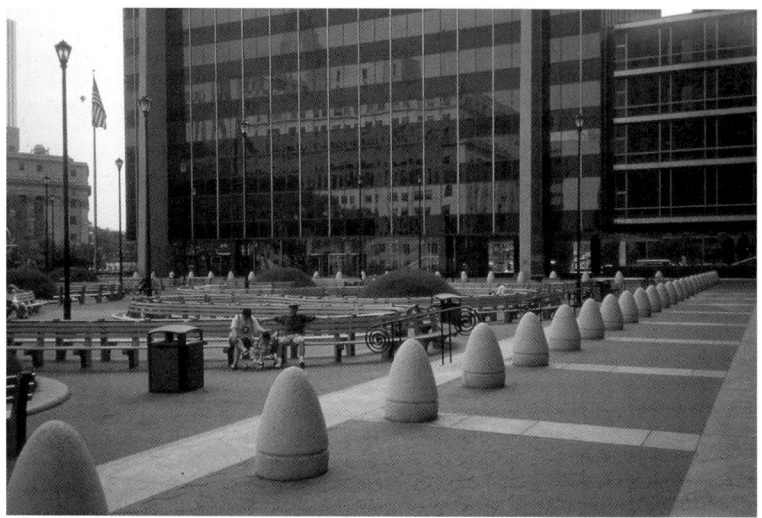

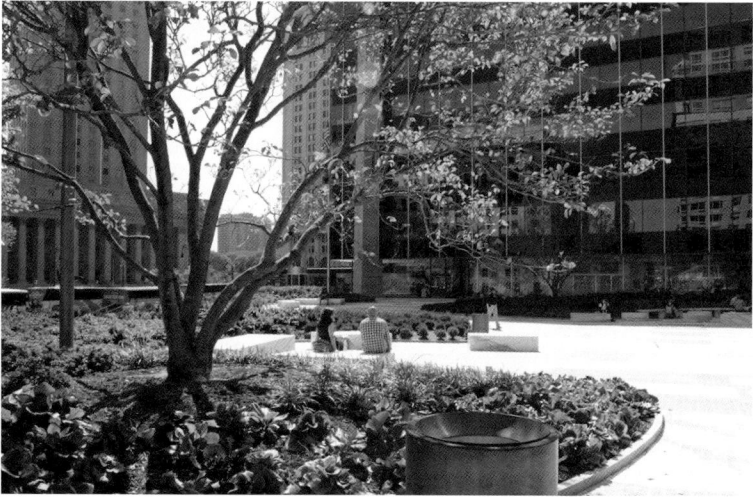

45, 46 Jacob Javits
Plaza, Manhattan,
designs by Martha
Schwartz, 1997, and
by Michael Van
Valkenburgh, 2013.

and indeed the same critic invokes the famous phrase of Gertrude
Stein that there is 'no there there'. In each of these New York spaces
there is now a unmistakable 'here there'.

I enjoy Teardrop Park, and can see how the neighbourhood
enjoys it, but my instinct is to find more satisfaction in places that
seem to have emerged from the sites themselves. This requires both

a recognition from the designer that what was there will somehow contribute to the new space, and the ability of users and visitors to grasp this. The wall in Teardrop Park is undoubtedly conspicuous, and presumably prompts the question of why it should be there at all. (On that last point: if visitors should find the door open at its southern end, they can glimpse a tiny and efficient room within the wall that houses the air-conditioning and other equipment for the surrounding apartments.)

IN ALL THREE CASES a particular nature, or natures of varying kinds (geology, dereliction, weeds, human infrastructure, cultural life), has been revealed through the skill of a designer. Now there is a long and fascinating tradition, alas rarely invoked in the theory of landscape architecture, that examines and explores the idea advanced by the Greek philosopher Heraclitus in the fifth century BC with his aphorism that 'Nature likes to hide.' That being so, subsequent philosophers and scientists have endlessly explored how, if they exercise their own specific skill, nature can instead be made to reveal herself, can be unveiled and can exhibit the genius of that place for the edification of others less learned or adept in that discovery. And landscape architects, like land artists, have joined in offering images of that process.

The tradition initiated by that aphorism of Heraclitus was explored and illustrated magnificently in 2004 by Pierre Hadot in his *Le voile d'Isis* (2004; translated as *The Veil of Isis*, 2006), in which he examines philosophical and scientific commentaries as well as artistic representations of how Isis (nature) can be unveiled. Yet among landscape designers only Francis Bacon and Goethe get brief appearances in Hadot's extensive and learned narrative. But similar unveilings were effectively espoused by early modern place-makers (that term coined by 'Capability' Brown long before his profession obtained the title 'landscape design'). Martha Schwartz saw a contemporary, postmodernist way of animating the 'nature' of Jacob Javits Plaza. And one of the ways designers do this is by revisiting earlier unveilings or recent contemporary perspectives when they engage with their own. This awareness of the usefulness of earlier practice in current design is an important topic, for it illuminates historical narratives without necessarily undermining the new.

A new work by a distinguished landscape architect, Georges Descombes of Atelier Descombes Rampini, is the project in 2018 to reformulate the River Aire, near Geneva, which had been canalized since the nineteenth century. It stirred memories of Vaux-le-Vicomte, where nearly four hundred years earlier André Le Nôtre had converted the small, meandering River Ancoeuil into a canal for the length of its passage through the garden.[6]

Both Le Nôtre and Descombes may suggest how Heraclitus' aphorism could be addressed. The seventeenth-century canal and its unveiling or disclosing of the natural stream were perfectly clear in Le Nôtre's own drawing (illus. 47) of Vaux-le-Vicomte, in which the colour blue designates both the straight canal and the tiny river; that is less clear in contemporary black-and-white engravings. But on the site itself the contrasting lines of canal and river are compelling. The formalization of the river has several motives. The slight presence of the river, which is otherwise unnoticed as it wanders through the neighbouring territory, turns to prominence as it is transformed into a canal, visibly engineered and with straight, stone-lined edges. This new, temporary form also partakes of the formalism of the surrounding garden, so it engages with its organization and is not an intrusion into unmediated nature. Furthermore, the canal was designed to accommodate boats and gondolas, and at one end it expands into a circle in which the craft can turn around. At this point the water drops out of the garden and resumes its wavering riverine way across the meadows (illus. 48).

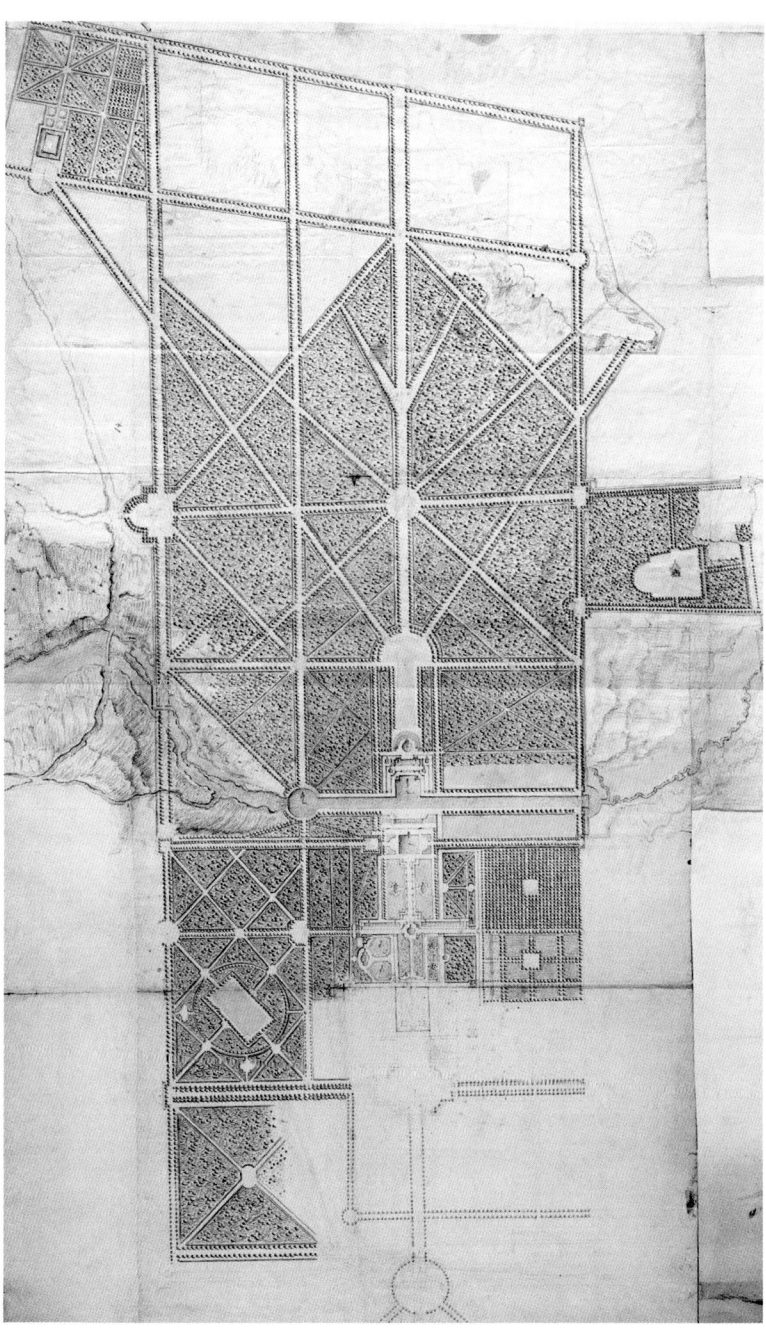

47 Le Nôtre's plan of
Vaux-le-Vicomte.

As such the river reveals its significance *qua* river by assuming, briefly, the form and uses of a canal. That is a surprise as one explores Vaux, particularly for those modernists who think French gardens are 'formal' (a term they tend to use with some disdain) and that everything there will be perfectly clear and evident, and who rely on aerial views or plans that seem to flatten the garden territory, rather than come to know it by walking there. But surprise was a crucial element of Le Nôtre's design, as F. Hamilton Hazlehurst demonstrated in his *Gardens of Illusion* (1980). At Vaux, for example, he recognized that visitors, starting from the chateau, cannot see what is at the bottom of the slope down which they are walking, but only the upper portion of the distant slope that climbs the far hillside, so the canal is hidden as they walk down towards it. It is only at the very end, when they emerge at a point above what will turn out to be cascades, that they realize that slightly below them at a lower level is a concealed stretch of water. The deceit or surprise becomes clear only when visitors go further and climb the far slope to reach the statue of Hercules, at which point, looking back towards the chateau, they realize how the visual trick has

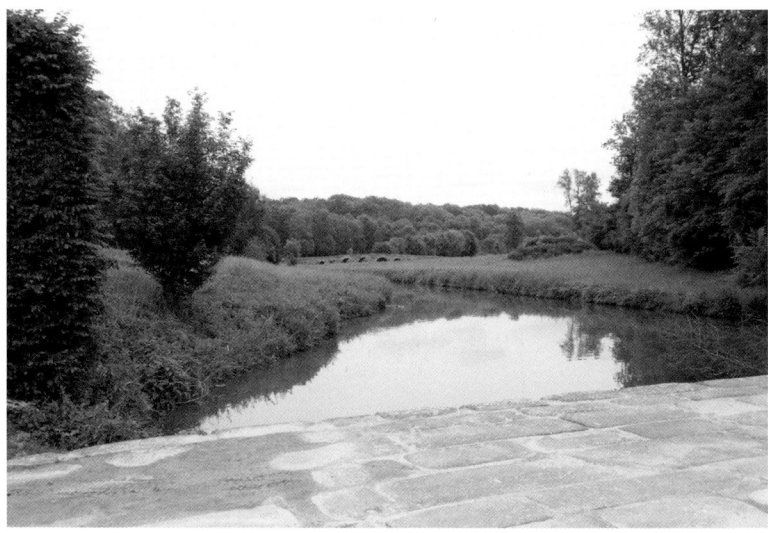

48 Vaux-le-Vicomte – the end of the canal as it falls into the meadow.

been organized, and see the cascades from the top of which they first saw the canal/river. This reveals much of the *genius loci* that Le Nôtre contrived on the topography there. It is also important to recognize that the colossal figure of Hercules is an apt presence there, for he was, among his other labours, a maker of gardens.

The River Aire, unused by the mid-twentieth century and criticized for being 'unnatural', has now been extensively *re-naturalized* (to translate directly from the French proposal for the site). But in this case, what transpired was the decision to leave the canal, although somewhat modified, and to reintroduce the old line of the river. This 'doubles' the river, what the subtitle of a book on the project, *Aire*, written in three languages (English, French and German), calls a double, *son double*, *Doppelgänger*. Instead of a river transformed for some metres into a canal, as at Vaux, this doubling invites and indeed ensures a comparison and contrast that carefully, yet emphatically, provide a before and after, a historical then and a now, and, as will become clear, some suggestions for its future.

One of the few clear examples of this effect in landscape design would have been Repton's Red Books, where a watercolour of the original state of a site is lifted to show the new proposal; of course, unlike with the River Aire, we see that transformation compared and contrasted only in the Red Book itself. If and when Repton had transformed the original landscape we would see some, little or none of what was originally there, unless with his Red Book in hand we explored the here and now with the then and there of the volume.[7] At the Aire, we have a chance to see both. The opportunity to seize such a comparison suits the modernist landscape project, which Vaux did not explicitly invite.

This deliberate effect allows visitors to see, understand and compare both the industrial, canalized format and a reanimation of the path of the river. That comparison was inscribed in a very early sketch by Julien Descombes (illus. 49) in which a straight line (the canal) is overlaid, confronted and occasionally crossed by a

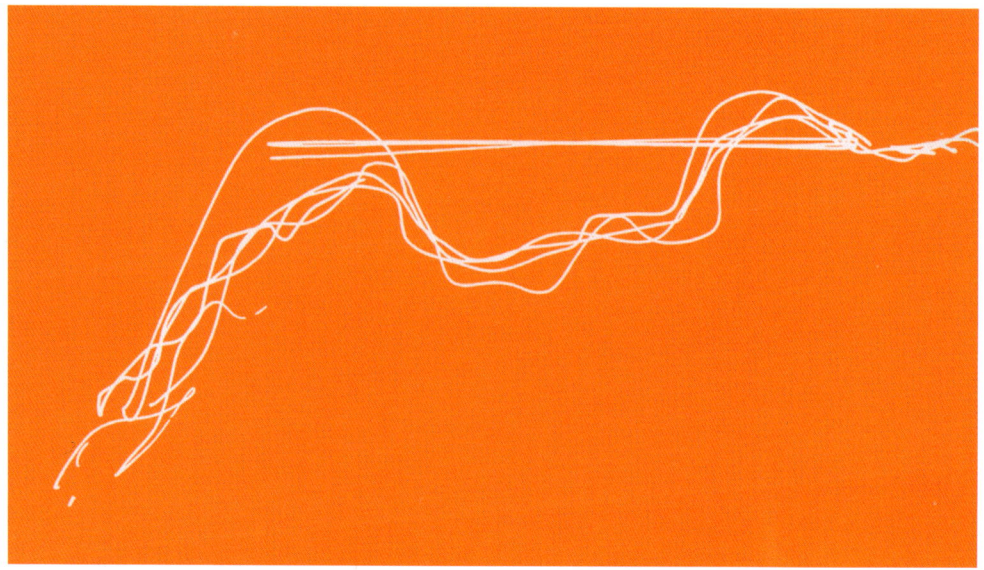

49 Julien Descombes, sketch of the River Aire.

meandering cluster of several lines (the river). That rapid sketch of what was envisaged has served as both an emblem of the project and a diagram of its construction.

It was in 2001 that the State of Geneva invited limited proposals from four teams to enter a competition to remake the canal, and the contest was won by an interdisciplinary group led by Descombes. The organizers of the competition told contributors in effect 'to demolish the canal and to make something new; to reinstall a new river where the old one had once been'. But Descombes demurred. For one thing, he had grown up in the area and knew it intimately, so his memory of it was powerful. He was also a designer who wished to ensure that what he found and confronted there would not be erased. The process of its transformation was to be memorialized, as well as new uses and meanings enabled.

The group won the competition, essentially, by refusing the state's invitation to recover a lost paradise, a 'pure nature' that no longer existed in the twenty-first century. They observed that you cannot turn back time, nor reinstate an ecology that no longer pertains to the surrounding agricultural territory or to the need to protect arable lands and the nearby city of Geneva from flooding. Instead, they embraced a dual approach. They would rework the canal rather than eliminate it. In addition, a 'new' river was constructed, one that meandered back and forth across the line of the canal. Furthermore, since rivers tend to flood, it was allowed or even encouraged to do just that. The visual contrast, the juxtaposition, of the two streams of water made visitors realize how the site had been understood and re-presented.

The canal, originally austere and straightforward in all respects, is now broken into a series of descending fragments, punctuated with small weirs, stairs descending from the canal-side pathways to the water, pedestrian bridges crossing it, and a pavilion on a new platform (illus. 50). It is now an enlarged and enhanced social space, with benches and tables, where the canal waters themselves can

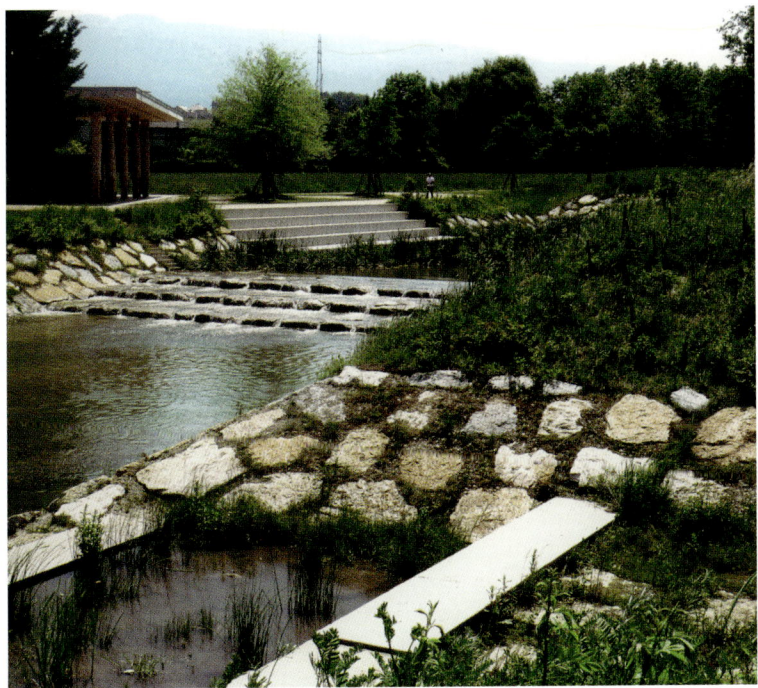

50 Canal of the Aire today with improvements.

be accessed and scrutinized and the surrounding arable land seen anew. The potential of flooding can be controlled in places and water diverted into retention ponds, and upright timbers inserted into the flow prevent clogging debris during storms. It has become what Descombes calls a 'rivergarden'.

Running alongside the canal for approximately 4 kilometres (2½ mi.) is the 'new' river, which is in a sense more imaginative, unexpected and intriguing. Basically, two moves were made along its length. Topsoil was removed along a meandering route that the designers reinvented, rather than seeking to reinstate its original trajectory. The process of this flow was both exaggerated and made visible by allowing the water to pass around and over a cluster of lozenge-shaped squares. These were created in the new riverbed and were based on an experiment – this is Switzerland, after all – where milk was allowed to flow over what looks like a bar of chocolate and found its way between the raised squares (illus. 51), sometimes deforming its precise geometry or even briefly

51 The chocolate-bar experiment.

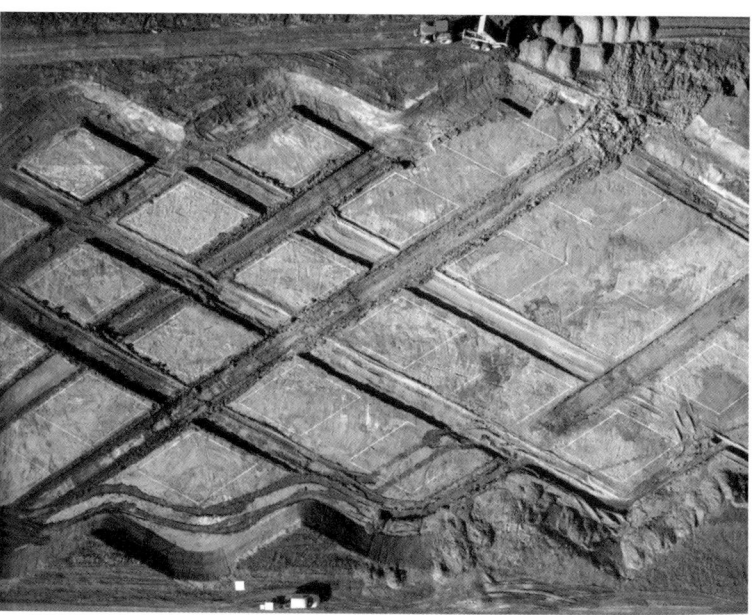

submerging one or two of them, as the water sought the quickest way forwards. Such 'deformations' created a fresh paradox, whereby what the designers inserted actually freed the river to create its own design. So the river, flowing past and sometimes over the lozenge shapes, reconfigures them, while on the raised oblongs a rapid growth of plants and shrubs – some local, some brought in – gradually began to change the appearance of this section, and will one day probably eliminate it for good.[8] Thus a hint of its future.

The comparison of river and former canal is also presented wittily in Descombes' *Aire* book, where the same small black-and-white images are repeated alongside the essays in three languages, giving us a strange sense of how we might look at them differently, culturally, through the lens of those linguistic perspectives. Inserted between the essays are uncaptioned sequences of images, and an anthology of drafting diagrams and sketches of the site, as it was thought through over several years.

This 'topographical imagination', in the words of one contributor to the book, the landscape architect Elissa Rosenberg, shows that responding to the problem of the canal does not erase what was there before. Equally, Descombes argues that the site is as much a place of questioning as it is one of pleasure. The new canal is marked by different materials, social opportunities, new pathways and new vistas, which raise questions about the relation of the former canal to the existing and original landscape and culture around it. Water, as another contributor, the philosopher Gilles Tiberghien, writes, needs the banks and lands around it if it is to make sense. Each augments or subverts and explains the other.

IT IS OF COURSE more than likely that it will be in modern designs that we visibly confront the unveiling of what natures were there before the current intervention, either because, as with the High Line, we still have material evidence of that, or because recent projects are documented. Pre-modern designs – the before-and-after images by Repton excepted – remain largely undisclosed on the site itself, simply because they were reworked for cultural or aesthetic reasons or for reasons of cheaper upkeep, so that little of the original layout would have survived. Archival plans can help us to envisage earlier versions; for the gardens of Chantilly, for example, we have a map from 1579 in Jacques I Androuet Du Cerceau's *Les plus excellens bastiments de France*, and a general map from between 1650 and 1662, at which time Le Nôtre took over.[9] When we compare these with a post-Nôtrean map of 1673, it is clear that a sense of the place has emerged significantly in the extensive layout of wooded rides and avenues through the northern park-land. Yet more subtly, but effectively, to the west of the chateau, the Nonette River, which flows into and through the immediate garden, is marked in blue in the newer map, and reveals that a similar canalization to that at Vaux was also used here. Thus an unveiling of another local nature.

When new layouts obliterate early designs, as with Van Valken-burgh's reformulation of Schwartz's plaza, it is harder to see how a new sense of place has been established. One of the key moments in the history of landscape architecture occurs in the long eight-eenth century, when in many respects new 'landscape' designs replaced and so eliminated older geometric, regular layouts. But this was often piecemeal and emerged over several years. Even then, the theoretical advice that Alexander Pope offers, by which a designer can respond to the given topography and yet honour its *genius loci*, is somewhat undermined when he finishes by sug-gesting that its model would be Stowe. Granted, that estate has examples of wonderful interventions during its early years, but the sense that it invoked 'ambitious hills', 'circling theatres' or soar-ing fountains was largely improbable in its topography, and not apparent in 1731, when Pope published his *Epistle*.[10] The disclosure of topographical incidence became much clearer at least with

'Capability' Brown's design, for example, of the Grecian Valley. But in many cases old layouts were entirely erased and a new nature unveiled; any revealing of the old did not receive much attention, hence the value of Repton.

When Repton decided in 1788 to assume the mantle of Brown, he inherited a landscape concept that privileged a neoclassical nature, seemingly unchanged and unchanging. Nature in its fullness was there, largely unveiled, although that disclosure was not immediately clear to everyone. Brown's son would also present Repton with maps of his father's best works. Those landscapes lacked many signs of antique reference, conspicuous references to a presiding deity, mythical figures, symbols or specific iconography. There were temples, seats and eye-catchers, to be sure, but few if any dedicated to a Diana or a Venus. Whatever ornaments there were consisted as much in flower gardens and flowering shrubs as in allegorical personages.[11] These new landscapes spoke of consumption and social prestige.

Repton accepted much of that legacy, but he was himself clearly interested in what he called 'character', which for him was a term more factual and analytical than *genius loci*. In fact, only rarely did he use the latter phrase, and then with some irony, as in his Red Book for Rhug in Denbighshire, north Wales. There he argued that

I am, however, restrained from indulging to *its full extent* my veneration for antiquity, by reflecting that modern comfort and convenience are the first objects to be consulted in the improvement of a modern residence; and therefore I trust I shall neither incur the censure of those who know and feel the comforts of the age we live in, nor offend the genius of the place, by 'calling from the vasty deep the angry spirits' of Owen Glendwra . . . who formerly inhabited this domaine.[12]

Repton was something of a conservative, as were many of his clients, and by the end of his career he despised 'new money' and the *nouveaux riches* who nevertheless sought him out. Yet he also realized that some modern sense of *genius loci* was necessary that did not rely on Celtic myth or Latin notions. It was 'modern comfort and convenience' that had to be consulted, and these in their turn were the foundation of a new sense of place.

Each Reptonian Red Book sets out the designer's proposal for the site by first listing the 'character', the central quality of its landscape, either found there and/or to be drawn out with his proposals. 'Character' is a word that Samuel Johnson used frequently in his *Dictionary* (first published in 1755), and the word itself is defined primarily as a 'mark, a representation', 'the private properties of any person or thing'. It is more than merely descriptive, for it gestures to more than the phenomena of something or somebody. It marks Repton's concern to identify and define the essence and then potentialities of place of a specific locality. He explained it himself in *Sketches and Hints on Landscape Gardening* (1795): 'All rational improvement of grounds is, necessarily, founded on a due attention to the CHARACTER and SITUATION of the place to be improved: the former teaches what is advisable, the latter what is possible, to be done.'[13] This is essentially what Pope's epistle to Burlington advised on the genius of place: to combine the topography of the site with what a careful review of it 'tells' the designer he might do. And that is precisely how watercolours functioned in Repton's Red Books: first, an image of the site as he found it, and then, with one flap or sometimes two lifted up, his view of what he would provide (illus. 52). While these watercolours present what Repton originally found and then sketched in anticipation, it is his text that specifies the hints to be taken up for devising a modern spirit of place.

Repton is an enormously important figure in landscape design, both for his own work and for what he proved by way of reformulating earlier garden designs for new clients and their new understandings of nature and its culture.[14] At many social levels, the ownership of parks was changing, as were their size and contents; deer parks, for example, largely disappeared, as did the extensive acreage required to accommodate them. But my focus is on what Repton understood and contrived as a fresh perspective on the ancient notion of *genius loci*. The elements of modernity, comfort and convenience were set out in the series of topics that were taken up in his Red Books, after the discussion of character. These included approaches to the mansion; walks and drives within the estate; vistas and viewsheds; plans that indicated some of the necessary adjuncts to rural existence such as greenhouses, vegetable gardens and even workers' cottages; and the presence and uses of water. He made no attempt to impose one mode or other, being instead content to rely on what the situation required; for example, at Glemham Hall in Suffolk he allowed a straight walk that the client requested, and also himself installed one on the terrace, but elsewhere he espoused meandering pathways.[15] In common with an increasing number of professional landscapers, he was drawn, inevitably, to smaller sites, and in 1826 he saw that it 'seldom falls to the lot of the improver to be called upon for his opinion on places of great extent'.[16] This flexibility would increasingly be apparent in his professional designs.

One of the most crucial modern elements in the establishment of character seems to have been an emphasis on movement, on how visitors and owners saw and appreciated the *domaine*, even a small one.[17] For Brandsbury in Middlesex from 1789, the meandering walks were a series of encircling and touching pathways that led through the site and in particular allowed views towards St Paul's Cathedral and the spires of London churches.[18] This, it must be noted, sits happily if somewhat paradoxically alongside Repton's picturesque appetite. He recalled that Brown had 'always [been] afraid of . . . a very fine situation', but he embraced such situations, even augmenting them with denser woods and enlarged rivers and lakes; many of his watercolours depict an artist sketching the scenery of the Repton proposal. In one amusing example in the Red Book for Rhug, a shepherd who is shown with his flock viewing the original, unreformed landscape now reappears (when the flap is lifted) and leans over the artist to admire his drawing of Repton's 'fine situation' (illus. 53, 54). Movement was by no means a project that only Repton urged; even the scholar Richard Payne Knight, who took exception to Repton's less than adequate picturesque, saw walks as central to exploration, and many wound through his own grounds at Downton Castle in Herefordshire. Stopping to observe, admire and understand set pieces and maybe sketch their picturesque invitations in extensive views did not hamper the insistence on exploration. In this, Repton drew on the fad for travel and exploration in Britain as well as on the Continent, where exploration could be combined with sketching.

For many clients Repton was keen on signalling the start of a visit by erecting gate lodges and often circuitous approaches to the

52 Humphry Repton, Red Book for Rivenhall, Essex, from his *Sketches and Hints on Landscape Gardening* (1795), reproducing the lost Red Book, with flaps raised at both sides.

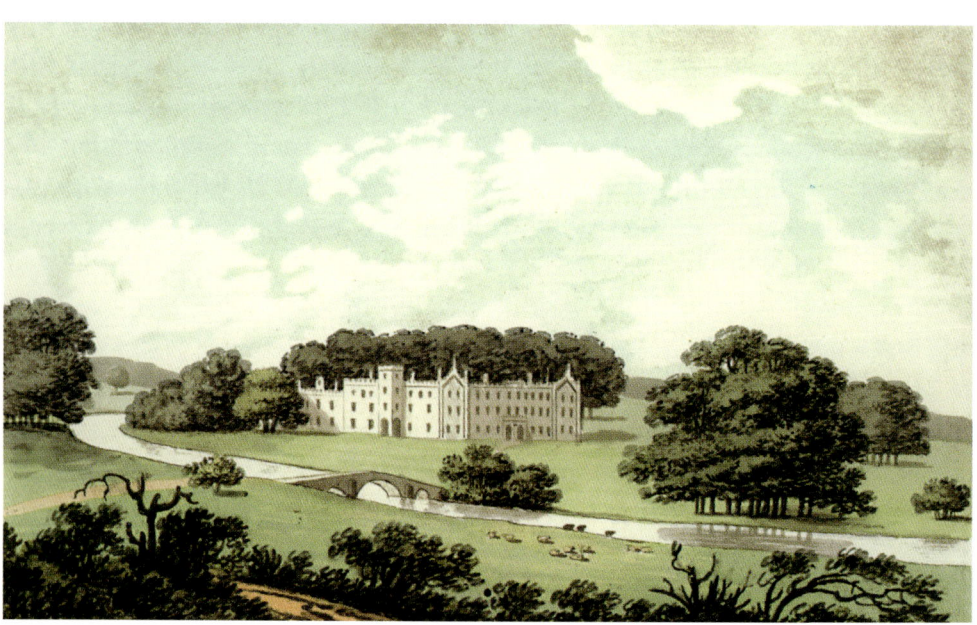

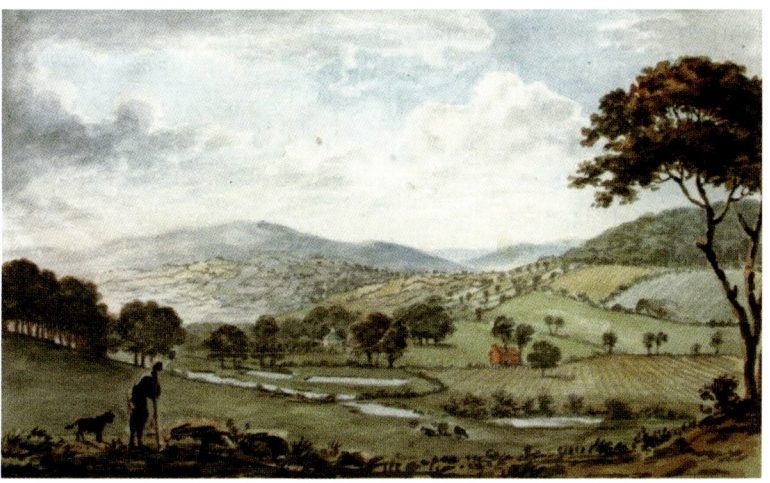

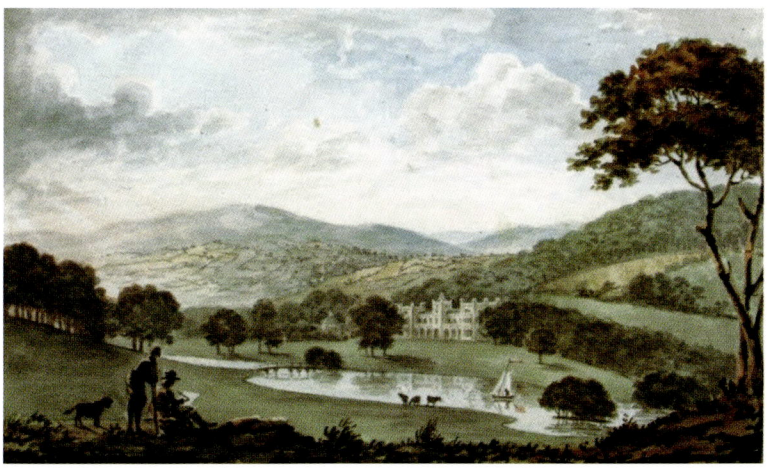

53, 54  Humphry Repton, Red book for Rhug, Denbighshire, North Wales, 1795, watercolour; note how the shepherd admires the artist's handiwork.

mansion that conducted visitor and owner alike through some of its best and most typical scenery; these would sometimes wish or need to respond to the exigencies of the topography. For Blaise Castle at Henbury outside Bristol in 1796, he found he could not approve of Grecian architecture for its lodge, since it would give the wrong impression of an approach to something called a castle; so he gave it a more Gothick appearance.[19] His coloured map marks the various ways of exploring what is in effect a very varied landscape; the coach route from the main road to the house is marked in orange, and other roads through the extensive woods in green, while further walks, which are deemed steep and required pedestrian access, are in brown. The River Avon, when Repton first saw it, was viewed through a perfect opening in the woods; he eliminated that picture frame with a road that allowed visitors a continuous view of the river as they explored. He was also concerned at Blaise that visitors would not feel, when at last reaching the classical mansion that declared clearly its 'elegance, cheerfulness and hospitality', that it committed violence to 'the Genius of the Place', especially when the route thither had taken them through dense woods and romantic prospects. But, once arrived at the mansion, visitors and owners were offered views of two edifices appearing in the woods, now seen at a distance: a cottage with smoke pouring from its chimney and the ancient 'Castle' (thirty years old!) emerging above the trees (illus. 55).

What is also clear, especially as Repton responded to newer clients, was that the various natures could best be invoked to suggest variety and their handling, which involved the use of much older elements of design that indicates that variety and its presentation. This heralded a fresh return to the older layout of a series of natures, where the immediate garden close to the mansion had been succeeded by more utilitarian areas and then, if the site allowed, an expansion into fields and woods. While he exploited and augmented much of Brown's neoclassical place-making – celebrating the formal qualities of woodland, water, individual trees and clumps, land and further vistas – Repton saw the modern importance of displaying, rather than hiding, the work and functions of an estate where comfort and convenience were visible.

Repton's legacy ought to be more visible than it is, especially since he has been invoked far less than 'Capability' Brown – especially his theoretical ideas, which Brown was largely unconcerned to propose. Repton's three main published treatises drew on the

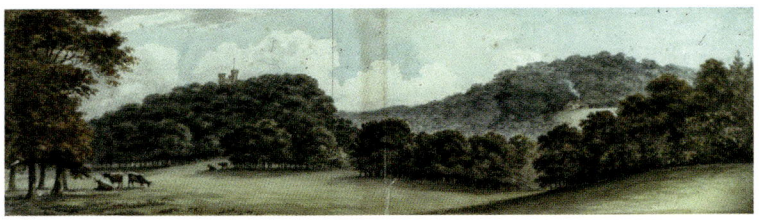

55 Humphry Repton, Red Book for Blaise Castle, 1796, watercolour.

many Red Books he created, whether these dealt with projects that had been implemented or not; his first publication, *Sketches and Hints* (1795), borrowed from fifty such Red Books, as did *Observations on the Theory and Practice of Landscape Gardening* (1803) and *Fragments on the Theory and Practice of Landscape Gardening* (1816). The substantial influence of Repton's landscape gardening was considered enhanced in 1840 when John Claudius Loudon gathered all those and other publications into a volume entitled *The Landscape Gardening and Architecture of Humphry Repton*; the original watercolours were not illustrated, black-and-white versions of them being used with his texts instead. The importance of that collection cannot be ignored. And, while it was not an *oeuvre* much cited by later designers, its substance was critical and arguably long-lasting.

THE IMPORTANCE OF REPTON – his afterlife – is less what he may have influenced through our knowledge of his specific works than in the parameters he set for later professional landscapers. His use of flaps to reveal a before-and-after of a site and yet suggest the continuing presence of essential topography and character has survived: Brenda Colvin's dual images for the hill at Gale Common in Yorkshire in 1967 reveal her sense of how poetry emerges in the re-creation of a site.[20] The scope of later designers would be much expanded, with their reliance on earlier gardenist forms considerably and yet patchily invoked, and the ability to take on a variety of different projects: if Repton had moved from country estates and smaller villas near towns to the organization of London squares, later professionals seized the chance or saw the necessity to extend their work to reformulate derelict sites, among others.

The thrust of almost all Repton's projects, as advanced largely in the Red Books and sometimes when he executed the sites, was his attention to place. And this seems to have been the central, if not always acknowledged, motive for much later professional work. One must suppose that a designed place is devised to give more meaning, more interest – for visitors, to be sure, but also for owners of that specific place; this will be the same whether it is created *ex nihilo* or restores an old one. That is the incentive of preservationists, who see that 'places enrich and enable in the best sense of the word [preservation]'.[21] Yet some contemporary landscape architects, sceptical of any atavistic invocation of a Latin *genius loci* that might detract from its modernity, nevertheless use the concept merely as a conventional gesture to what they are in fact doing more rigorously or by other means.

An interesting example is the use of the phrase by Ian McHarg in his *Design with Nature* (1960).[22] It is deployed specifically in his final chapter, 'The City: Process and Form', as the marker of what he calls 'the inventory of values' when discussing Amsterdam, Venice and Paris. He sees 'form' as insufficient in analysing the 'locational factors that explain the sites of cities – tidal limits, fords, bridge crossings, mineral and agricultural resources, propitious climates and the like'. Absent any consideration of such factors, this convinced and determined environmentalist puts his finger on it when he says that 'when cities are built upon beautiful, dramatic or rich sites, their excellence often results from the preservation, exploitation and enhancement, rather than obliteration of this genius of the site.' For those three major European cities, that demonstrates the excellence of their creations, which then 'enter the inventory of values, the genius loci'. That the Latin phrase is rendered here in English signals McHarg's acknowledgement of past cultures, yet I am disturbed by the implications of that word 'exploitation', and his book is somewhat ambiguous in its attention to those inherited cultures.[23] His basic argument that 'nature' rather than 'design' must derive environmental concerns (not the other way around) is admirble, but loses much of what people can bring today from their experience in a complex and culturally determined world.

If Repton had also needed to respond to an enlarging commercial and industrial era in Britain, with money passing to the bourgeois who then wanted a place of their own, by the mid-twentieth century it was the decline of those very industrial and commercial enterprises that was leaving empty spaces to be re-envisaged. Peter and Anneliese Latz made a large impact in Europe by addressing that, starting with their rethinking of large, abandoned infrastructure. The former steelworks at Duisburg-Nord, Germany, was transformed into a public park, much frequented, with some dramatic performances in an amphitheatre formed of large steel plates, and wonderful gardens created within the former bunkers; all the while its visitors were wholly aware of the remains of the former steelworks and its re-formulation. Like the High Line, it seemed to promise a model for other such devastated sites, and with Peter Latz then teaching at the University of Pennsylvania, it was an iconic model for his students. Yet it was clear to those who thought it through that these new designs could not simply be replicated on different sites, and I recall James Corner saying that it was not so easy 'to do the High Line' elsewhere; for a start, it would be impossible to replicate the New York milieu. Latz, too, saw that his later works needed a fresh response: 'each conversion project is different,' he wrote, 'the preliminary decisions are complexly different and the prevailing site conditions are completed different.'[24]

Indeed, Latz & Partners' other projects are clearly and obviously different from each other. The practice's repertoire of effects is at once eclectic, inventive and superbly alert to the cultural resonance of place, past, present and even future, as the designers relied

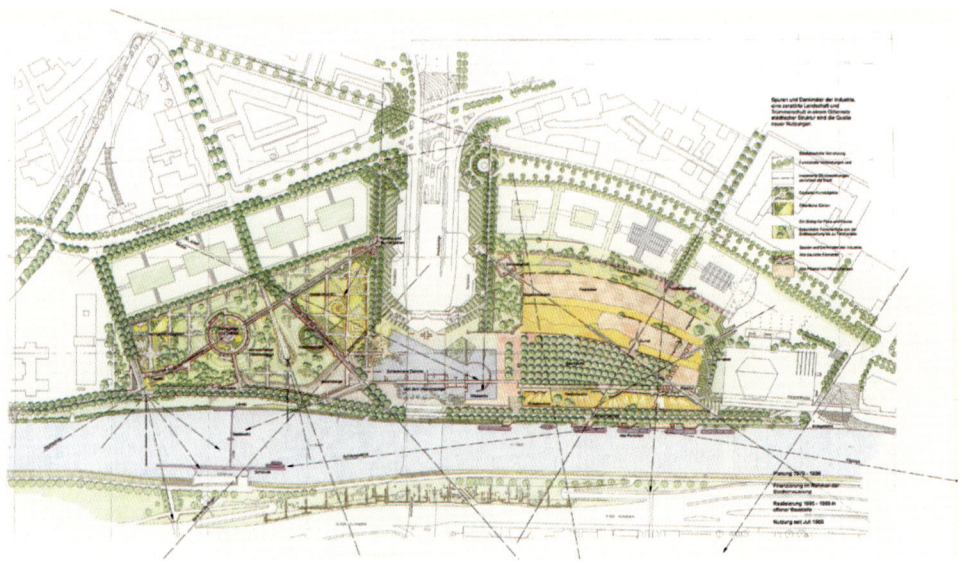

56 Peter Latz, detail
of final design for
Saarbrücken River
Port Island, 1985–9.

creatively on previous landscape forms and insertions. Saarbrücken River Port Island (1985–9; illus. 56), created after the old harbour's basins were filled in, is an intricate array of geometric forms and sightlines, access points, groves of trees, flora growing in rubble plots, and a huge new water gate (*Wassertor*) like a Roman ruin, through which all surface and drainage water is pumped and purified before feeding the lake below the road that passes the gate. The noise of the falling waters drowns out the din of passing traffic. The little Arab town of Hiriya on the outskirts of Tel Aviv, abandoned in 1948, had by 1952 become the largest rubbish dump in the world, known as 'Trash Mountain', emitting methane gas, containing polluted water and smouldering garbage, and attracting flocks of birds that created a hazard for planes using the nearby Ben Gurion Airport. Many artists – 28 in all – sought to rethink this 'navel of the country', and eventually eight international teams were invited to take part in a competition. This was won in 2004 by Latz + Partners, and for them it became an Ayalon Park, an astonishing transformation with a cluster of landscape features: a wadi or dry ravine, agricultural terraces at the base of the mountain, the cliffs that Latz determined not to remove, an inner oasis fed with recycled water, and secret gardens at the summit with spectacular views. It is a new cultural place with a new identity, inspired by visionary landscape thinking with a preservationist instinct, attentive to its past and the many possibilities of its future. In all these Latz designs, out of the existing location is drawn a new sense of the place, often

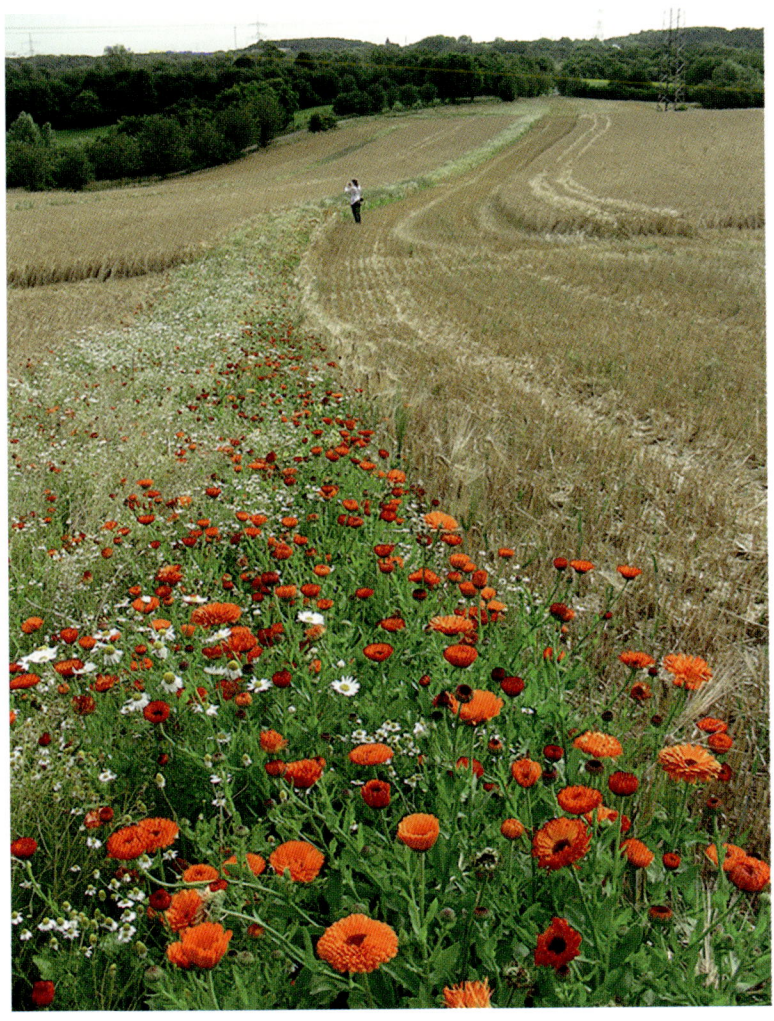

57  Paolo Bürgi, fields replanted by farmer.

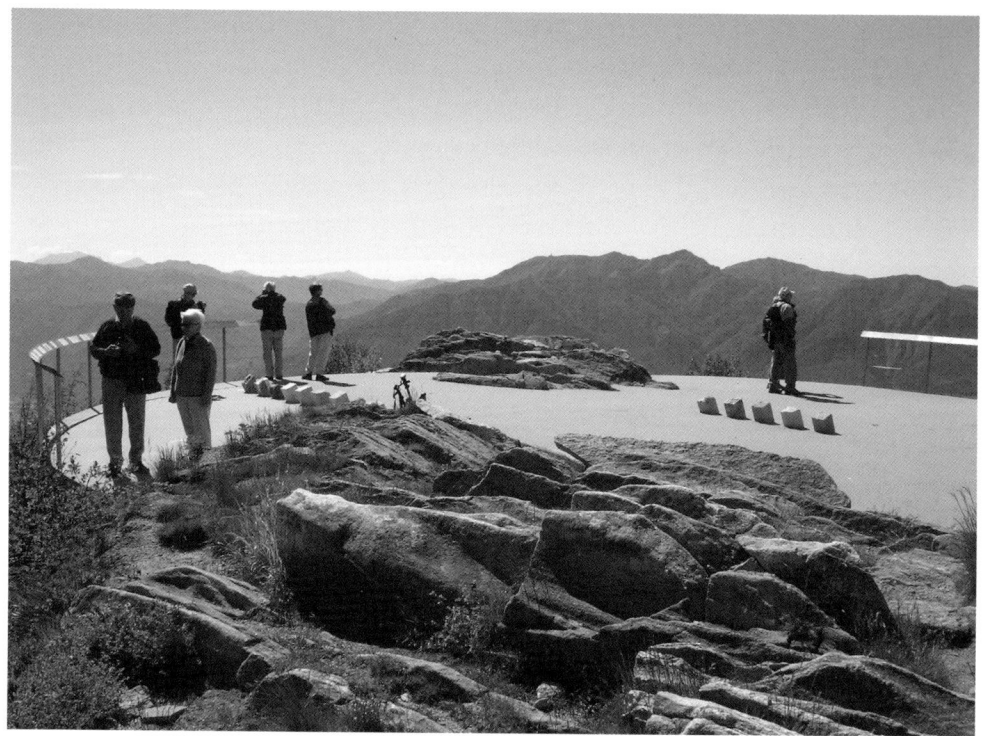

58 Paolo Bürgi, Geological Observatory, Cimetta, overlooking Lake Maggiore, from where both the lowest and highest points of Switzerland can be viewed.

respecting the history of industrial decline, and in the Tel Aviv case a determination to retain the human stories and imagine a parkland that promises a useful future for all.

But it is not only dereliction that attracts new designs. Paolo Bürgi in particular has made both alpine mountains and agricultural fields as sites of new ideas about how people respond to and rethink new places for themselves. Agricultural land can be extremely boring or incomprehensible for urban folk, especially those who move into newly built houses that intrude on farmed land. But if the farmer, guided by Bürgi, transforms the fieldscape slightly by ploughing into his crops bands of multicoloured flowers (illus. 57), he begins to make the neighbours understand what he does, especially as it changes from month to month and year to year, and it pleases him that they might learn to appreciate his world. A similar move to invoke a flowery mead took over the perfectly manicured lawn in front of the chapel and Fellows' building at King's College, Cambridge. An eloquent yet empty space between those wonderful buildings and the River Cam was unused except by senior members of the college. Now the area below the west end of the chapel is filled with a mass of blue-purple cornflowers, red poppies and white ox-eye daisies, through which a path will lead visitors. It is at once an ecological effort to control the loss of biodiversity in the United Kingdom, an almost immediate creation of habitat for insect-feeding birds and an invitation to others to 'inhabit' a previously privileged site.

An alpine project is, understandably, more elaborate than a field, for it must compete with its remarkable setting. Bürgi's 'Geological Observatory' near Cardada in the Swiss canton of Ticino (illus. 58) is approached first by a funicular, then a walk through woodland to a chairlift that takes visitors up the mountain, where a final short path leads to a circular concrete platform set in the rocks. Two parallel lines of small, shaped stones mark the centre, and their meaning dawns on visitors as they comprehend the vast arc of mountains on the far side of the valley up which they have come. For the far view clearly reveals a huge cleft in the hillside. This slippage marks the Insubric Line, which was created millions of years ago when the European and African tectonic plates slipped past each other and ruptured the geology. On the baluster of the observatory are detailed schemes and instructions for what we are looking at, and the stones behind are now understood as formal chunks of African and European stone. If Switzerland provides endless belvederes from which to view its scenery, here the 'observatory' transfigures the view by this careful organization of space – a small moment amid the vast mountain experience, with actual rocks punctuating the otherwise perfect circle of concrete. This is also an *haut lieu* (literally!) where the approach is part of the final experience.

Another Swiss design that involves a belvedere is Georges Descombes' design for the Swiss Way. Originally proposed as a path around Lake Uri (Urnersee) to mark the seven-hundredth anniversary of the Swiss Confederation, it was only the Geneva segment that was completed. Designed to draw attention to the richness of the site, and drawing on a series of maps from 1894 to 1947, this 2-kilometre (just over 1 mile) stretch from Morschach to Brunnen very simply invites the walker to see and feel the topography. Some glacial boulders were cleaned of grass and lichen to reveal the white stone and to make their erratic natural placement more noticeable. The edges of paths were reinforced in places with concrete, and wooden steps were strengthened with metal strips. This left 'a mark of one time', wrote Descombes, 'to overlay an unequivocal trace' of contemporary landscaping. A former railway line was linked to the new path with wooden steps, which also served as seats from which to take in the view. A belvedere at the edge of the path was positioned to look down over the lake, with its circular steel framework open to the whole surrounding landscape, but with one gap facing the water. The Chanzeli belvedere embraced the whole experience of this segment of Switzerland.

Many landscapists are cognizant of being contemporary as well as tied to past practices. Yet, as Van Valkenburgh is quoted as saying, 'We often lack the capacity to read landscape as contemporary because we don't often expect modernists to use natural materials.'[25] That remark in itself is complex. Natural materials are these days often the result of horticultural invention and development; reading them is complicated in that the sites chosen – urban plaza, ocean or river parklands where land and water meet, college campuses, factories or art centres – reveal the same mix of natural and cultural or made. Van Valkenburgh himself is clearly alert both to the prominent use of natural materials and to the role of artists in the composition of meaningful places. At the Allegheny River Trail Park in Pittsburgh, native reeds are pressed into concrete surfaces and thin slices of Van Valkenburgh's favourite bluestone pave the higher levels; he uses rock work, with running water, in Bailey Plaza at Cornell University; and black-locust logs are embedded in the floors of the Tahari Courtyards in Millburn, New Jersey. That he finds proper occasion to involve amphitheatres in larger sites, as Latz + Partner did at Duisburg, implies the performative aspect of so much good modern landscaping. It performs, too, for him the element of the sublime that these natural materials allow. Yet the mechanical and technological input is something that also matters: the huge bluestone wall at Teardrop Park, noted above, actually has a hollow interior, not mentioned at all in the article on it, where a pristine room services the heating and cooling equipment for the surrounding apartments. Modern technology is hidden within a culturally conceived natural topography!

Almost all these moves towards finding a modern, useful and exciting meaning for place involved drawing on older elements. They deliberately mix old and new, and the ancient dialogue between them and between nature and culture is complicated. With land-scape, there is also the need to see older forms as doubly aware of the past – gardens can be essentially nostalgic – and of a recog-nizably contemporary world. Latz's large roof garden at 120 Fenchurch Street in London has an open pergola of steel, and glass balustrades (illus. 59, 60); gardens are featured alongside the sur-viving steel structures of the Parco Dora on formerly derelict land in Turin; while at Willy-Brandt-Platz in Bremerhaven a series of raft-like surfboards are etched into the promenade. All such ref-erences to earlier design ideas are surely in the spirit of Ezra Pound's famous injunction 'Make It New', where the modern 'new' was necessarily based on an earlier 'It'.

Some modernists have seized on the contemporary fashion for garden festivals, either permanent, such as that at Chaumont-sur-Loire in France or the Métis Festival in Canada, or established for specific horticultural events.[26] Gardens are and have been generally

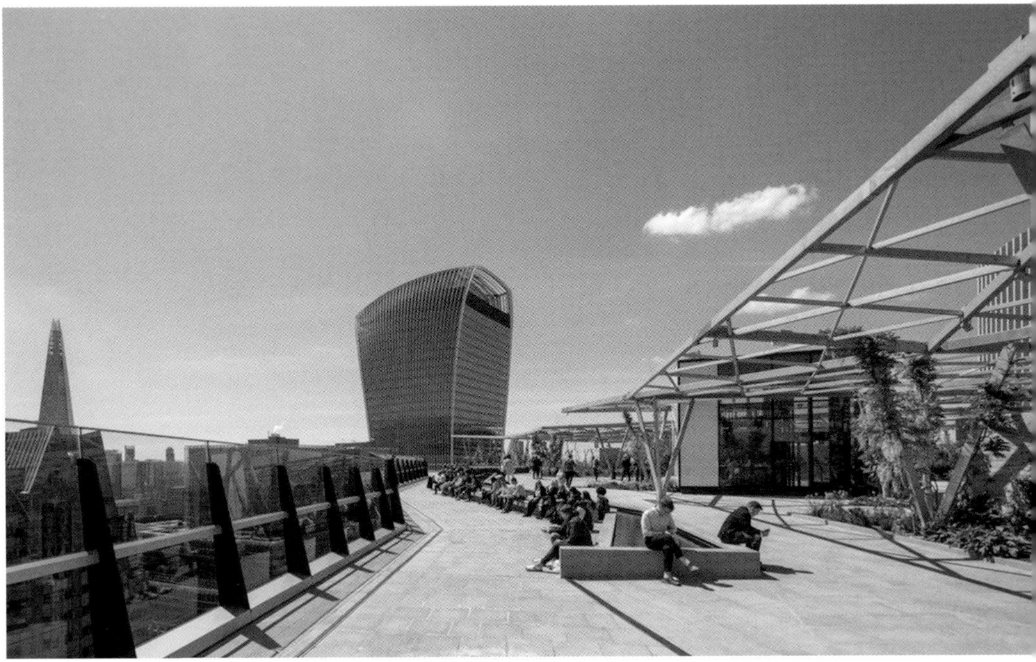

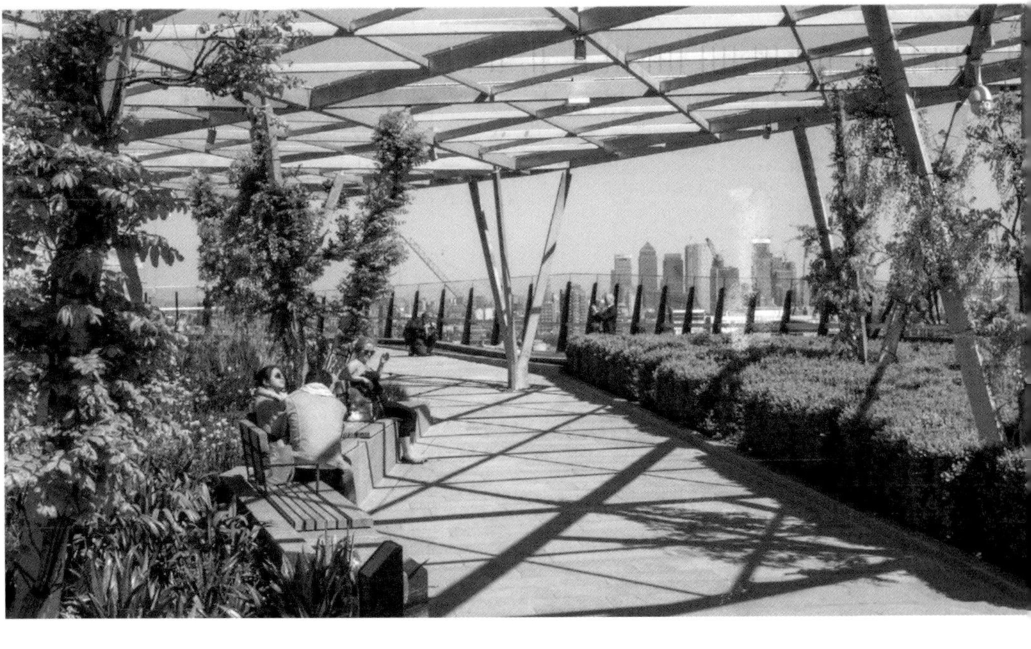

designed for some person or situation and have an indefinite life, whereas garden festival exhibits are short-lived and conspicuously experimental, eliciting interesting and less plausible versions of gardenness. Their main challenge is to find, in a limited space and for a short period, a clear sense of meaning and spirit there, although some might find a more permanent location elsewhere. There are also more deliberate attempts to find new, modern forms and ideas. In Peter Latz's 'Fog Garden' for Chaumont (illus. 61), fog rose between large slabs, themselves brought in from outside and to be returned afterwards. It was strangely impressive, mysterious and unusual, and the sunshine through the mist transformed stone and plants in ways that would be far less impressive in a large public space.

Devised also for an empty space, these garden exhibits at their best seek a simple meaning, although increasingly they have become more complex and demanding of their visitors. Exhibits at the Shanghai International Horticultural Exposition in 2011 were both simple – the 'Scent Garden' and its adjacent 'Aromatic Pavilion', where turbines wafted the aromas from conifers and bottled perfumes filled a greenhouse – and baffling, such as the 'The Labyrinth and the Mountain', in which paper canaries hung in wicker cages, presumably to mimic the real ones used to alert miners to destructive gases, but for no clear reason.[27]

At Chaumont in 2019, Bernard Lassus offered his 'Jardin des Hypothèses', in some sense a review of earlier proposals. He regrouped three of his earlier 'perennial' gardens, all of which took up his long-standing interest in the debate between what was natural and what artificial, and all of which (as he argued) examined how 'a space could become a place, respecting, protecting and understanding what surrounded and was part of it, and how would it evolve'. The natural elements would be monitored by instruments for measuring humidity, acidity, wind, water, temperature, light, sound and geological activity, while perforated metal shapes

59, 60 Peter Latz, rooftop garden at 120 Fenchurch Street, London.

*overleaf:*
61 Peter Latz, Fog Garden, Chaumont-sur-Loire, 1998.

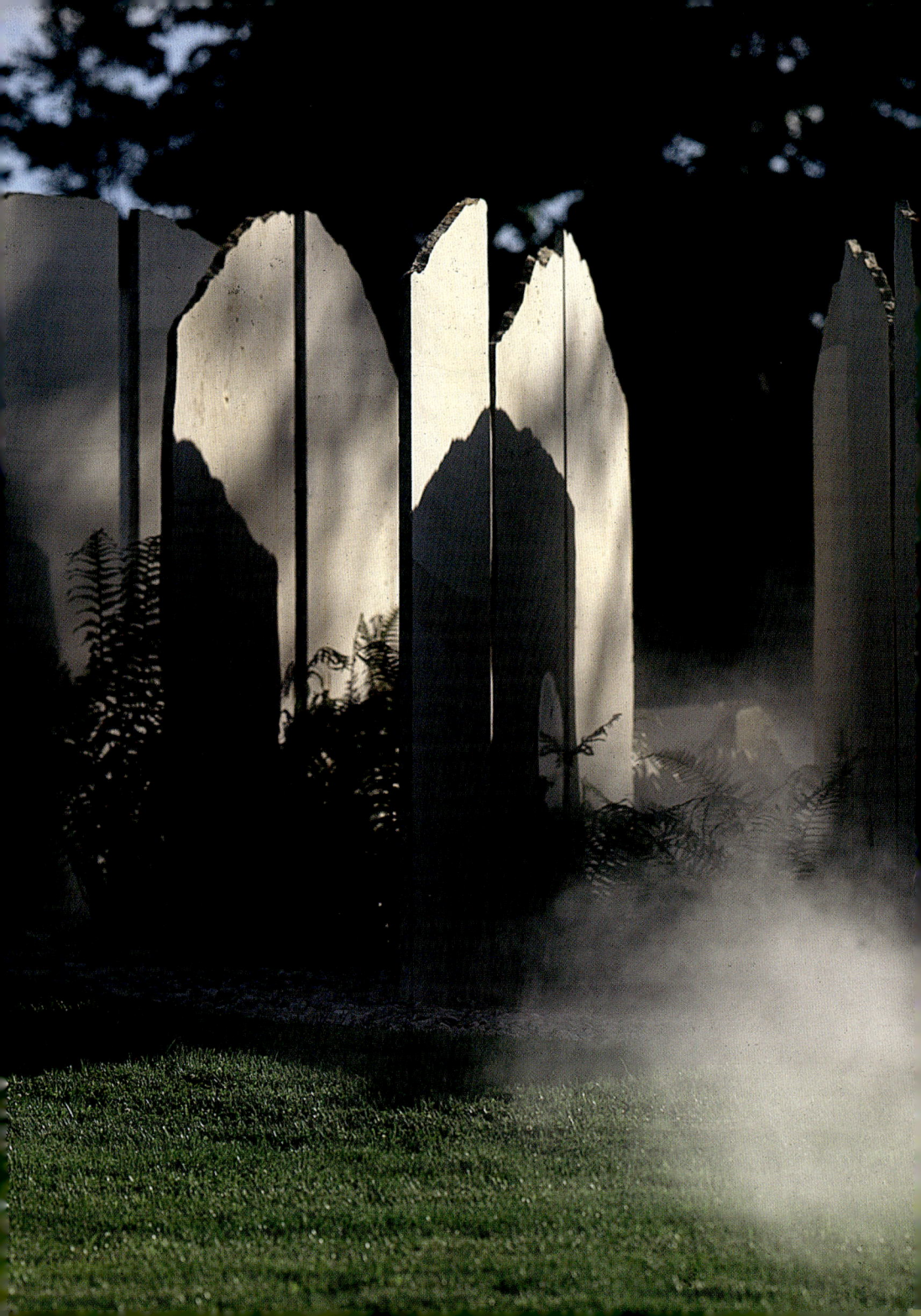

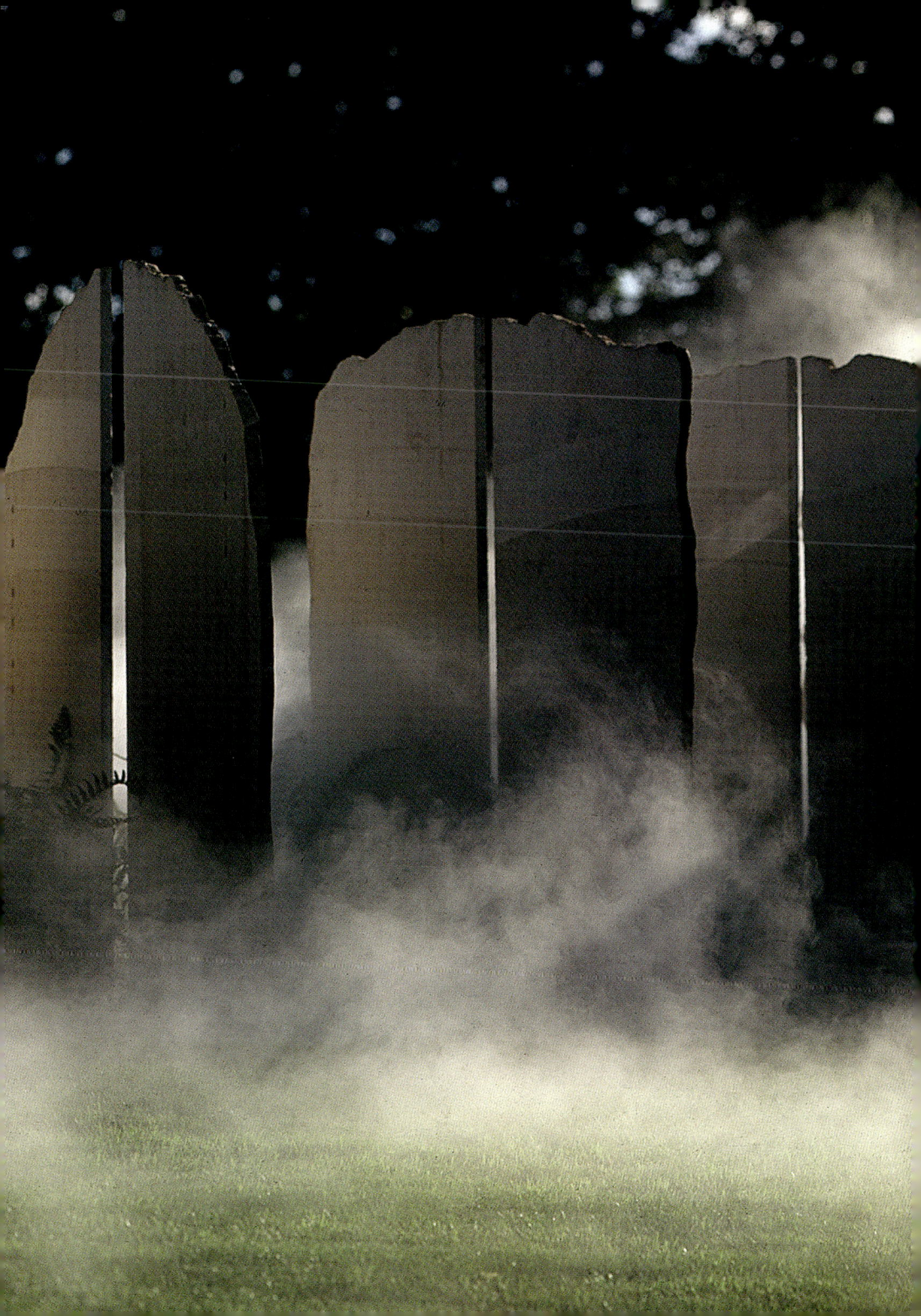

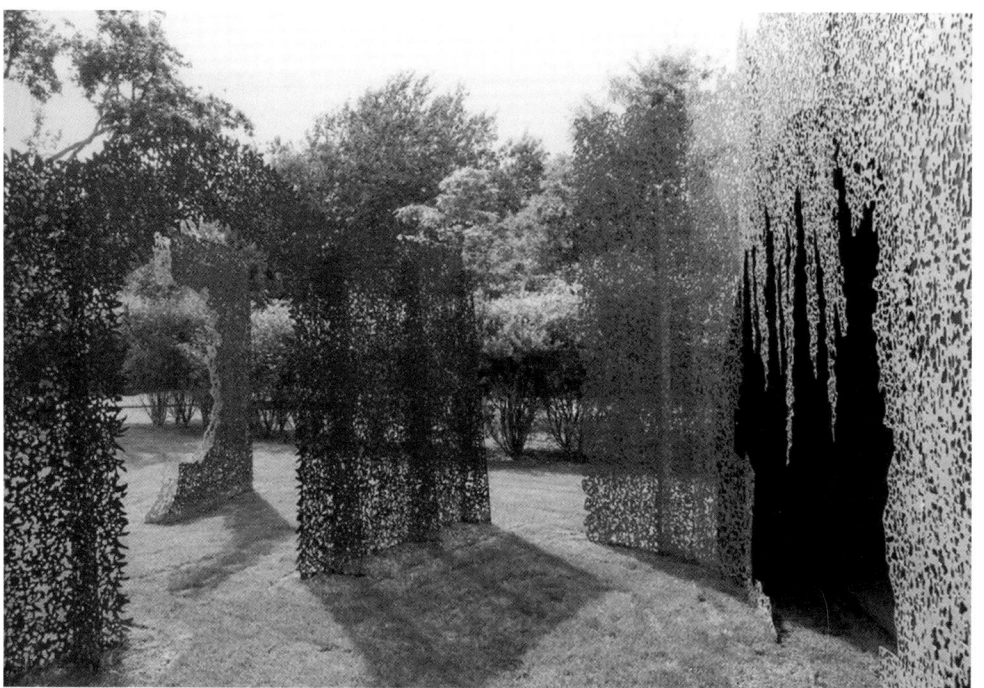

62 Bernard
Lassus, Le Jardin
des Hypothèses,
Chaumont-sur-
Loire, 2019.

represented trees and shrubs, which would be changeable to signal
different seasons from those outside – spring could flourish in
winter, or snow not melt in summer. There was also a 'Théâtre de
Verdure' (Green Theatre), where grottoes, also in perforated metal,
would tell the story of the unmeasurable and incommensurable,
alongside natural bouquets of flowers, to make manifest, as in many
gardens, the drama of hypothetical challenges to what a garden
could be (illus. 62).[28]

GENIUS LOCI has a special role to play in creating gardens and
landscapes where meaningful and sometimes challenging ideas
are defined anew, or can be drawn from an understanding of
the place itself. This experience can be gained by visiting these
designed landscapes, and these days by watching television or

visual exchanges on social media. It is unlikely that anybody has not had that experience. Yet it is also more than ever true that people get to explore places where design has not occurred, as in excursions to wildernesses of all kinds; equally, we all have to live in places that have been shaped by large cultural forces. But many people live, work and play in sites that are not designed, or, if they are, have been the result of centuries of cultural accumulation of buildings, vistas and landscape elements. Many people will not be aware of any design or cultural formation, but their responses and reactions are formed instinctively and unconsciously by what they have absorbed elsewhere. Alain Roger may see *genius loci* as something that only we each bring to a landscape, but that is a fundamental aspect of the way we relate to places. It is a matter of some subtlety how we can and do respond and register our attention to places we know well and to those that we see for the first time. This is therefore the topic of the last chapter: namely, how is our sense of the identity of a *genius loci* formed?

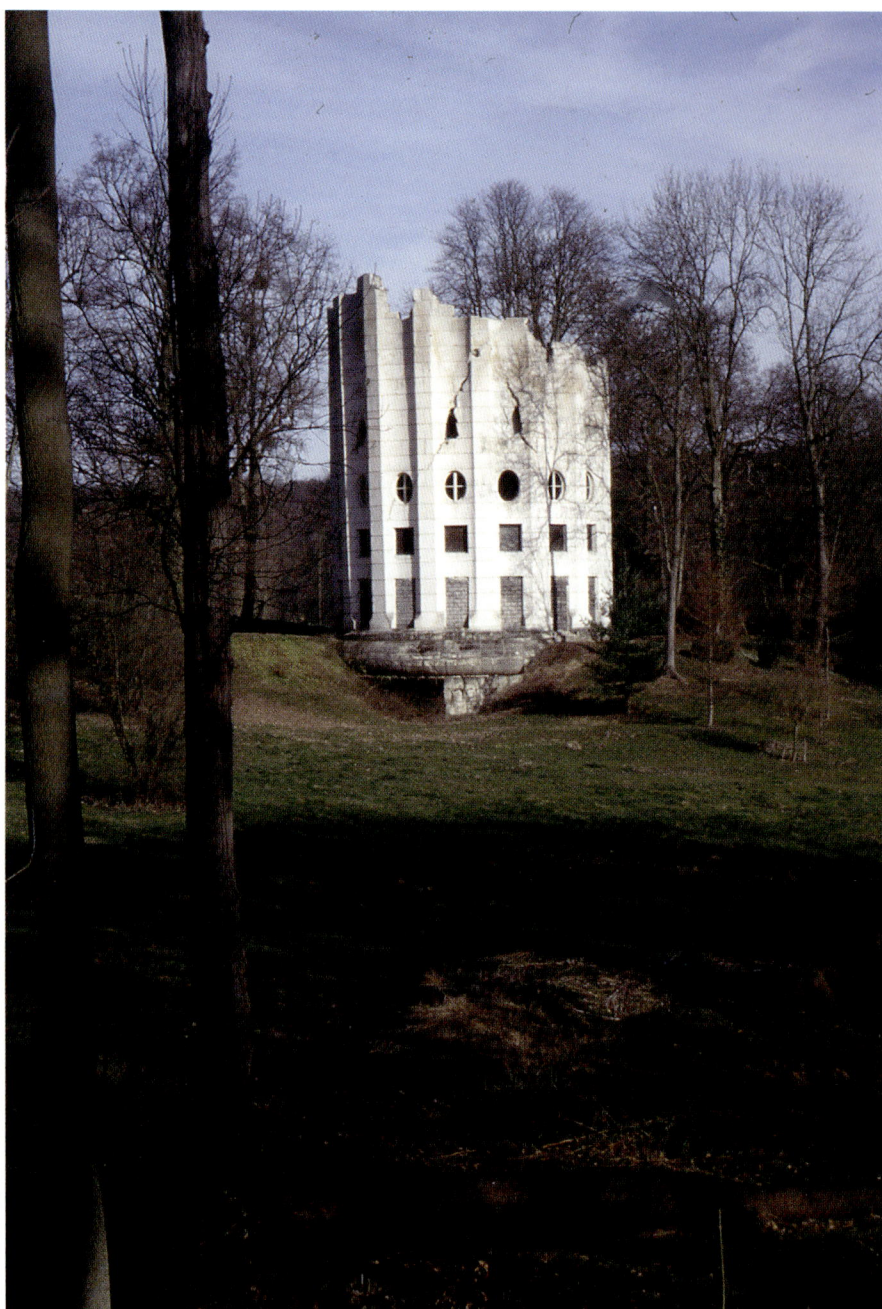

EIGHT

# By Way of Conclusion

Place is not simply an intellectual perspective, it is an emotional
experience ... [it] encounters the world first from the place of the
heart, and brings me to the notion of nature, for example, only
through a secondary effort of thought.

Yves Bonnefoy

Place, needless to say, becomes more, not less, precious within
a landscape of infinite disorientations.

Alasdair Forbes

These comments on the importance of place may help its
better definition. While Marcel Proust advised writers
that 'Il faut jamais conclure' (Never conclude) – a wise
recommendation when matters are complex – the idea of *genius
loci*, simple in itself, has been complicated or even deniable over
the years. Yves Bonnefoy insists that place is not wholly susceptible
to intellectual explanation, while Alasdair Forbes also sees that
the recognition of place can become a precious need when we are
faced with disorientation in the modern world.

Both have written about sites: Bonnefoy about the Désert de
Retz, Chambourcy, and Forbes about the landscape he has been
creating at Plaz Metaxu in north Devon since 1992.[1] What they

63 'Colonne brisée'
(ruined column),
Désert de Retz,
1782.

*177*

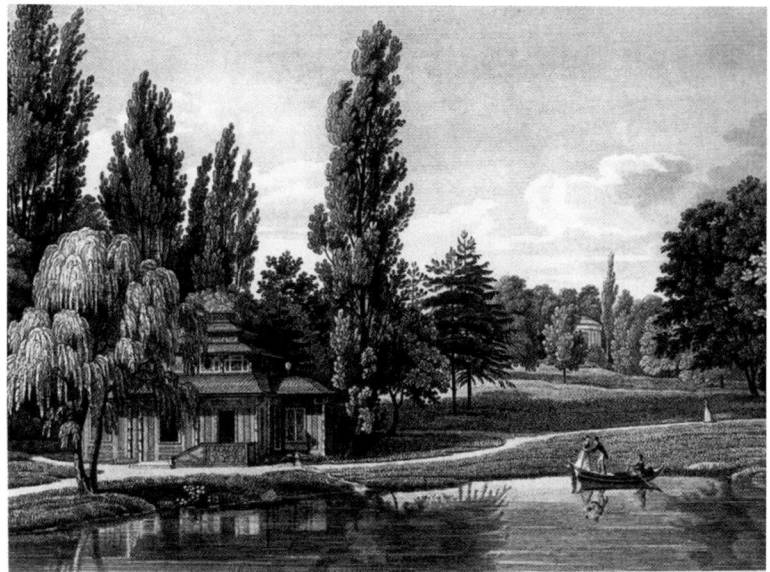

64 Chinese House at
Retz, now destroyed,
engraving from
Le Rouge, *Jardin
Anglo-Chinois Cahier*,
13 (1785).

make of those two designed places can suggest ways in which genius of place can provide a legitimate perspective in responding to places that are not the result of designers' intervention. In different ways, they elicit ideas on *genius loci*, and the opportunity that provides the wherewithal to articulate it. Bonnefoy brings to the eighteenth-century design in Retz a useful historical perspective, and thus a grasp of its cultural context in the years before the French Revolution. Forbes has far less historical distance from his own garden creation, yet he brings to it what he himself has found formative in a bold review of modern culture.

At Retz was gathered a cluster of strangely assorted structures – a Chinese House, a Temple of Pan, a gothic ruin, a pyramid, a theatrical platform, a Tartar tent and a huge ruined tower (illus. 63, 64) – all items that, even in the late eighteenth century, existed at the antipodes of everyday life. Bonnefoy argues that Retz has little coherent or determined 'centre', yet still a '*puissance invisible*'. This less visible hinterland of ideas is explored by moving from the place itself (*le lieu proche*) to the larger world of the French

Enlightenment, and then to a confidence that, he writes, the god of this place can be explained only by recourse to the category of the place itself (*'le dieu a son lieu, le dieu n'est approchable que par le recours à la catégorie de lieu'*). An additional factor, although Bonnefoy does not allude to this, was the strange celebration of the place in a new era by the Surrealists in the 1920s, and its subsequent rediscovery and conservation.

The mystery that surrounds Retz was captured by the architectural writer John Harris, who found his way into it in 1952, first, after reading about it in the *cahiers* of French garden designs by Georges-Louis Le Rouge (1776–87), and then by braving notices that warned trespassers away. Harris wrote about this in *Echoing Voices: More Memories of a Country House Snooper* (2002), finding on that occasion the remains of its astonishing Chinese House, made of teak imported from China, and then on a subsequent visit lamenting that it had disappeared. It was clearly that early visit that spurred his research, through which he sought to learn more about the picturesque and European imitations of Chinese originals from books by Sir William Chambers and the contemporary Swedish critic Osvald Sirén. In short, both his own experience of an astonishing scene and what he then gathered from his readings form the basis of his understanding of that scene's *genius loci*. He found its subsequent and dedicated restoration, as he later confessed in a 'naughty note', was 'at the expense of the romance of decay and ruin', which then coloured his own response.

At Plaz Metaxu, it was precisely Forbes's readings, his own intellectual context, that shaped the complex landscape, and these may indeed 'disorientate' the visitor. Yet Forbes invites responses on at least two levels. On the one hand we can appreciate the way the valley is shaped, how its materials are formed, the simple pleasures of the lake, the slopes, light, sound, hedges, paths, enclosures and groves, all of which take time to walk around as we find the various routes (illus. 65). This is straightforward, requiring an alert and sensitive eye, but with no need to grasp what it might mean. On another level, Plaz Metaxu incites, or requires, what Forbes terms 'orphic spatiality'.

The main title of Forbes's book is *On Psyche's Lawn*; this is clear, for we know what a lawn is, and we should know that Psyche was the goddess of the soul (in any case, the author soon reminds us of that). And Psyche lends herself to the term and approaches of *psych*ology. The subtitle needs explanation beyond it being, obviously, the place where the lawn is. 'Plaz Metaxu' is Greek (not the Welsh *plas*) and means the place that is in between, and we are soon told what that betweenness may mean. First, it is the landscape between two sloping hills that descend to form the valley, its lawns, stream and lake. But it is also – and this is already hinted at in the main title – between an actual territory and topography (a body of lawn) and the ideas and notions Forbes has devised and articulated for it (its soul). So we have the Orphic world of song and poetry, and its physical spaces.

The first images in the book are of those lawns. The caption of the first names the view as 'Orexis', and the other alludes to a cluster of upright steel shafts overlooking the valley as the 'Dragon's Teeth' (see illus. 8.3). But as we proceed through the analysis, the captions give many other classical names and insist on the classical nomenclature and the meanings of objects inserted there.

That betweenness is both in the book and in the landscape, and the former will unpack the mysteries as well as the physical ingredients of place in a sequence of carefully chosen foci – of the lawn, but also of many other aspects of the landscape. It is a remarkable and challenging folio volume. Immediately following the title page is a simple one-page 'physical description of Plaz Metaxu', and then a chapter entitled 'Plaz Metaxu and its Arrière-pays'. The French phrase can mean 'back country', hinterland or the 'background of the place', but it is more illuminating if you know that it was borrowed by Forbes from Bonnefoy and his book *L'Arrière pays* (2003, published with the same title in an English translation by Stephen Romer in 2012).

Bonnefoy is fascinated by crossroads (another place that is 'between'), and considers whether the path not taken may lead to an *arrière-pays*, a 'place of greater plenitude and of more authentic being'. Forbes finds that *arrière-pays* in the works of the American psychologist James Hillman, who (Forbes writes) 'reads the myths into our lived experience today with moving acumen and insight, but holds bravely out (against scientific orthodoxies) for a "poetic basis of mind", as well as privileging a polytheistic temper' (p. 12). This polytheist for Forbes is the classical world of gods and goddesses: Psyche, Narcissus, Hermes, Hesperos, Mnemosyne and Syrinx, to name the ones I recognized immediately. Forbes structures his design and thus the book by using each deity, or sometimes a place (Hades, Epidauros), to designate each section of his garden.

65 'Dragon's Teeth' overlooking the Valley at Plaz Metaxu.

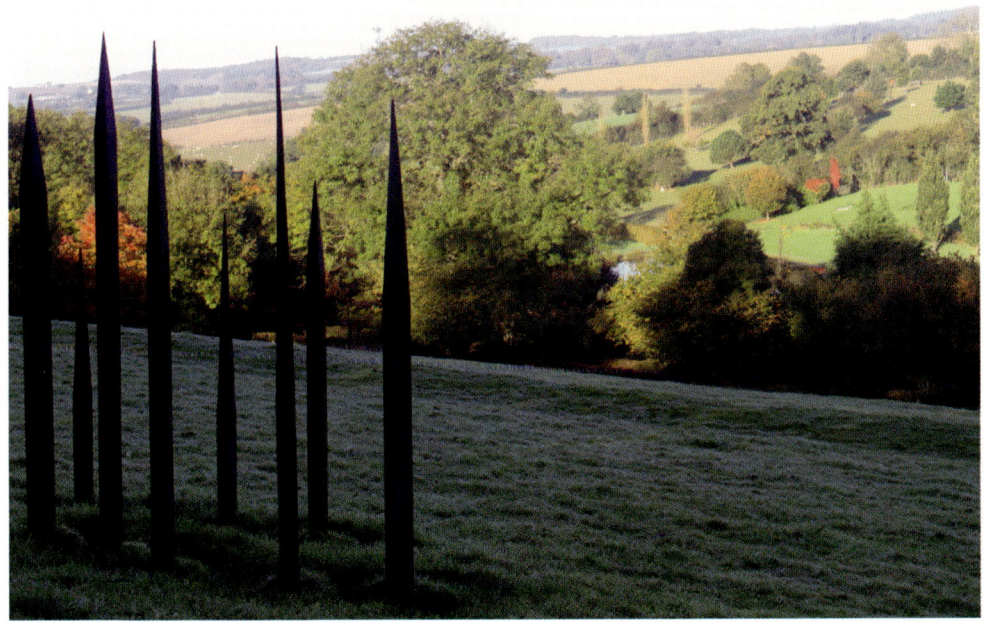

The gods, we might say, are metaphors for place, although I suspect Forbes himself might find that word insufficient. Yet metaphors *are* a prime basis of the poetic mind, and metaphors are yet other crossroads or places in between.

Forbes expands on his personal 'education in literature, psychology, myths, "wisdom teachings", philosophy and goodness knows what else!', specifically the many works of Hillman. That is doubtless more than many who attend to gardens would argue for. But it is a very useful version of a *genius loci* that has been denied or rejected as a useful term or concept today. It is more rigorous than Maurice Barrès's rather weary appeal to our experience at the edges of a wood or a simple grassy space (see Chapter Two), and, more strenuously, is a means to rebut Alain Roger's denial of the existence of *genius loci*.

Forbes writes in the first chapter of his book that the gods he invokes are those who might have functioned thus in classical times:

> So when I came to make the garden the gods, by a series of 'spatial epiphanies', fell into their allotted places, often it seemed, without recourse to me, though I must, at least, have been their filter. What mattered was the eloquence with which they entitled the spaces to 'speak'. The god in adopting the space, drew on the space's inherent character to further invest it with a meaning – or a set of meanings (inseparable from the way the space 'behaved').

He notes that this does not involve statues, as happened in Renaissance gardens: 'the god simply became the space, the space a divine gesture. For me to be able to recognize this, I had to revere both space and god, and to be familiar with their attitudes and sympathies.' In this he appears to be echoing Bonnefoy's identification of *dieu* and *lieu*.

Forbes is quick to recognize that other moderns less 'reveren-tial' than himself also invoked the antecedents of this polytheistic agenda: Friedrich Nietzsche, Sigmund Freud, Friedrich Hölderlin, Rainer Maria Rilke. But few addressed themselves directly to spe-cial events such as a garden landscape. The French evolution of *haut lieu* to signal a place of special signification and noumena does it better, simply because it privileges both place and the reception of place; Anne Cauquelin describes this when she sees nature as a fragment of nature ('*c'est-à-dire qu'il tient lieu*'), that it holds that nature *in place*, gives it a meaningful space. As in most gardens, a nature can be at once general and topographically situated, and is condensed there in its fullness.[2]

In this Devon landscape there are resources to draw on, but they are far less immediately available; its modernity is not perhaps as discernible as French Enlightenment ideas could be. Forbes provides his visitors with written notes, his own scattered and published remarks on what was in his mind during the creation and development of Plaz Metaxu, and now his book. The accumu-lation of ideas makes the place more, rather than less, precious, for, as Forbes says, two things are necessary: walking and reading. Walking allows responses to everything that is there, including the objects that puzzle or disorientate. Reading can enlarge a visitor's response as it did originally for Forbes, with his invocation of classical writings, such as Virgil's and Ovid's story of Orpheus, his ascription of Greek names to the whole territory (Hermes, Artemis, Eos and others), and his debt to writers such as Carl Kerényi, or Hillman's Jungian anthology of psychological texts, *A Blue Fire* (1989).

How, then, do we interpret the inscribed quotations of Plaz Metaxu (from Wallace Stevens, among others; illus. 67), and what meanings should we attach to a strange configuration of nine upright rocks, a large figure of Pan carved into a north-facing slope, twin megaliths or the ¶ (pilcrow, which in writing signals a new paragraph) erected at a bend along a path (illus. 66)? In the middle of the courtyard behind the house, named the Hermes courtyard, is a large terracotta urn lying on its side; since Hermes was the messenger of the gods, the open mouth of the urn pointing towards a visitor suggests that it conveys a message.[3]

Both Retz and Plaz Metaxu, like all gardens, but particularly strongly so, refuse any simple, 'central' view. Yet this sequence of wondrous and puzzling clues and invitations recalls Ian Hamilton

66 The Pilcrow at Plaz Metaxu.

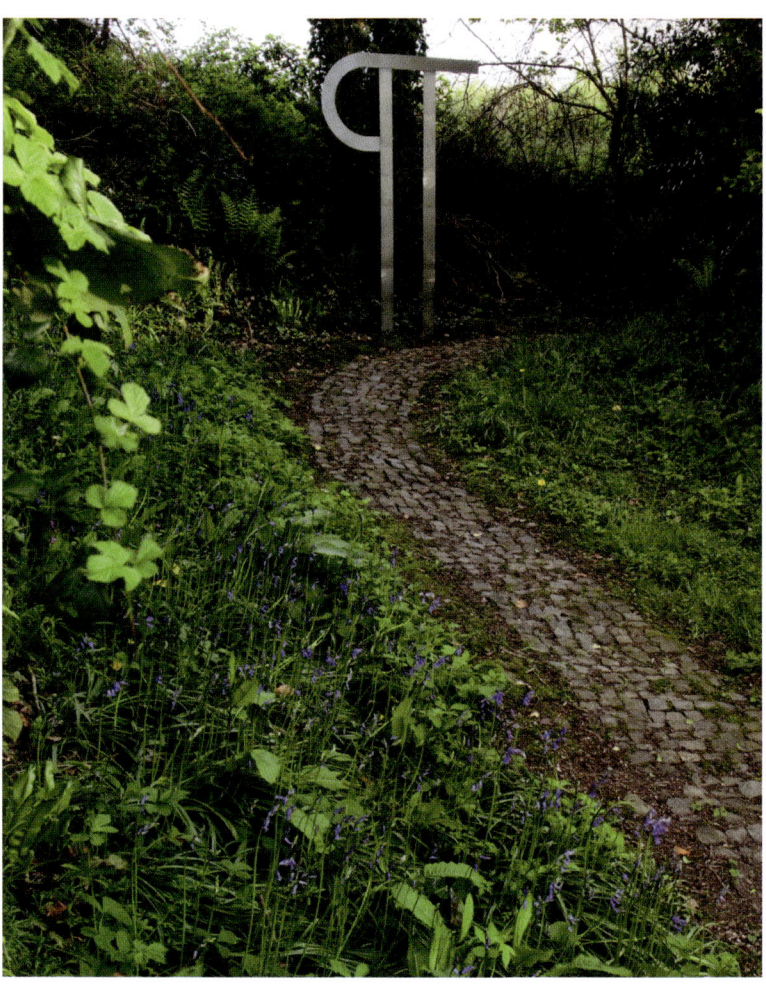

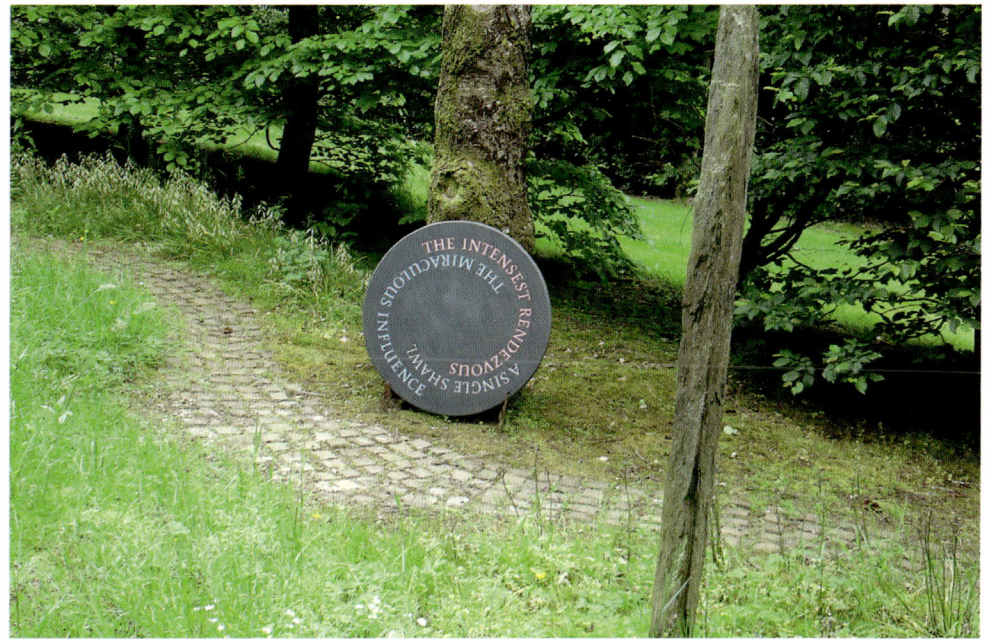

Finlay's aphorism, from one of his 'Unconnected Sentences', that 'consecutive sentences are the beginning of the secular,' for Plaz Metaxu has the feel of something poetic and potent that derives from its 'disorientations'. With Forbes, we are closer to the rich arsenal of ideas that has shaped him and continues to shape his landscape. For the commentary on Retz, it takes a poet and a historian with a considerable intellectual grasp of the ideas that were around at this moment of the French Enlightenment, which (given our own distance from those times) are more accessible. Yet it allows an understanding to emerge with some sense of its mystery that, if not explained, is also strangely dominant, and that itself might encourage further enquiry.

What we derive from the experience of knowing designed landscapes may carry over into our intuitive response to other places. An intriguing example of that influence was suggested by Kathryn Gustafson's Les Jardins de l'Imaginaire in the previous

67  Plaz Metaxu, inscribed quotations by Wallace Stevens.

*185*

chapter, where lessons might be drawn from the different scenarios to apply them to other less deliberate sites. They may stir our imaginations as to what to discover in larger, cultural places.

During Roman times, places would be given meaning by deities or dedicated to famous humans, and even after the establishment of Christianity in Europe metaphorical purpose was still found in dressing in Roman dress, erecting statues of the older gods and heroes in gardens and inserting inscriptions from their works. This happened rhetorically, too, in the form of *prosopopoeia*, where at a moment in the landscape a voice indicates its significance to the passer-by. Hence Finlay's plaque, or maybe tombstone, at his famous garden, Little Sparta near Edinburgh, that declares 'MAN/ A PASSERBY' (illus. 68). It either addresses one who has passed away from a landscape that still exists, or hails the person who simply walks that way.

Gardens are occasions that set themselves distinctly within a different context, and usually the approach to them – through less pleasing or uninteresting surroundings, finally taking the visitor to the more meaningful site – renders contrast and approach the dominant triggers of any new understanding. The journey across the Venetian lagoon to Torcello, the way up the mountain at Cadarda to the Geological Observatory, the avenues that often lead towards houses and parklands: all these prepare one for the places within. Visitors on the dirt road to Little Sparta glimpse a distant cluster of trees in the otherwise barren topography, yet when they open the gate at the summit, it leads them into a wholly different terrain. It is dense in more ways than one, and once we are inside, the sense that it is set apart from any earlier surroundings prompts reflection on why that should be so.

But approaches to and contrasts between places are not everything. For almost everyone, the significance of a place is a question of what they bring with them – preconceptions, associations – and whether they choose to recognize features that are somehow special: for example, is it a tombstone in Little Sparta, or just an inscribed stone? Just as certain manuscripts are palimpsests, so too are places where our minds are layered to the extent that we dip into them when we need to respond to a place.

Both Michel Collot and Francis Ponge found their titles, themes and topics by 'taking' them from places and things, *des partis pris des lieux – ou choses* (The meanings from places – or things). Skill in grasping what the world offers is a central requirement in the search for *genius loci*. Gilbert Highet wrote of the 'presences' that classical writers found in the places they wrote about, so these days the same need is there, although telltale signs may be lacking. That is why Barrès finally offered the edges of a wood, a mountain summit, a spring or some grassy space as more simple opportunities to find a place from which we could 'take' a special sense of occasion. Much of the world is a 'show' or theatre, which is why gardens used amphitheatres or platforms (as at Retz) to remind visitors of performance and its reception.[4] But one early use of 'theatre' was as a collection, a conspectus, which a designed garden may accomplish, but which in an undersigned space will not be likely to occur with such density; there, an individual attention to its possibilities must come into play.

Roger Cardinal writes of Paul Nash's 'hidden qualities of natural things'. The natural world does communicate much, variously, to almost everyone, but it takes longer and perhaps more practice to pull out the hidden aspects. Pulling aside the veils of Isis, as Pierre Hadot made clear, can be a strenuous but exciting activity. He offers many examples, and more sources of inspiration and discernment are everywhere. To the contribution of reading, looking at art and listening to music can be added not only visits to designed landscapes and cultural sites, but the resources now available on the Internet, on television programmes, at garden centres and on social media. I am struck by how much television thrillers or detective stories deploy landscapes to hint at meaning, as well as providing 'atmosphere' (I am thinking here of ITV's series *Vera* and the BBC's Shetland). Kathleen Raine, in 'Stonypath' (1977), her poem on Little Sparta, sees there a 'contained image' of 'wood, water, wind', but then finds them 'Restored to mental space/ Which is the world's true place'. That slippage from a specific place, or garden, to mental space is larger than the specific stimulus and can now be part of the bigger world. And it recalls Ruskin's remark, quoted in Chapter Three, that looking gives 'the far higher and deeper truth of mental vision'.

Absent a person's total inability or lack of concern to register where she or he is in the world at any one moment, we are all liable to be conscious of this 'mode of perception' that is central to our attention to the world. We bring to it what we have acquired over the years: a cluster of skills, habits, prejudices, memories and associations (Coleridge thought the last on this list prevailed over fancy, but its role in imaginative response is crucial). Our regard of the world about us is indeed a 'living power' (Coleridge again) as we negotiate it. In an age of much more distraction and 'disorientation' than was obtained in the past, a respect and grasp of the facts and meanings of our surroundings are both needed and inspiring. *Prosopopoeia* and *genius loci* are not actually there on the ground, speaking to us and directing us. But they can serve us well.

68  Ian Hamilton
Finlay, 'MAN/
A PASSERBY'
at Little Sparta.

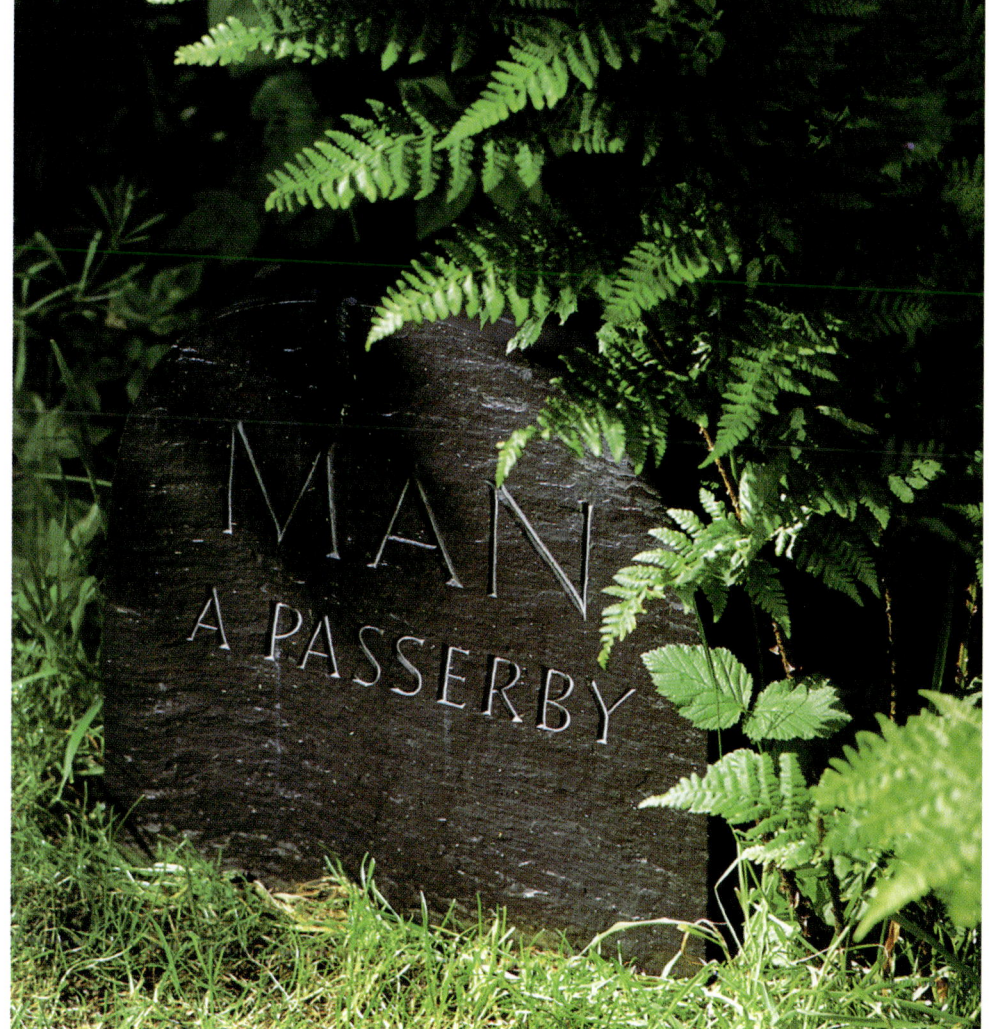

# References

**Preface**

1  In *Nones* (London, 1962), pp. 11–15.

**1 The *Genius Loci* of the Ancients and Its Modern Revisions**

1  Gilbert Highet, *Poets in a Landscape* (1957), p. 1. The 'landscape' Highet explores is both topographical and literary.
2  The topic has been extremely well covered, beginning with Pausanias, the first-century Greek traveller and geographer who explored ancient Greece mainly to interpret Greek culture for a Roman audience. This was handled extensively by Jane E. Harrison in *Mythology and Monuments of Ancient Athens* (1890) and again in her *Themis: A Study of the Social Origins of Greek Religion* (1912).
3  See Dorothy Kent Hill, 'Roman Domestic Garden Sculpture', in *Ancient Roman Gardens*, ed. Elisabeth B. MacDougall and Wilhelmina F. Jashemski (Washington, DC, 1981), pp. 81ff. Stefano de Caro, 'The Sculptures of the Villa of Poppaea at Oplontis', in *Ancient Roman Villas*, ed. Wilhelmina F. Jashemski (Washington, DC, 1987) catalogues a range of sculptures that include Aphrodite, Dionysos and Artemis. Wilhelmina Jashemski, *The Gardens of Pompei*, vol. XI (Appendices) (New Rochelle, NY, 1993) has many references to how those gardens were peopled and their meanings suggested.
4  See Otto Kurz, '*Huis Nympha Loci*', *Journal of the Warburg and Courtauld Institutes*, XVI (1953), p. 171. A sense of how even in the eighteenth century an inscription was needed becomes more palpable for present-day designers who do not invoke quotations; J. B. Jackson is 'inclined to believe that when a designer relies on inscriptions to make his point he is tacitly admitting artistic incompetence' (*The Necessity of Ruins*, 1980, p. 96).
5  There is good evidence of the presence of women as being in charge of gardens: see, for example, Charles Evelyn (a pseudonym maybe of John Lawrence), *The Lady's Recreation; or, The Art of Gardening Improv'd* (1717),

or Thaisa Way, *Unbounded Practices: Women, Landscape Architecture, and Early Twentieth Century Design* (Charlottesville, VA, 2009). The incidence of women as designers appears largely in the late nineteenth and twentieth centuries, for which see Chapter Eight below.

6 Margaret Atwood, *The Blind Assassin* (London, 2000), p. 27. J. B. Jackson is also sceptical about the use of the Latin phrase (see Chapter Two below).

7 Susan Stewart, *The Ruins Lesson: Meaning and Material in Western Culture* (Chicago, IL, 2020). Stewart's third chapter is particularly rich in references to beings who haunted and gave meaning to ancient ruins.

8 Highet, *Poets*, p. 201. The previous allusion to Virgil is at p. 80, and to Horace, p. 135.

9 See Harriet I. Flower, *The Dancing Lares and the Serpent in the Garden* (Princeton, NJ, 2017). I am grateful to Kathy Gleason for this recommendation.

10 Mark Akenside in *British Poets*, ed. R. Anderson (London, 1854), vol. IX, pp. 797–8, 803. See also Akenside's *Poetical Works*, ed. Robin Dix (London, 1996). I owe this discussion to John Gage, who discussed Turner's debt to Akenside in his *Colour in Turner: Poetry and Truth* (London, 1969), pp. 142–5.

11 I review his Italian contacts in my *William Kent: Landscape Garden Designer* (London, 1987), specifically pp. 15–29.

12 See Liz Bellamy, 'Designing Gardens in English Novels of the 1790s', *Studies in the History of Gardens and Designed Landscapes*, XL/3 and 4 (2020), pp. 227–38.

13 *Works*, I.132. I consider Ruskin's sense of place in some sections of my *The Art of Ruskin and the Spirit of Place* (London, 2021).

14 References in the main text are to the standard, revised translation (New York, 2007) and its editorial commentaries.

15 Kelly Drake (a pseudonym), '*Genius Loci*: Akrai, Sicily', in *The Oxford Book of Garden Verse*, ed. John Dixon Hunt (Oxford, 1993), p. 230.

## 2 Does *Genius Loci* Exist?

1 Besides the references offered in the text that follows, both Roger and Berque have been excerpted and contextualized in Thierry Paquot, *Le Paysage* (Paris, 2016), in particular section 2, 'L'apport des disciplines'. Neither has been translated.

2 I am quoting from *Essais* (Paris, 2004), vol. III, chap. 5, p. 874. The English by M. A. Screech puts it thus: 'If I were in the trade, I would treat art as naturally as I could, just as they make nature artificial, I would make art natural.' *The Complete Essays* (London, 2003), p. 988.

3 From the Preface to his *Local Knowledge: Further Essays in Interpretative Anthropology* (New York, 2000), pp. ix and xi. Geertz later argues wryly (p. 77) that 'common sense is both a more problematical and a more profound affair than it seems from the perspective of a Parisian café or an Oxford Common Room.' And he worries about the excessive focus on the personal that some writers – including Merleau-Ponty – have pursued in 'the so-called phenomenology of everyday life'.

4 He discusses this in *Modern Painters*, vol. IV. I take this topic up in my book *The Art of Ruskin and the Spirit of Place* (London, 2021), and again here in the next chapter on Torcello.

5 The specific role of designers in charting and making places is the topic of the previous chapter.

6 The proceedings of the *seminaire* are online at https://geographielit-teraire.hypotheses.org. Collot has himself written *Pour une géographie littéraire* (Paris, 2014), *La Pensée-paysage* (Arles, 2011) and *Le Parti pris des lieux* (Brussels, 2018).

7 In *Pour une géographie littéraire* (pp. 191ff). All quotations, translations and references are from this essay, not from Butor. Four volumes of Butor's collected work are dedicated to 'Genius loci', as well as a smaller anthology that he edited himself, *Michel Butor par Michel Butor* (Paris, 2003).

8 *Michel Butor par Michel Butor*, p. 69.

9 Quoted in Collot, *Pour une géographie littéraire*, p. 200.

10 See Fernand Braudel, 'Géohistoire: La société, l'espace, le temps', in *Les Ambitions de l'histoire* (Paris, 1997), p. 114.

11 See for instance Udo Weilacher, *Between Landscape Architecture and Land Art* (Basel, 1996), one of the earliest explorations of this connection; and Gilles A. Tiberghien, *Nature, Art, Paysage* (Paris, 1993).

12 See the very personal approach to Jackson in Helen Lefkowitz Horowitz, *Traces of J. B. Jackson: The Man Who Taught Us to See Everyday America* (Charlottesville, VA, 2020). Cited in my text as *Traces*. There is also an extensive, very useful survey of Jackson's idea in the review essay by Mark Treib in *Studies in the History of Gardens and Designed Landscapes*, XX (2002), pp. 147–52, where Horowitz's collection of his writings is frequently cited.

13 See Douglas Adams's essay in *Drawn to Landscape: The Pioneering Work of J. B. Jackson*, ed. Janet Mendelsohn and Christopher Wilson (Staunton, VA, 2015).

14 In the significantly titled *A Sense of Place, a Sense of Time* (New Haven, CT, 1994), pp. 157–8. In the quotation that follows Jackson emphasizes celebration, a term we often use about things that we like or cherish, as well as about rituals that can involve more than celebration.

15  *Entretiens sur la poésie* (Paris, 1990), pp. 352–9, where he too expands '*lieu*' into '*haut lieu*'.

### 3  Torcello and the Expression of Place

1  See John Hayman, *John Ruskin and Switzerland* (Waterloo, Ontario, 1990), John Hayman, ed., *John Ruskin: Letters from the Continent 1858* (Toronto, 1982), quoted p. 34, and Ian Warrell, *Through Switzerland with Turner* (London, 1995). In his diaries (Oxford, 1956; pagination continuous through three volumes), Ruskin frequently admires the environs of Lucerne and comments on its geology (p. 37) and its beauty (p. 43), yet he can also be frustrated by his efforts to paint it (p. 554). I discuss Ruskin's understanding of place at length in *The Art of Ruskin and the Spirit of Place* (London, 2021).

2  Harold I. Shapiro, ed., *Ruskin in Italy: Letters to His Parents 1845* (Oxford, 1978), p. 206. The second volume of *The Stones of Venice* was published in 1853, with the chapter on Torcello.

3  Ruskin had done much reading about Venice, as well as endless exploration on foot and by gondola. I myself relied on several books about the city, including that by Hugh Honour, *The Companion Guide to Venice* (London, 1967), and the detailed information in the TCI *Venezia* in several and augmented editions (3rd edn, 1985).

4  These are illustrated in Hugh Honour and John Fleming, *The Venetian Hours of Henry James, Whistler and Sargent* (London, 1991), pp. 29 and 30.

5  Quoted ibid.; the passage on Torcello (quoted below) is on pp. 28–31.

### 4  Places: J.M.W. Turner, Paul and John Nash

1  Henry James, 'French Pictures in Boston', in John L. Sweeney, *The Painter's Eye* (London, 1956), p. 48; Paul Nash, *Outline*, p. 27, extracted from a long passage about 'my first authentic place' that he discovered as a boy in Kensington Gardens, London; in that same passage he found he could 'escape from myself' there. I use *Outline: An Autobiography*, edited and with an introduction by David Boyd Haycock (London, 2016), which also includes a memoir by Nash's wife, Margaret.

2  As written to Herbert Read, quoted in David Fraser Jenkins, with essays by David Boyd Haycock and Simon Grant, *Paul Nash: The Elements* (London, 2010), p. 27.

3  Claude Colleer Abbott and Anthony Bertram, eds, *Poet and Painter: Being the Correspondence between Gordon Bottomley and Paul Nash* (Oxford, 1955), pp. 59–60. They first got to know each other in 1910 and

conducted their growing friendship most often by post and the exchange of parcels of books and drawings, punctuated by ill health on both sides. I also suspect that Bottomley, writing so much to Paul, did not give his full attention to John; his few comments on John are both somewhat condescending and less focused on John's work, which he derived almost entirely through the correspondence with what Paul sent him.

4 Jack Lindsay, ed., *The Sunset Ship: The Poems of J.M.W. Turner* (Lowestoft, 1966).

5 Nash, *Outline*, pp. 27–8.

6 Abbott and Bertram, *Poet and Painter*, p. 230.

7 The range of Turner's paintings that concern places is vast and has been much discussed. Some sense of that topic can be seen in Andrew Wilton, *The Life and Work of J.M.W. Turner* (London, 1979) or Frederick Ogee, *J.M.W. Turner: Les Paysages absolus* (Paris, 2010).

8 See Roger Cardinal, *The Landscape Vision of Paul Nash* (London, 1989), p. 118.

9 I am relying a little here on one of my earliest attempts to grapple with Turner, '"Wondrous Deep and Dark": Turner and the Sublime', *Georgia Review* (Spring 1976), pp. 139–64.

10 Nash also drew designs for arches; see cat. 55 and figs 55 and 56 in the Tate catalogue (n. 15 below).

11 I use this phrase again at the start of the next chapter, when Gerard Manley Hopkins borrowed the term from Duns Scotus to describe subjects about which he wrote.

12 Cited in Ogee, *J.M.W. Turner*, pp. 148–9.

13 Cardinal, *The Landscape Vision of Paul Nash*, p. 118.

14 Martin Price, *To the Place of Wisdom* (New York, 1965).

15 Paul Nash's equally large commitment to landscape has more recently been explored in two catalogues: that edited by Andrew Causey, *Paul Nash* (Oxford, 1980), with the catalogue on pp. 343–485; and Emma Chambers, ed., *Paul Nash*, in connection with an exhibition at the Tate in 2017 (London, 2016). Both also contain very useful essays on Nash's work. For John, an early book by Allen Freer, *John Nash: 'The Delighted Eye'* (Farnham, 1993), and more recently Andrew Lambirth, *John Nash. Artist and Countryman* (Norwich, 2019). This large and detailed book is biographically based, which helps to distinguish John from Paul, but the many images offer a large window into the younger brother's graphic imagination, which is as powerful as Paul's. The range and excitement of John's images are impressive. Alas, Lambirth dislikes footnotes, as 'I make a point of not including them in my books' (p. 335). At the end of the book is a 'Gallery' (pp. 323–32) of other

works that the author has found during the course of his research, 'largely of unknown paintings and drawings'.

16  Chambers, *Paul Nash* has sections on both themes, respectively pp. 140–51 and 128–39.

17  Abbott and Bertram, *Poet and Painter*, p. 60. Paul's oil painting from a private collection is illustrated in Chambers, *Paul Nash*, plate 29. Its somewhat anonymous pond was in fact one near John's new home in Buckinghamshire (see Simon Grant in Jenkins, *Paul Nash: The Elements*, p. 39).

18  Quoted in Lambirth, *John Nash*, p. 86, and p. 90 for the next reference.

19  Most usefully and critically by Cardinal in *The Landscape Vision*. See also Freer, *John Nash*, and Lambirth, *John Nash*. An essay by Sarah Fill, 'Surrealism and Prehistoric Dorset', appeared in Chambers, *Paul Nash*. Jenkins, *Paul Nash: The Elements* also touches on his place within Surrealism; but the more he is situated among such artists – Giorgio de Chirico, René Magritte – and he certainly took encouragement from some of them, the more he seems to find his own role, 'stretching normality to the limits' (p. 27).

20  See Jenkins, *Paul Nash: The Elements*, cat. 47 and commentary, to which I am indebted here, and to the essays by David Boyd Haycock and Simon Grant.

21  Ibid., cats. 28 (Leicester Museum and Art Gallery) and 32 (Aberdeen Art Gallery). This catalogue makes, indeed, a strong case for the surrealism of Nash with its selection of images for the Dulwich Picture Gallery exhibition with which it was associated.

22  These remarks by Nash are cited in Cardinal, *The Landscape Vision*, pp. 15, 122, 23, 64. Nash's love of 'winter country' was also instinct for seeing pure forms of natural objects.

23  Abbott and Bertram, *Poet and Painter*, p. 241.

24  Jenkins, *Paul Nash: The Elements*, cat. 39. A letter by Nash is quoted in the catalogue entry. In *Outline* (pp. 100ff) he discusses this famous landmark.

25  Lambirth, *John Nash*, n. 16.

26  *Outline*, pp. 100–101. It is unlikely that clumps were an ancient British topographical marker; Tom Williamson advises me that they were first seen in the early eighteenth century, and thinks that the idea of clumps may have been derived from Kent's interest in transforming estates for his clients.

27  Interestingly, Nash's friend Gordon Bottomley also wrote a poem about Pan, 'The Dairymaids to Pan', in *Poems of Thirty Years* (London, 1925), pp. 12–13: 'Goatfoot,/ we know you/ Though we cannot see you.'

28  Abbott and Bertram, *Poet and Painter*, p. 46.

29  Ibid., p. 212, and subsequent quotation.

30  Illustrated in Lambirth, *John Nash*, p. 22, presumably in a private collection, but not credited in his checklist. His text notes how John loved the house's garden of flowers, orchards, croquet lawn and vegetable garden, but these do not appear in the watercolour at all.

31  Illustrated respectively ibid., pp. 10 (private collection), 42 (Museum of Modern Art), 289 (Art Galleries Harlow) and 311 (private collection).

32  Jenkins, *Paul Nash: The Elements*, cat. 13. A cluster of interpretations of this, in the Tate, are gathered in the commentary. John also painted war scenes.

33  Ibid., cats 15 and 9.

34  Bottomley was sometimes disappointed that Nash did not involve people in his scenery; see Abbott and Bertram, *Poet and Painter*, p. 40. Nash himself was somewhat defiant about people who suggested that he 'should draw people in landscapes' (p. 233). John Nash's *The Edge of the Orchard* (1919) did not include any figures, although the nearest branches are greatly animated. For earlier instances of inserting people into landscapes, see the discussion in Donald Wesling's section 'Peopling the Landscape', in *Wordsworth and the Adequacy of Landscape* (London and New York, 1970), pp. 59ff.

35  The index of Abbott and Bertram, *Poet and Painter* chronicles those artists, and also their concern for English placefulness (see pp. 106, 116, 189).

36  Cardinal, *The Landscape Vision*, fig. 12.

37  Abbott and Bertram, *Poet and Painter*, p. 187.

38  Ibid., p. 241.

39  Ibid., p. 37.

40  It is very different in the making of gardens, where both sounds and scents are calculated; see various discussions of those in D. Fairchild Ruggles, ed., *Sound and Scent in the Garden* (Washington, DC, 2017).

41  See Bottomley, *A Stage for Poetry: My Purposes with My Plays* (Kendal, 1948), which contains illustrations by Nash for these dramas. Nash writes of starting to illustrate Bottomley's *The Crier by Night* in *Outline*, p. 67.

## 5  Poets on *Genius Loci: Ut natura poesis*

1  See the recent analysis by Michael Leslie, 'The "Usurping Sense": Site, Sight, Space, and Meaning in John Denham's *Cooper's Hill*', *Studies in the History of Gardens and Designed Landscape*, XXXIX (2020), pp. 278–95. For what follows, see *The Collected Poems of Brian Morris* (Minehead, 2001), notably pp. 157 and 36–7, and many others.

2 On 'significant form', see n. 4 below. There is also a large discussion of this in modern French poetry and criticism, from some of which I have derived stimulus and knowledge; see in particular works by Michel Collot and his essay on Michel Butor cited in Chapter Two.

3 Interestingly, Nash was also fascinated by the falcon or hovering hawk; see *Outline*, pp. 89–90, 92.

4 Quoted by W. H. Gardner (the editor) in his introduction to *Gerard Manley Hopkins Poems and Prose* (London, 1953), p. xx, where Hopkins is compared to Clive Bell's notion of 'significant form'. Other poems that address aspects of 'realty' are 'Ash-Boughs', p. 82; 'Duns Scotus' Oxford' is on p. 40.

5 J. Shawcross, ed., *Biographia Literaria* [1817], 2 vols (Oxford, 1962), vol. 1, chapter 23, specifically p. 202.

6 Quoted here from the early (1805–6) version of *The Prelude*, ed. Ernest de Selincourt, 2nd edn revised by Helen Darbishire (Oxford, 1959), p. 158; the same passage was used in the 1850 version.

7 See James D. Kornwolf, 'David Meade II', *Journal of Garden History*, XVI (1996), p. 265, for the American example, and for the Tuileries see Evelyn's *Elysium Britannicum; or, The Royal Gardens*, ed. John E. Ingram (Philadelphia, PA, 2000).

8 The literature is large, but Wordsworth's Dove Cottage held an exhibition in 1983, with a catalogue, *The Lake District Discovered 1810–1850: The Artists, the Tourists, and Wordsworth*, with notes and commentary by Peter Bucknell and Robert Wolf (Grasmere, 1983). See also William Roberts, *A Dawn of Imaginative Feeling* (Carlisle, 1996). There is a much more focused view of place in Peter Dale and Brandon C. Yen, *Wordsworth's Gardens and Flowers: The Spirit of Paradise* (Woodbridge, 2018).

9 London, 2018. Subsequent quotations are also taken from here. Davidson uses his own experience of the Lakes, and the key modern guides to them by Alfred Wainwright, who himself uses words and sketches to describe each of his climbs and walks. Davidson's early chapters narrate some of the earlier approaches to the Lakes before reaching Coleridge's, where his text and maps seek to follow Coleridge's original walks, as far as is possible.

10 It went through three editions, somewhat revised, until 1810, and was republished by Preston Publishing in 1990; it has also been issued online. Its author became a Fellow of the Society of Antiquaries in 1795.

11 I use the illustrated edition, Peter Bicknell, ed., *The Illustrated Wordsworth's Guide to the Lakes* (Exeter, 1984).

12  *The Collected Poems* (New York, 1982), p. 76. Subsequent discussions focus on 'The Idea of Order at Key West' (pp. 128–30, 23, 47–8, 117–18, 94), and on New Haven, pp. 465–88.

13  *The Oxford Book of Local Verses* (Oxford, 1987), p. xi. Examples here from pp. 193, 221 and 263.

14  'Hermes, Shapeshifter', in *Ruins*, with a foreword by V. B. Price (Albuquerque, NM, 2011), pp. 90–91.

15  The French is hard to put into English, but asks colloquially what 'your take' is on some person, thing (*'choses'*) or place, that is, what do you make of it? It therefore seems that things can be part of places, and each can alert the other.

16  Michel Collot, *Le Parti pris des lieux* (Brussels, 2018), p. 35; my version of *'les cimes peu à peu ressortent des ténèbres, phosphorescentes sous la lune. Une lueur blueit la page. Une rumeur sourd du silence. La neige crisse sous l'écriture'*. Other references are taken from pp. 40, 105.

17  I discovered Darwish's poetry in Ursula Lindsey's review of works by and about him, 'This Land Is Mine', *New York Review of Books*, 27 February 2020.

## 6  Travel Writers on Place

1  'Landscape and Character', *New York Times*, 12 June 1960.

2  I shall quote from James, *A Little Tour* in the Tauchnitz edition (1954), Lawrence in Penguin Books of 1960, Ford in the Echo Press edition of 1935, Durrell from the Faber paperback of 1959 and Theroux in the Houghton Mifflin Harcourt edition of 2020. With James, who titles each essay with the place visited, I have not given page numbers, since the references can be found in my chapter.

3  It is obvious for any writer that his or her personality determines much of the way places are viewed. Ford's partner, Stella Bowen, saw Provence more straightforwardly as a paradise of light, warmth, good and simple food, a simplicity of thought that cleared the mind, like sunlight, and somewhere reason wins.

4  'To Ford Madox Ford in Heaven', *The Collected Later Poems* (New York, 1963), pp. 60–61.

5  It is interesting that Lawrence Durrell too in *Bitter Lemons* thinks that 'snake-lore here [in Cyprus] would be worth investigating' (see p. 107).

6  For readers unacquainted with the area, a map would have made sense in this book to track Theroux's zigzagging across the border; toponymical names are frequently in Spanish, so he must occasionally note that Del Rio is 'Del Rio, Texas'.

7 All quotations from *The Songlines* (New York, 1988). Much of what I draw on from that book has uncanny parallels with the Romans' idea of *genius loci*.

### 7  Landscape Architecture and the Fabrication of Place

1 *New York Times*, Book Review, 26 August 2012.

2 I consider this project, and illustrate several of its gardens, in my conclusion to *The Making of Place: Modern and Contemporary Gardens* (London, 2015). See also Kathryn Gustafson and Jane Amidon, *Moving Horizons: The Landscape Architecture of Kathryn Gustafson and Partners* (Basel, 2005).

3 *Historical Ground: The Role of History in Contemporary Landscape Architecture* (New York, 2014). The brief references in that book to the term *genius loci* are on pp. 12–14 and 28. I will review certain of my earlier remarks here, but the examples now discussed, with a couple of exceptions, invoke fresh examples of *genius loci*, and are drawn also from earlier projects.

4 Jay Gould saw man as always *homo narrator* in 'So Near and So Far', *New York Review of Books*, 20 December, 1994, p. 26.

5 For the High Line, see *The High Line Foreseen Unforeseen* (London, 2015), a huge and wonderful compendium of drawings, drafts, materials, commentary and photographs that document the site, compiled by James Corner Field Operations and Diller Scofidio + Renfro. See also a collection of reflections on the High Line, Udo Weilacher, ed., *Inspiration High Line* (Munich, 2018). For Teardrop Park, see Erik de Jong, 'Teardrop Park Elective Affinities', in *Reconstructing Urban Landscapes: Michael Van Valkenburgh Associates*, ed. Anita Berrizbeitia (New Haven, CT, 2009), pp. 172–91. For Jacob Javits Plaza, see below.

6 I draw here on F. Hamilton Hazlehurst, *Gardens of Illusion: The Genius of André Le Nostre* (Nashville, TN, 1980), pp. 17–46, and, for Descombes, his *Aire: The River and Its Double* (Geneva, 2018) and Marc Treib, *The Landscapes of Georges Descombes* (Novato, CA, 2018).

7 I was once allowed to take a Red Book into the grounds and compare it with what was there.

8 The project took ten years to complete. Along the way, research, propositions and crucial commentary were published by the interdisciplinary design group Superpositions in a tabloid-like newspaper, the *River Chronicle*, first in October 2014 (48 pp) and again in June 2016 (56 pp). This contains essays (some in English) and many images, serial shots of the *étape* (stages) of the project, notes for a

projected film, dialogues between Descombes and a colleague, articles, sketches, and essays by Elissa Rosenberg on imagining a topography; other essays include a comparison between this larger surrounding landscape and Peter Latz's Duisburg-Nord by Jean-Marc Besse, a piece on the formation and deformation of the lozenges by Thomas Juel Clemmensen on 'nature restoration', and Marc Treib's discussion of how the river was itself the co-designer. Some of these essays were regathered in the *Aire* book (Zurich, 2020) and *Laisser faire la rivière* (Superpositions, 2021).

9 These and other plans are available in Nicole Garnier-Pelle, *André Le Nôtre (1613–1700) et les Jardins de Chantilly* (Paris, 2000), figs 3 and 4, with a later layout (fig. 13) representing Le Nôtre's work in 1673.

10 See the discussion and reference in Chapter One.

11 This is a central point in the chapter 'Landscape and Modernity' in David Brown and Tom Williamson, *Lancelot Brown and the Capability Men: Landscape Revolution in Eighteenth-Century England* (London, 2016).

12 In a private collection, and I am grateful to Tom Williamson for directing me to it. This is not the only reference to *genius loci* in Repton – he invoked it in his Red Book for Blaise Castle – but the note of irony here suggests at least his scepticism about simply relying on it. The reference to the Welsh nationalist leader more usually spelled Owain Glyndŵr may signal the fact that Repton knew Thomas Gray's poem 'The Bard' (published 1757) and its debt to the current idea of Celtic sublimity, and bards in the Gwedir family.

13 An excellent limited-edition facsimile of this was published in Paris in 2006; p. 1.

14 Most importantly Stephen Daniels, *Humphry Repton: Landscape Gardening and the Geography of Georgian England* (Cambridge, 1999), André Rogger, *Landscapes of Taste: The Art of Humphry Repton's Red Books* (London, 2007) and Tom Williamson, *Humphry Repton: Landscape Design in an Age of Revolution* (London, 2020). To all these I am much indebted, even as I focus primarily on how Repton reconsidered ideas of *genius loci*.

15 These can be seen in the Red Books at Dumbarton Oaks, Washington, DC, an edited facsimile of which was published as *Humphry Repton: The Red Books for Brandsbury and Glenham Hall*, with an introduction by Stephen Daniels (Washington, DC, 1994).

16 *Fragments*, p. 69.

17 From the late eighteenth century onwards, movement was both encouraged and considered as a topic to be discussed. See Andreas

Mayer, *The Science of Walking: Investigations into Locomotion in the Long Nineteenth Century* (Chicago, IL, 2020) and Lucius Burckhardt, *Why Is Landscape Beautiful? The Science of Strollology*, ed. Markus Ritter and Martin Schmitz (Basel, 2015), especially pp. 223–310.

18  See n. 14 above.

19  The text of the Blaise Castle Red Book, with one illustration, is reprinted in John Dixon Hunt and Peter Willis, eds, *The Genius of Place* (Cambridge, MA, 1988), pp. 359–65. I also discuss this particular Red Book in 'Humphry Repton and Garden History', *Journal of Garden History*, XVI/3 (Autumn 1996), pp. 215–24.

20  See Trish Gibson, *Brenda Colvin: A Career in Landscape* (London, 2011), especially the chapter 'Industry in the Landscape'.

21  Emily T. Cooperman, writing for the Preservation Alliance for Greater Philadelphia on the preservation of a major Frank Lloyd Wright building, the Beth Sholom Synagogue in Elkins Park, Montgomery County, Pennsylvania.

22  I use the edition of 1992, p. 175.

23  David Leatherbarrow and Richard Wesley, who in *Three Cultural Ecologies* (London, 2018) discuss McHarg (pp. 4–6), query whether he sufficiently accepts the process and rewards of 'inherited culture', and cite his own description of it in the chapter on vales as a 'ragbag of ancient views, most of them breeding fear and hostility, based on ignorance, certain to destroy, incapable of creation'.

24  Quoted in Udo Weilacher, *Syntax of Landscape: The Landscape Architecture of Peter Latz and Partners* (Basel, 2008), p. 135, to whose book, imagery and discussions with him I am indebted. This book shows several of his projects.

25  Quoted in Berrizbeitia, *Reconstructing Urban Landscapes*, pp. 181–2. That collection of essays on a variety of works by Van Valkenburgh is a remarkable enquiry into their design, implementation and use.

26  I discuss festival gardens in *The Making of Place*, pp. 63–77. The Chaumont site sets aside a series of spaces, designed by Jacques Wirtz, to be used by visiting designers; it is illustrated there as fig. 32.

27  This Xi'an exhibition is discussed by Karl Kullmann in 'De/framed Visions: Reading Two Collections of Gardens at the Xi'an International Horticultural Exhibition', *Studies in the History of Gardens and Designed Landscape*, XXXII/3 (2012), pp. 183ff.

28  For further images and brief descriptions of this exhibit by Lassus, see his 'Le Jardin des Hypothèses', *Studies in the History of Gardens and Designed Landscape*, XL/3–4 (2020), pp. 194–6. The same gesture towards a hypothetical landscape was made, although for different reasons, in

a design by Martha Schwartz for a site in Florida: when lack of funds prevented the replacement of large palm trees, she invented fake ones.

## 8  By Way of Conclusion

1  *Le Nuage Rouge* (Paris, 1977), pp. 367–82; Alasdair Forbes, *On Psyche's Lawn* (London, 2020).
2  Anne Cauquelin, *Petit traité du jardin ordinaire* (Paris, 1996). I am grateful to Bernard St-Denis for this reference.
3  I illustrate this courtyard and the designs by Gustafson in *The Making of Place: Modern and Contemporary Gardens* (London, 2015), pp. 37 and 261–5 respectively.
4  A colleague who teaches in theatre told me long ago that one of her teachers, Judith Malina (founder of the Living Theatre), said, 'When a certain place on the stage has harboured a powerful scene, or soliloquy, or discovery, that place holds its traces for the rest of the performance.' That is also apt for mental responses to place, where one 'powerful scene' can colour others elsewhere.

# Select Bibliography

Bonnefoy, Yves, *L'Arrière pays* [2003], trans. Stephen Romer (London and Kolkata, 2012)

Bucknell, Peter, and Robert Woof, *The Lake District Discovered 1810–1850: The Artists, the Tourists, and Wordsworth*, exh. cat., Dove Cottage, Grasmere (Grasmere, 1983)

Cardinal, Roger, *The Landscape Vision of Paul Nash* (London, 1989)

Chatwin, Bruce, *The Songlines* (London and New York, 1988)

Dale, Peter, and Brandon C. Yen, *Wordsworth's Gardens and Flowers: The Spirit of Paradise* (Woodbridge, 2018)

Davidson, Keir, *O Joy for Me! Samuel Taylor Coleridge and the Origins of Fellwalking in the Lake District, 1790–1802* (London, 2018)

Descombes, Georges, *Aire: The River and Its Double* (Geneva, 2018)

Friedman, Avi, *The Nature of Place: A Search for Authenticity* (Princeton, NJ, 2012)

Geertz, Clifford, *Local Knowledge: Further Essays in Interpretative Anthropology* (New York, 2000)

Hunt, John Dixon, *The Making of Place: Modern and Contemporary Gardens* (London, 2015)

Jackson, J. B., *A Sense of Place, a Sense of Time* (New Haven, CT, 1994)

James, Henry, *English Hours* (1905)

——, *Italian Hours* (1909)

Kurz, Otto, 'Huis Nympha Loci', *Journal of the Warburg and Courtauld Institutes*, XVI (1953), pp. 171–7

Lambirth, Andrew, *John Nash: Artist and Countryman* (Norwich, 2019)

Mayer, Andreas, *The Science of Walking: Investigations into Locomotion in the Long Nineteenth Century* (Chicago, IL, 2020)

Owens, Susan, *Spirit of Place: Artists, Writers and the British Landscape* (London and New York, 2020)

Norberg-Schulz, Christian, *Genius Loci*: *Towards a Phenomenology of Architecture* (New York, 1991)

Roberts, William, *A Dawn of Imaginative Feeling* (Carlisle, 1996)

Roger, Alain, *Court traité du paysage* (Paris, 1997)

Stilgoe, John R., *What Is Landscape?* (Cambridge, MA, 2015)

Tiberghien, Gilles A., *Nature, Art, Paysage* (Paris, 1993)

Weilacher, Udo, *Between Landscape Architecture and Land Art* (Basel, 1996)

# Photo Acknowledgements

The author and publishers wish to thank the relevant organizations and individuals listed below for authorizing reproduction of their work.

Abbott Hall Art Gallery, Kendal, Cumbria: 18; Aberdeen Art Gallery and Museum: 35; Art Gallery of New South Wales, Sydney: 28; Bibliothèque de l'Institut de France, Paris: 47; William Blake, from *The Marriage of Heaven and Hell*: 6; Böhn Collection, Venice: 14; Bridgeman Images/© Estate of John Northcote Nash. All rights reserved 2022: 33; Bridgeman Images/Photo © The Fine Art Society, London/© Estate of John Northcote Nash. All rights reserved 2022: 32; Bridgeman Images/Leeds Museums and Galleries, UK/© Estate of John Northcote Nash. All rights reserved 2022: 21, 22; Bridgeman Images/© Tullie House Museum & Art Gallery, Carlisle/© Estate of John Northcote Nash. All rights reserved 2022: 26; Bristol Museums, Galleries and Archives: 55; © The Trustees of the British Museum: 1, 20, 25, 34; Buckinghamshire County Museum: 7; courtesy of Paolo Bürgi: 57, 58; Cobham Hall, Wormsley Library: 52; S. T. Coleridge, from *Notebooks*: 39; Emily Cooperman Photos: 42, 43, 44, 65, 66, 67, 68; courtesy of Georges Descombes: 50, 51; Courtesy of Julien Descombes: 49; John Evelyn, from *Elysium Britannicum; or, The Royal Gardens*, ed. John E. Ingram (Philadelphia, PA, 2001), p. 229: 38; Ford Madox Ford, *Provence* sketch, 1933: 40; courtesy of Professor Helen Horowitz: 9; John Dixon Hunt: 3, 8, 10, 11, 41, 45, 46, 48, 63; courtesy of Bernard Lassus: 62 (photograph by Eric Sander, Domaine de Chaumont-sur-Loire); courtesy of Peter Latz: 56, 59, 60, 61; engraving from *Le Rouge, Cahier 13*: 64; Leeds City Galleries, Leeds Art Gallery: 19; Leicestershire County Council Artworks Collections: 30; Lady Lever Art Gallery, Liverpool: 5; Paul Mellon Centre, Yale University: 13; © Estate of John Northcote Nash. All rights reserved 2022: 29, 31, 36; National Archaeological Museum, Naples: 2; courtesy of Lord Newborough:

53, 54 (photographs by Joe Cornish); John Ruskin, from *Modern Painters* IV: 15, 16; Sheffield Museums: 12; Tate Gallery: 24, 37; Tullie House Museum & Art Gallery, Carlisle: 27; J.M.W. Turner, from *Liber studiorum*: 17; Walker Art Gallery, Liverpool: 4; York City Art Gallery: 23.

# Index

*Italic* numbers refer to illustrations